Attitudes and
Social Adaptation

A PERSON-SITUATION INTERACTION APPROACH

INTERNATIONAL SERIES IN EXPERIMENTAL SOCIAL PSYCHOLOGY

Series Editor: Michael Argyle, University of Oxford

A Related Pergamon Journal

LANGUAGE & COMMUNICATION*

An Interdisciplinary Journal

Editor: Roy Harris, *University of Oxford*

The primary aim of the journal is to fill the need for a publicational forum devoted to the discussion of topics and issues in communication which are of interdisciplinary significance. It will publish contributions from researchers in all fields relevant to the study of verbal and non-verbal communication.

Emphasis will be placed on the implications of current research for establishing common theoretical frameworks within which findings from different areas of study may be accommodated and interrelated.

By focusing attention on the many ways in which language is integrated with other forms of communicational activity and interactional behaviour it is intended to explore ways of developing a science of communication which is not restricted by existing disciplinary boundaries.

*Free specimen copy available on request.

NOTICE TO READERS

Dear Reader

An invitation to Publish in and Recommend the Placing of a Standing Order to Volumes Published in this Valuable Series.

If your library is not already a standing/continuation order customer to this series, may we recommend that you place a standing/continuation order to receive immediately upon publication all new volumes. Should you find that these volumes no longer serve your needs, your order can be cancelled at any time without notice.

The Editors and the Publisher will be glad to receive suggestions or outlines of suitable titles, reviews or symposia for editorial consideration: if found acceptable, rapid publication is guaranteed.

ROBERT MAXWELL
Publisher at Pergamon Press

Attitudes and Social Adaptation

A PERSON-SITUATION INTERACTION APPROACH

by
LYNN R KAHLE
University of Oregon, U.S.A.

PERGAMON PRESS
OXFORD · NEW YORK · TORONTO · SYDNEY · PARIS · FRANKFURT

U.K.	Pergamon Press Ltd., Headington Hill Hall, Oxford OX3 0BW, U.K.
U.S.A.	Pergamon Press Inc., Maxwell House, Fairview Park, Elmsford, New York 10523, U.S.A.
CANADA	Pergamon Press Canada Ltd., Suite 104, 150 Consumers Road, Willowdale, Ontario M2J 1P9, Canada
AUSTRALIA	Pergamon Press (Aust.) Pty. Ltd., P.O. Box 544, Potts Point, N.S.W. 2011, Australia
FRANCE	Pergamon Press SARL, 24 rue des Ecoles, 75240 Paris, Cedex 05, France
FEDERAL REPUBLIC OF GERMANY	Pergamon Press GmbH, Hammerweg 6, D-6242 Kronberg-Taunus, Federal Republic of Germany
First edition 1984

British Library Cataloguing in Publication Data

Kahle, Lynn R.
Attitudes and social adaptation —
(International series in experimental social psychology v.8)

1. Attitude change
I. Title   II. Series
303.3'2   PM291
ISBN 0—08—026074—8 Hardcover
ISBN 0—08—030835—X Flexicover

Printed in Great Britain by A. Wheaton & Co. Ltd.

To my Parents

Introduction to the series

MICHAEL ARGYLE

SOCIAL psychology is in a very interesting period, and one of rapid development. It has survived a number of "crises", there is increased concern with external validity and relevance to the real world, the repertoire of research methods and statistical procedures has been greatly extended, and a number of exciting new ideas and approaches are being tried out.

The books in this series present some of these new developments; each volume contains a balance of new material and a critical review of the relevant literature. The new material consists of empirical research, research procedures, theoretical formulations, or a combination of these. Authors have been asked to review and evaluate the often very extenstive past literature, and to explain their new findings, methods or theories clearly.

The authors are from all over the world, and have been very carefully chosen, mainly on the basis of their previous published work, showing the importance and originality of their contribution, and their ability to present it clearly. Some of these books report a programme of research by one individual or a team, some are based on doctoral theses, others on conferences.

Social psychologists have moved into an increasing number of applied fields, and a growing number of practitioners have made use of our work. All the books in this series have been of some practical application, some will be on topics of wide popular interest, as well as adding to scientific knowledge. The books in the series are designed for advanced undergraduates, graduate students and relevant practitioners, and in some cases for a rather broader public.

We do not know how social psychology will develop, and it takes quite a variety of forms already. However, it is a great pleasure to be associated with books by some of those social psychologists who are developing the subject in such interesting ways.

Preface

WHEN I completed the comprehensive examinations for my Ph.D. degree, one of the questions asked me to present my own theory of attitude change. I believe the time allotment for that question was 12 minutes, give or take a few seconds. It was with great surprise that I later learned that some of the faculty members evaluating my answer considered it to be incomplete. Since that time I have been forced to live with the nagging sense of guilt over a task unfinished, as if cursed by Zeigarnik himself. It is with great relief, therefore, that this manuscript and another step down the road of elaborating social adaptation theory is nearly ready to share with others.

The need for an attempt to bring together the various theories of attitude change has been present for some time. My colleague, Vaida Thompson, likes to invoke the old story about the elephant and the blind men when describing the state of theory in the attitude change literature. The blind men, when brought to the elephant, began to describe what they were able to feel. One reported encountering a large, hanging snake. Another equated the elephant with a tree. Yet another claimed that the elephant must be kin to the spear. Each blind man, of course, only captured part of reality. One felt the trunk, another the leg, the third the tusk. Each captured an important part of the real elephant, but the total picture eluded the men because of the limitations of their methodology for perceiving the elephant. Likewise, attitude theorists mostly have captured some of the nature of attitudes and attitude change, but the broad picture has escaped theoretical capture. Until the ways of perceiving attitudes expand, we will be limited to partial perceptions. It is the hope behind this book that we will begin to consider new ways soon.

Any major project necessarily spills over into the lives of people near it, and this book is no exception. Several of my colleagues commented on parts of this manuscript at various stages of its completion, most notably Chet Insko, John Thibaut, and Vaida Thompson. Likewise, a number of students provided helpful comments on some sections of the manuscript: Mark Alicke, Sarah Drenan, Robert Crawford, Bruce McCleary, Gerry Mitchell, Rupert Nacoste, and John Wittenbraker. All of these people deserve special thanks, although any errors in the manuscript clearly cannot be attributed to them. By far the biggest supporter of this entire project has been Debi Eisert, who has given me emotional support, intellectual criticism, proofreading help, and even collaborative help, especially on Chapter 6.

Lynn R. Kahle

Contents

CHAPTER 1

Introduction

The Emergence of the Concept of Attitude

WHAT is an *attitude*? We encounter the term almost daily in contemporary life. A local tavern promises reduced prices during "Attitude Adjustment Hour". On a late night television movie a gangster threatens a turncoat with "attitude re-arrangement". A ground hog[1] who refuses to budge from his hole on Ground Hog's Day unless an attractive female ground hog awaits him from above has his behavior attributed to a "bad attitude". A pamphlet promises that we will learn life's secrets if we enroll in "Adventures in Attitudes". A space physicist tells us that Skylab would not have spewed debris across Australia if, prior to the crash, it had been possible to "change its attitude". We even encounter a meaning of the term *attitude* that is quite similar to the social science conception when the newspaper reports on the attitudes of Germans toward nuclear proliferation.

Attitude apparently first crept into the English language around 1700, according to a recent review of the history of the concept (Fleming, 1967), as a jargon term for artists to describe body position in a painting. Its initial spread throughout the art world included the adopting of the concept for the drama equivalent of body position, calculated pose, by around 1725. In this sense the word implied a phoniness characteristic of actors and actresses pre-tending to be something other than their "real" selves. Some contemporary social psychologists (Tedeschi, Schlenker, & Bonoma, 1971) have advocated a return to the theatrical metaphor reminiscent of this early use of the term.

Charles Darwin introduced *attitude* into the literature of science in his 1872 book, *Expression of the Emotions in Man and Animals*. Darwin removed both the pretend aspect and the theatrical aspect from the concept, replacing these

---

[1] A ground hog, or woodchuck, is a marmot native to North America. February 2 is Ground Hog's Day, a mock-holiday in the United States. Tradition says that if the ground hog sees his shadow when he ends his hibernation on February 2, winter will continue for six more weeks. If the ground hog does not see his shadow (i.e. the day is cloudy), winter's end is near.

meanings with a concept implying a behavioral reality. For Darwin *attitude* implied stereotypic motoric responses associated with the expression of an emotion, usually in the sense of the posture of the entire body. Attitudes in this sense evolved, according to Darwin, in order to initiate an equilibrium-restoring function. Emotion for Darwin upset equilibrium, necessitating the attitude.

Sir Charles Sherrington in 1906 wrote *Integrative Action of the Nervous System*. This book continued the Darwinian concept of *attitude* as a behavioral, motoric response, but it reversed the figure and the ground. It viewed *attitude* as a continuous state, not as an occasional outburst. Whereas Darwin viewed the attitude as evidence of being upset, for Sherrington attitudes indicated normal pose. Attitudes reflected the stable nature of body position.

A concept very similar to the contemporary social science idea of attitude developed independently in German language psychology, particularly among proponents of the Würzburg school of psychology. The term frequently seen in Würzburger writings, *Aufgabe*, was usually translated *mind-set* rather than *attitude*, but it implied something quite similar to the word attitude as it is used today. In spite of the translation difference, Margaret Washburn attempted to integrate Sherrington's concept of attitude with the concept of *Aufgabe* by proposing a theory of incipient action, of learning by doing. This development helped to establish one element of the eventual concept of *attitude*.

A second element of the eventual concept of *attitude* emerged from a phenomenological critique of Sherrington's thinking written by Kurt Goldstein. Goldstein lashed out at Sherrington's attitude concept and its failure to consider imagination, creative thinking, and the ability of humans to be concerned with the possibilities of life. What is uniquely human in Goldstein's perspective should be part of the concept of attitude but is missing in Sherrington's definition. A contemporary psychologist might reinterpret the debate as one of whether the concept of attitude should or should not include what Piaget calls formal operational abilities (see Flavell, 1963). Goldstein would probably argue that formal operational thought must be included in any adequate concept of *attitude*. Goldstein did link his writing to some of the most articulate defenders of formal thought in his day, the existentialists and the phenomenologists. Goldstein defined human nature as attitudinal when he contemplated the phrase "attitude toward the possible". He argued that the concept of *nothingness* in the existential literature means lack of an attitude.

In this climate the various elements of the attitude concept were combined into a concept recognizable by modern social scientists. William Thomas elaborated on Darwin in *Sex and Society* (1907). He claimed that natural selection had favored those people who organize "habitually recurrent" situations under "fixed mental attitudes". In this book he linked affect and cognition in the *attitude* concept, and he conveyed the notion that attitudes have implications for behavior. In the social science classic, *The Polish Peasant in Europe and America* (1915, with Znaniecki), the concept of *attitude* Thomas held was elaborated further: "By attitude we understand a process of individual consciousness which determines real or possible activities of the individual in the social world" (p. 22). Thus, the ongoing state of Sherrington's definition, the tension between mental and behavioral components of Washburn's definition, and the emphasis on the uniquely human capacity to contemplate possibilities and think with formal logic of Goldstein's definition all were integrated into the formal definition presented in Thomas and Znaniecki's classic book.

Although Thomas thus formulated a vision of the attitude concept that more or less persists until today, he perhaps unwittingly removed the physiological element and therefore the observable element of an attitude. Without a manner in which an attitude could readily be empirically observed, its scientific usefulness could be questioned. A number of social scientists quickly corrected this problem, most notably L.L. Thurstone (1928), in his appropriately titled article, "Attitudes Can Be Measured", and Rensis Likert (1932). We will discuss attitude measurement later in the book, but for now suffice it to note that many contemporary definitions of attitude are operational, rather than strictly conceptual, in that they define an attitude as what attitude scales measure, nothing more and nothing less. Even when authors do not formally and officially identify their concept of attitude as operational, the reader should be wary of conceptual definitions that radically diverge from operational definitions. What a particular researcher claims to measure and what a researcher in fact measures (i.e. the operational definition) may not always conform.

Charles Osgood and his associates (e.g. Osgood, Suci, & Tannenbaum, 1957) developed perhaps the best known empirically-formulated definition of attitude. Through the use of their semantic differential technique, which we will discuss in the chapter on methodology, they have conducted a number of factor analytic studies in which they have rather consistently discovered three components of attitudes. The most important of the three statistically is the affective or evaluative dimension (e.g. good-bad, like-dislike). The other two dimensions are the activity or behavioral dimension (e.g. active-passive) and the potency (third) dimension (e.g. strong-weak). Many contemporary authors prefer to define a different third dimension, such as a cognitive, knowledge, or belief dimension. Most attempts to measure attitudes today directly assess only the affective or evaluative dimension. That is, attitudes are operationally defined as preferences; hence, Bem's (1970) definition — "attitudes are likes and dislikes" (p. 14) — is probably a good rough and ready definition. Most researchers assume, however, that the evaluative information provides insight into probable behaviors and into the social knowledge that a person holds.

Contemporary trends in the definition of attitudes include the drift toward more theoretically-based definitions and the drift toward emphasizing social cognition. The former trend involves authors who define the attitude concept to fit more clearly a specific theoretical position. For example, some proponents of self-perception theory have defined attitudes as what we infer from our behavior. The other trend has developed from the ascendency of the cognitive aspect of attitudes in research volume. Cognition has become an increasingly important force in contemporary psychology, growing from the influence of Lewin and Piaget, among others, to the point that some authors have implied that cognition may be the long-desired unifying theoretical force across all of psychology (Kruglanski, 1979; Weisz & Zigler, 1979). This optimistic assessment of the importance of cognition is not without some basis in fact, although ascribing universality to it is a bit premature (see, e.g. Sampson, 1981).

Many definitions of *attitude* include as a defining component the notion that an attitude is a "predisposition to respond" in a certain way (e.g. Allport, 1935; Campbell, 1950). Such conceptual definitions, however, have not always corresponded well with results of empirical research based on more operational definitions of attitude, such as the view that an attitude is "a tendency or predisposition to evaluate an object or symbol of that object in a certain way" (Katz & Stotland, 1959). For example, some writers believe that attitudes hardly ever lead to behavioral responses (Deutscher, 1966; Wicker, 1969), and others cite evidence that in some cases attitudes (as predispositions to evaluate) are actually postdispositions derived from responding rather than predispositions to respond (Bem, 1972). Unless one assumes that a cognition that fails to lead to behavior is by definition not an attitude (Triandis, 1979), the "predisposition to respond" definition clearly fails to encompass a number of important empirical manifestations of "predispositions to evaluate". For example, an attitude such as "dislike of rat meat" may never lead to any behaviors toward rat meat for most middle and upper class people, who never have an opportunity to eat or to refuse rat meat. A more adequate conceptualization of *attitude*, then, should specify more precisely the functional relationship between attitudes and behaviors in such a manner that it is possible to incorporate: the insights of self-perception theory (Bem, 1972), evidence that sometimes behaviors and attitudes appear not to be related (Deutscher, 1966; Wicker, 1969), and other more classic views of attitudes (e.g. Allport, 1935; Campbell, 1950).

One possible starting point for the framing of a more encompassing conceptualization of *attitude* would be to recognize that social cognitions, such as attitudes, are indeed cognitions and that much of the existing theory and research on other types of cognitions may therefore also be applicable to attitudes (see Kahle, Kulka & Klingel, 1980). That is, we use our attitudes to help us know about our social worlds. One of the best known theories of cognition, which has only recently received much attention in areas of social cognition other than moral development, is that of Piaget (e.g. 1929, 1930, 1952). In Piaget's view a function of cognition is to facilitate the process of adaptation to one's environment. "There is adaptation when the organism is transformed by the environment and when this variation results in an increase in the inter-changes between the environment and itself which are favorable to preservation" (Piaget, 1952, p. 5). This transformation consists of equilibration with the environment via ongoing assimilation of new information into existing mental structures and via complementary ongoing accommodation of existing mental structures to incorporate new, discrepant information. A complementary function of external adaptation is internal organization, which is the tendency to systematize processes into coherent, coordinated systems (see Flavell, 1963; Ginsburg & Opper, 1969; Tomlinson-Keasey, Eisert, Kahle, Hardy-Brown & Keasey, 1979).

In addition to adaptation, a second function of cognition is abstraction. "Psychological models for visual perception (Minsky, 1975; Posner, 1969), sentence completion (Bransford & Franks, 1972; Schank & Abelson, 1977), verbal memory (Bartlett, 1932; Mandler & Johnson, 1977), visual memory (Mandler & Parker, 1976), and decision making have emphasized the abstraction of prototypes, data structures, semantic products, deep structures, schemata, and themes as the central component of cognitive information processing" (Dreben, Fiske & Hastie, 1979, p. 1758). Through experience, vicarious experience, and thought, cognition serves to reduce the infinite number of stimuli that constantly impinge on a person to a manageable number of abstract propositions. During formative or transformative stages in the history of an abstraction, the abstraction will be tested, refined, and clarified. As the abstraction becomes more stable, when a specific instance dictates a behavioral response, the abstraction may be applied to that instance.

Where, then, do attitudes fit in this view of cognition? The Katz & Stotland (1959) definition quoted above specified in part how attitudes *differ* from other cognitions. What many have failed to recognize, however, is what attitudes have *in common* with other cognitions, which are not formed as predispositions to evaluate. A primary function of attitudes, as of other cognitions, is to facilitate the process of adaptation to the environment. We may then define *attitudes*: Attitudes are adaptation abstractions, or generalizations, about functioning in the environment, especially the social environment, that are expressed as predispositions to evaluate an object, concept, or symbol. This abstraction process emerges continuously from the assimilation, accommodation, and organization of environmental information by individuals, in order to promote interchanges between the individual and the environment that, from the individual's perspective, are favorable to preservation and optimal functioning. For example, you at one time knew that, in the year of your 5th birthday, on June 30, July 4, July 7, July 19, August 3, and August 6 you ate chocolate ice cream with good consequences (sweet, cold taste). Cluttering the storage capacity of your mind with all of the dates and details of each ice cream event is cumbersome, however, and it is far more efficient to summarize the details with the one statement, "I like ice cream".

Other Types of Social Cognition About People

Attitudes, of course, are not the only type of social cognition nor the only type of adaptation abstraction. They simply are the ones formulated as preferences. A variety of other types of social cognition have also been studied by psychologists. How people come to know their social worlds and the devices used for remembering the knowledge once obtained have occupied a good deal of attention in the social psychological literature in recent years.

One of the most specific types of social cognition is the *attribution*. In the social cognition literature attributions are defined as the particular reason or reasons for the occurrence of a particular behavior. When we seek to explain the behavior of someone, we may attribute the behavior to a person's trait (e.g. he broke the world's record because he is strong), to a temporary characteristic of a person (She broke the world's record because she was "fired up"), to the temporary situation (She broke the world's record because the crowd cheered her on with uncommon enthusiasm), or to the more long-term situation (He failed to break the world's record because the existing record is unbreakable). Attributions may also be nonsocial, as in the instance of calling ice cream "sweet". In a sense attributions are the building blocks of the other types of social cognition we will discuss, since they are the most specific of the types we will discuss in a system in which abstraction is a key goal.

Beliefs represent the information a person has about an object of attention. Fishbein & Ajzen (1975) define a belief as something that "links an object to some attribute" (p. 12). Beliefs generally summarize several attributions. A person holding a belief recognizes that the belief varies along a dimension of probability or factuality. "The sun is bright during the day when no clouds are in the sky" would be a belief most people hold with a high degree of certainty. "It will rain tomorrow" would also be a belief, although one held with less certainty. Beliefs may also be negative, or held with no certainty. "President Reagan and Prime Minister Thatcher are communists" is a belief most people would hold with a very small probability of factuality. Attitudes, according to Fishbein & Ajzen (1975), are simply beliefs with an evaluative component; hence, attitudes define the third rung on this ladder of abstraction after attributions and beliefs. Several attributions (He picked up the log because of his strength; He threw the ball far because of his strength) combine to form a belief (He is a strong person), which in turn is linked with an evaluation (Strength is good) to form an attitude (I like him).

Attributions to relatively enduring characteristics of a person lead to a special class of beliefs called *traits* or personality (Fishbein & Ajzen, 1975). A number of traits have captured the interest of social psychologists recently: aggressiveness, androgyny, authoritarianism, developmental levels, dogmatism, introversion-extraversion, locus of control, Machiavellianism, needs for achievement, affiliation, and power, neuroticism, outgoingness, self-concept (including especially self-esteem), and self-monitoring. All of these traits presumably reflect fairly stable personality characteristics or behavioral styles that are relatively unchangeable. Yet many have been changed experimentally, have been shown to vary from situation to situation, and have displayed a certain volatility. Most involve some type of outlook or life philosophy, which would imply that traits such as these to some extent are beliefs, social cognitions, and adaptation abstractions. If a trait is attributed to self or to others, that trait becomes an attitude when linked with an evaluation just as surely as any other belief becomes an attitude when linked with an evaluation. Traits should therefore not be viewed as entirely independent of a person's cognitive life (Mischel, 1973). They are simply a special case of social cognition. It is interesting to note that many of the same methodological and theoretical controversies have developed in independent, parallel forms within the attitude and within the trait research traditions.

The *value* is the most abstract of the types of social cognition about which we will talk. Like attitudes, values are social cognitions and adaptation abstractions (see Kahle, in preparation). Like attitudes, values involve preferences or evaluations. The two major differences are that values lack objects and are more abstract. Attitudes are directed *toward* some object, person, or idea (I have a favorable attitude toward roller coasters), whereas values are not (I value fun). The highly abstract nature of values implies that we hold very few values — Rokeach (1973) estimates that we hold thousands of attitudes but only a few dozen values.

Types of Social Cognition About Situations

All social behavior occurs in a situation or context. Behaviors that are appropriate for one type of situation are inappropriate for another situation. Laughter at a party elicits a different set of social sanctions than laughter at a funeral. Situations have received less classification attention than traits and attitudes as sources of influence on behavior, at least in the literature of social-personality psychology, perhaps because situations are far more complicated than persons. Many situations include more than one person, include physical or environmental limitations, and include aspects of many diverse, more distal influences on behavior, such as culture, history, economics, and language.

Social cognitions about situations may be considered to parallel social cognitions about persons since situations are objects of perception just as are persons. Situation *attributions*, for example, are frequently discussed. Jones & Nisbett (1971) have proposed that situational attributions are ventured predictably more often when a person is describing his or her own behavior than when describing the behavior of others, for example. *Beliefs* in the personal sphere have a parallel in the concepts of norms and roles. People develop theories of behavioral expectations, or facts, about situations. It is a fact from the perspective of the individual, held with some ascertainable probability, that the teacher occupies the lecture role and the student occupies the note-taking role, rather than the opposite. Fishbein & Ajzen (1975) describe the situational equivalent to attitude as the *subjective norm*, which is the combination of perceived norms and motives to comply with those norms. Just as people have traits, situations have *dynamics*. Situations also differ in the opportunity they avail for manifesting values.

Preview of Next Chapters

Any adequate theory of attitude change, it would seem, would necessarily examine the relationship between situations and persons. The cognitions about both, as well as factors about both not perceived, undoubtedly interact to produce most important social behavior. Yet most theories tend to overemphasize one source of influence at the expense of the other, as well as at the expense of the interaction between the two.

In the next two chapters we will examine the major theories of attitude change presently under active debate. The theories can be classified according to whether they emphasize the person or the situation as the major source of influence in the change process. Although at times this classification system may strain a bit to include one theory or another in a specific category, the system is basically plausible. An interactive theory will then be presented in Chapter 4, after the need for such a theory is established in Chapters 2 and 3.

Several cautionary notes may aid the reader in utilizing these sections optimally. The discussion of these theories is aimed at demonstrating that *the proposed classification system is viable* for categorizing the major change mechanisms rather than at providing a comprehensive explanation of all of the nuances of the theories. In each case the root metaphor or key concepts of the theory's change mechanism will be discussed, one example of a study sometimes cited as evidence of its viability will be presented, and a summary of some of the key criticisms of the theory will be given. Only one study will be given because one empirical success, it is believed, justifies further exploration of a theory. Since no theory has universal admiration, it can be assumed that every theory explains at least some data in a manner that at least some researchers find unsatisfactory. Criticisms most salient from the present perspective have been selected. Others have provided more comprehensive evaluations for readers seeking detailed considerations (Insko, 1967; Kiesler, Collins & Miller, 1969; McGuire, 1968a; Oskamp, 1977; Petty & Cacioppo, 1981; Reardon, 1981).

CHAPTER 2

Person-oriented theories of attitude change

PERSON-ORIENTED theories, as their name implies, deal with the subjective experinece of the individual. They maintain that attitude change occurs when the subjective experience of the individual changes. The thoughts of the individual are of primary importance in any understanding of the directions of attitudes. Whether a person accurately perceives the world or not, the perceptions the individual possesses and the relationships among them dictate what attitudes will be manifested.

Although the theories selected for inclusion in this chapter are few in number, their importance is unquestionable. Balance and dissonance theories have shaped the direction of attitude research since they were proposed, each generating a number of spin-off controversies and theories, as well as a number of direct tests. Cognitive response theory has not equalled the heuristic impact of balance and dissonance theories yet, but its history spans a much shorter time frame. If the early promise of the theory accurately indicates its future potential, we can expect this theory to be one of the most important of the next decade.

Balance Theory

Theory Summary

Although Heider (1946, 1958) is generally given credit for initiating balance theory, a number of other researchers have made important contributions to the relevant theoretical literature by proposing similar ideas, by extending Heider's ideas, or by refining the theory in one form or another (e.g. Cartwright & Harary, 1956; Insko, 1981; McGuire, 1960; Newcomb, 1953; Osgood & Tannenbaum, 1955; Rosenberg & Abelson, 1960; Wiest, 1965). Each theory in one form or another assumes that consistency among cognitions is an important motive or pull.

The key elements in balance theory as presented by Heider are (1) a person, p; (2) another person of interest to person p, o; and (3) a third element, x, which may be an idea, thing, or other object of judgment. Two types of relationships between these elements may exist — unit and sentiment. An example of a unit relationship, which deals with association, is ownership. An example of a sentiment relationship, which deals with evaluation, is liking. If p perceives that a relationship is balanced, it will tend to be stable. If p perceives imbalance, however, the relationship among the elements will tend to change. The easiest way to determine whether a relationship is balanced is to compute the sign that would result from multiplying the three relationships in a triad together (Cartwright & Harary, 1956). For example, assume that p likes (+) o and x and that p perceives that o also likes x. The product of three positive letters is positive. Since positive products imply balance and negative products imply imbalance, this example is balanced. If p likes (+) o and x but perceives that o dislikes (−) x, the implied product of the two positive and one negative values would be negative, suggesting that this triad is not balanced. Of the eight possible combinations of positive and negative sentiment relationships among p and o, p and x, and o and x, respectively, four are balanced and stable (+++, +−−, −+−, and −−+), and four are not balanced and therefore are likely to lead to change (−++, +−+, ++−, and −−−). The same applies for unit or combined relations. The key thing to note in this theory is that change depends upon the perceptions of the person, p. The perceptual influence of Gestalt psychology contributed much to Heider's thinking, including the perceptual metaphor on which he bases his predictions.

Research Example

Perhaps the best-known direct test of balance theory, cited by such noteworthy secondary sources as Insko (1967) and Kiesler, Collins & Miller (1969), was a dissertation directed by Heider and carried out by Jordan (1953). Jordan took each of the eight combinations of relationships mentioned above and crossed them with the combinations of unit or sentiment relationships. He found that, overall, research participants rated balanced triads as more pleasant than unbalanced triads, thus supporting balance theory. Most of the pleasantness, however, apparently resulted from only two (+++ and +−−) of the four balanced situations, with unexpected unpleasantness resulting from two balanced situations (−+− and −−+). The reasons for this unexpected finding have been the subject of some controversy.

Evaluation

After nearly three decades of research the basic balance hypothesis still appears to be essentially plausible. Some research, such as the Jordan study mentioned above, has revealed dents in the armor, but balance theory continues to generate research and increasingly sophisticated theorizing (e.g. Insko, 1981). Perhaps the greatest difficulty with the theory is its lack of falsifiability (Insko, 1981). When one deals with a "real life" relationship and all of its complexity, the exact elements to consider often escape identification. Consider, for example, a college dorm room-mate assigned to you at random. After a year of sharing a room, you probably would know hundreds of attitudes of this person, enter into hundreds of unit relations, and have a long list of attributes of this person, both favorable and unfavorable, all of which come into play in determining balance in a particular issue. How would you know when your list of relevant units and sentiments was complete when trying to predict a particular response? A faulty prediction would indict your specification of the elements, not the theory.

Other objections also have been raised. Some triads are probably not germane to the experience of balance or imbalance, but which triads these are, the theory does not specify. For example, the imbalanced triad: "I dislike Nixon" (−), "I like ice cream" (+), and "Nixon likes ice cream" (+); does not intuitively generate a strong motive to revise my sentiment toward either Nixon or ice cream. Finally, Heider's theory does not allow for degrees of relationships (Kiesler, Collins, & Miller, 1969). Certainly the true believer will experience imbalance differently than the lip-service follower. Contemporary balance theorists have overcome this problem (Insko, 1981).

Cognitive Dissonance Theory

Theory Summary

Cognitive Dissonance Theory (Festinger, 1957) has undoubtedly generated more research than any other theory of attitude change. The musical metaphor struck a chord in the symphony of social psychology that continues to produce overtones and harmonics. The theory, another type of cognitive consistency theory quite similar to balance theory, assumes that harmonious cognitions are music to our minds but that discordant and cacophonous cognitions drive us to seek a different channel or concert. In spite of the different metaphors, dissonance theory and balance theory overlap enough that Heider was able to define a balanced state as "harmonious" (Heider, 1958, p. 180). When a person realizes that two cognitions or sets of cognitions that the person holds imply the opposite of each other, the person experiences an aversive state known as cognitive dissonance. Exposure to information, decision making, disagreement with other persons, or "forced" compliance may all create the experience of dissonance. A person experiencing dissonance will be motivated to restore cognitive consonance through changing cognitions or behaviors, changing the importance of cognitions, or adding new cognitions. The important point is that all of the ways to alleviate dissonance involve modifying cognitions, thoughts changing, or minds changing — "intrapsychic" change, in the word of Tedeschi et al. (1971). In spite of the large number of experiments that have changed attitudes within the dissonance tradition through manipulating situations, any explanation of these results faithful to the original theory must fall within the confines of a person-oriented explanation.

Research Example

Festinger & Carlsmith (1959) promised either $1 or $20 to subjects who would lie to another "subject" (actually a confederate) by describing a dreadfully boring experimental task as enjoyable, fun, interesting, intriguing, and exciting. They hypothesized, based on dissonance theory, that attitude change would be greatest when a person is induced to behave counterattitudinally with the minimum necessary inducement. One might predict the opposite — that a larger inducement would lead to more change — from reinforcement theory. The results tended to support dissonance theory in that, after the experiment, subjects offered $1 reported greater actual enjoyment of the experiment than the $20 group.

Theoretical Specifications

A number of theoretical specifications, modifications, or clarifications have transformed dissonance theory, even among its proponents, into a somewhat different theory today. This trend of evolving and refining the theory as more about the phenomenon is learned certainly follows scientific tradition.

One variable apparently necessary to obtain the dissonance results rather than the reinforcement results obtained in some conceptual replications of Festinger & Carlsmith, such as by Rosenberg (1965), is perceived choice. When a subject is induced into performing a counterattitudinal behavior, he or she must believe that the decision was an internal one he or she truly selected, not one based on experimenter force (Linder, Cooper, & Jones, 1967). When the subject perceives excessive situational pressure from the experimenter, no attitude change as predicted by dissonance theory is likely to take place. One of the spin-off theories from dissonance theory, reactance theory (Brehm, 1966), deals with exactly this phenomenon. An additional theoretical spin-off from this notion of choice has emphasized the importance of commitment for locking a person into a behavioral pattern (Brickman, Coates, & Cohn, 1977; Kiesler, 1971).

Another important condition that seems to be necessary for the dissonance effect is that the subject feel some personal responsibility for a significant consequence (see Calder, Ross & Insko, 1973; Collins & Hoyt, 1972). If the participant believes that the counterattitudinal behavior that generated the dissonance did not lead to any noteworthy undesired consequence, or that it was not the subject's fault if it did, dissonance again can not be expected to be aroused.

Aronson (1969) has claimed that a conflict between self concept and counterattitudinal behavior is necessary in order to experience dissonance. He explains the Festinger & Carlsmith (1959) study as resulting from the conflict between the subject's telling a lie and believing himself (all subjects were male) to be an honest person. With very little justification for the lie, as in the $1 condition, the pressure to change is especially great. Dissonance results from conflict between cognition about self and cognition about behavior. Several researchers from other perspectives have also recently proposed that the self-concept is important in understanding social behavior (e.g. Eisert & Kahle, 1982; Markus, 1977; Rokeach, 1979).

Kahle (1978) found evidence consistent with this interpretation in a study in which subjects were asked to write prosmoking counterattitudinal essays (nearly everyone, even smokers, dislikes smoking) that would be used to convince junior

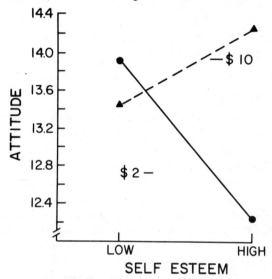

Figure 2–1. Interaction between self-esteem and justification for determining attitude change in study by Kahle (1978).

high school students to smoke. Subjects were offered either $2 or $10. Subjects with high measured self-esteem changed their attitudes more in the $2 condition, while subjects offered $10 were more likely to change their attitudes if they had low measured self-esteem. The implication is that subjects with low self-esteem behaved like attitudinal mercenaries, changing their attitudes for the highest bidder.

Each of these extensions preserves the person-orientation of dissonance theory regardless of whether they unify or fragment the theory. Whether dissonance necessarily involves cognitions about freedom, cognitions about commitment, cognitions about responsibility, cognitions about consequences, or cognitions about self, the locus of change still lies within the head of the person experiencing dissonance. As we shall see in the next chapter, not all explanations that have been proposed to account for the results of dissonance theory research ignore situations.

Evaluation

Dissonance theory has generated more research than any other attitude-change theory mentioned in this book. Whether one supports or opposes dissonance theory, its contribution in the form of attracting the attention of an army of bright researchers to the area of attitude change cannot be denied. Discussion of just the major topics of debate easily fills an entire book (Wicklund & Brehm, 1976). The intuitive plausibility of dissonance theory results in frequent descriptions of it even in the popular press.

Some of the criticisms of dissonance theory echo criticisms of balance theory. At times the theory is vague, leaving predictions imprecise (Chapanis & Chapanis, 1964). At other times the multiplicity of ways of resolving dissonance makes falsifying the theory impossible (Greenwald, 1975). Yet the theory does specify to some degree and predict to some degree several outcomes; almost universal agreement has been given to certain experiments characterized as supporting or not supporting dissonance.

Probabilogical Theory

Theory Summary

McGuire (1968d, 1981) has proposed one of many consistency theories that contains more quantification than most other consistency theories and has several interesting and provocative twists relative to other consistency and attribution theories. He proposes that humans think and form their attitudes by integrating logical thought and probabilistic thought, with Bayes' Theorem providing an approximation of the basic processes involved.

Several definitions are necessary to follow McGuire's theorizing. First, propositions are "statements that assign objects of thought to positions on dimensions of judgments" (McGuire, 1981, p. 292). Examples of dimensions of judgment are probability and desirability. Secondly, beliefs and attitudes are "responses that assign objects of thought to dimensions of judgment in such propositions" (McGuire, 1981, p. 293).

Some force exists that tends to maintain connectedness and interrelatedness among the propositions in one's mind. In part logical connectedness is sought. An operational definition of logic is the syllogism, with its major premise (e.g. Vegetables require fertilizer in order to grow), minor premise (e.g. Peas are vegetables), and conclusion (e.g. Peas require fertilizer in order to grow). The syllogism is somewhat flawed, however, in that it assumes that the major and minor premises are either true or false, when in fact often times propositions such as the major or minor premise are held with some equivocation (e.g. Vegetables *usually* require fertilizer in order to grow). If one explicitly recognizes this probabilistic element, then it is possible to consider the effects of probability on cognitive logic and to predict what changes might take place in related attitudes when "cognitive inertia" forces ideas to filter through a cognitive system. If, in the above syllogism, a prediction of the conclusion from the two premises were desired, the following formula would predict the effects of the force for connectedness!

$$p(c) \geqslant p(a)p(b)$$

where:

$p(a)$ = probability of the major premise

$p(b)$ = probability of the minor premise

$p(c)$ = probability of the conclusion

At least two tendencies toward the irrational distort inferences from their probabilogical optimum. First, *wishful thinking* is the tendency for more desirable events to become more probable over time. Secondly, the *rationalization* effect refers to the reverse phenomenon that desires are rated as more probable over time (McGuire, 1981). Basically, however, the theory assumes that people tend toward the rational within Bayesian logic, although research has not always supported this conclusion (e.g. Dillehay, Insko, & Smith, 1966).

Attitude change in this theory results primarily from the introduction of new information and new propositions. As time passes, other attitudes related to the one most directly influenced by the information will change as well. The change is, as in other cognitive consistency models, within the person's mind and field of perception. Situations are not discussed as important influences on attitudes.

Research Example

Wyer & Goldberg (1970) provided one example consistent with McGuire's theory, as have McGuire and his students. In the typical experiment subjects rate a number of propositions, are influenced by information to change one proposition, and then rate the propositions again to supply researchers with evidence of any filtering down of the counterattitudinal information.

Evaluation

This theory shares many of the strengths of other consistency models and has in addition several explicit and quantifiable hypotheses. Two major flaws, however, are the facts that much of the research has not been easily replicated (e.g. Bernstein & Kahle, 1982) and that much new evidence suggests that people are far less logical than the theory would suggest, even in its qualified form (see Nisbett & Ross, 1980). This second criticism may itself be tenuous, however (Henle, 1962).

Cognitive Response Theory

Theory Summary

Cognitive response theory (Greenwald, 1968; Petty, Ostrom, & Brock, 1981) has recently generated a renewed interest in the concept of attitude among social psychologists, particularly ones associated with Ohio State University. The theory assumes that all of the thoughts that pass through a person's head prior to, during, and while later considering a persuasive communication will contribute to a person's response to that communication and eventual attitude that results from it. Examples of someone's thoughts that might result from listening to a persuasive communication on capital punishment, provided by Petty, Ostrom, & Brock (1981, p. 6), include: "The thought of killing another person makes me sick", "How is capital punishment different from abortion, which is disgusting?", "The electric chair is the most economical way to deal with repeat criminals, though", and "Only racists and Republicans favor capital punishment". Presumably the more favorable the thoughts generated, both directly and indirectly, by the communication, the more the communication will change the person in the advocated direction. Obviously this theory is person-oriented in it's change mechanism.

Research Example

Petty & Cacioppo (1977) tried to persuade a group of introductory psychology students to accept the counterattitudinal position that all Freshman and Sophomore students ought to be required to live on campus. Half of the students were forewarned of the content of the persuasive communication, half not. Further, during the 3 minutes after the warning (or lack of it), half of the students were told to write all of the thoughts that had recently occurred to them, the other half to write only arguments related to the anticipated persuasion attempt. A measure of attitude after the actual persuasion attempt showed that only the subjects who did not know about nor think about the topic beforehand were at all influenced by the persuasion attempt. These subjects also were the only ones who did not generate any thoughts relevant to the communication. The implication of this manipulation is that the cognitive responses of the subjects enabled them to resist a persuasive attempt.

Evaluation

This theory certainly has a number of strengths. Over the short length of time that it has been formally proposed as a theory of persuasion, it has generated a significant amount of quality research. Note that this theory implies very active information processing of new information, which is certainly compatible with the view of attitudes as adaptation abstractions. Likewise, it provides a supplementary perspective that unifies a number of diverse theoretical discussions on topics previously thought to have little to do with persuasion, such as the "risky shift" phenomenon (Burnstein & Vinokur, 1975) and other socially important behaviors (see Petty, Ostrom, & Brock, 1981).

On the negative side very little has been published, in part because the theory is relatively new. We can suggest places where the theory has room for improvement. Once again we see in some cases unclear predictions. The sources of cognitive responses, especially irrelevant ones, are not always clear. The theory seems to have little room for unconscious or unaware attitude change, in spite of evidence that such attitude change can take place (see Brock, 1968). Perhaps most important, however, is the question of whether cognitive responses ought to be weighted in terms of their importance for some factor such as adaptive significance. For example, if someone tried to persuade you to eat a poison, you might generate the following cognitive responses: "It might taste sweet", "It would certainly taste unique and perhaps interesting", "Many people who now impolitely ignore me would notice me for sure", "The speaker obviously believes that it would be fun", and "I'll die". Cognitive response theory would predict conversion to eating the poison with these cognitive responses, but it may be that the one response with the largest weight in terms of adaptive significance, "I'll die", would have more impact than all of the others combined.

Functional Theory

Theory Summary

One of the most explicitly person-oriented theories of attitude change is the functional approach that has been proposed by Katz (1960), who argues:

> The functional approach is the attempt to understand the reasons people hold the attitudes they do. The reasons, however, are at the level of psychological motivations and not of the accidents of external events and circumstances. Unless we know the psychological need which is met by the holding of an attitude we are in a poor position to predict when and how it will change. (Katz, 1960, p. 170)

The functional approach assumes that different attitudes are based on different motives. Attempting to predict where and when to observe the attitude or how to change it necessitates understanding the underlying function or motive of that attitude. According to Katz (1960), attitudes may serve any of four functions, each one corresponding to one of the major philosophies of psychology: adjustment or utilitarian (behaviorism), ego defensive (psychoanalysis), value expression (humanism), and knowledge (cognitive). Table 2—1 reproduces the list Katz has provided of the origin and dynamics, arousal conditions, and change conditions of each of the functions. As is evident, Katz has proposed an "it-depends-on-the-person's-motive" theory that mirrors "it-depends-on-the-situation" theories. Ironically, however, once at least some of the motives have been identified in terms of their function for the person, the actual change condition

TABLE 2—1

Katz's Functional Approach to Attitudes

ADJUSTMENT

(A) origin & dynamics: utility of attitudinal object in need satisfaction. Maximizing external rewards and minimizing punishment.

(B) arousal conditions: 1. activation of needs. 2. salience of cues associated with need satisfaction.

(C) change conditions: 1. need deprivation. 2. creation of new needs & new levels of aspiration. 3. shifting rewards & punishments. 4. emphasis of new & better paths for need satisfaction.

EGO DEFENSE

(A) origin & dynamics: protecting against internal conflicts & external dangers

(B) arousal conditions: 1. posing of threats. 2. appeals to hatred & repressed impulses. 3. rise in frustrations. 4. use of authoritarian suggestion.

(C) change conditions: 1. removal of threats. 2. catharsis. 3. development of self-insight.

VALUE EXPRESSION

(A) origin & dynamics: maintaining self identity; enhancing favorable self-image; self-expression & self determination.

(B) arousal conditions: 1. salience of cues associated with values. 2. appeals to individual to reassert self-image. 3. ambiguities which threaten self-concept.

(C) change conditions: 1. some degree of dissatisfaction with self. 2. greater appropriateness of new attitude for the self. 3. control of all environmental supports to undermine old values.

KNOWLEDGE

(A) origin & dynamics: need for understanding, for meaningful cognitive organization, for consistency & clarity.

(B) arousal conditions: 1. reinstatement of cues associated with old problem or old problem itself.

(C) change conditions: 1. ambiguity created by new information or change in environment. 2. more meaningful information about problems.

From Katz (1960), p. 192.

may be either personal or situational, implying that in some respects functional theory is interactive. A similar theory has been proposed by Smith, Bruner & White (1956) and, although somewhat less similar, by Kelman (1958, 1961).

Research Example

No single research example exists that simultaneously demonstrates all of the four functions that Katz has hypothesized. What research does exist almost uniformly examines only one function at a time (Kiesler, Collins, & Miller, 1969). Perhaps the best data supporting the Katz theory comes from the book by Smith, Bruner, & White (1956), who interviewed ten men in depth when formulating their theory, which is highly similar to that of Katz (1960). Smith, Bruner, & White found that attitudes do serve different functions for different people, although they tended to emphasize social functions more than Katz appears to do. Highly conservative experimental social psychologists tend to frown on such in depth, clinical-style data (see Kiesler, Collins, & Miller, 1060). Certainly the data pleases no one who believes that truth can only be found on a Likert-type scale. This type of research in the right hands, however, can at the very least be provocative and intriguing, even if it requires more than the usual dose of skepticism when interpreted.

Evaluation

The lack of experimental evidence pertinent to functional theory underscores at least one major flaw: functional theory is not heuristic. If one views functional theory as descriptive or integrative, this shortcoming is not too serious; however, as a predictive theory, functional theory fails, which is why it has failed to stimulate research. This second flaw results from the postulation of multiple motives without sufficient information about how to identify the applicable motive in any given instance or how to predict what motive will emerge from the conflict of two or more motives as the paramount. Since one attitude may serve one function for some people and another function for other people, knowing the attitude of interest will not help in knowing which function it serves. Thus, one can never identify where on Table 2–1 to start when attitude change is sought. If Katz had identified one motive as the prime moving motive, it would be easier to formulate predictions.

CHAPTER 3

Situation-oriented theories of attitude change

SITUATION-ORIENTED theory focuses on what is outside of the person's skin in trying to understand and predict attitude change. Some aspect of the physical, social, or external environment, rather than the person per se, leads the way in changing attitudes. Much of experimental social psychology, with its manipulation of situations (independent variables), implicitly is situation-oriented.

Classical Conditioning

Theory Summary

Classical conditioning theory, also known as respondent or Pavlovian conditioning, was introduced by Russian physiologist Pavlov. The theory holds that repeatedly pairing an eliciting or unconditioned stimulus, which is capable of producing some desired response, with an originally neutral stimulus, which cannot initially produce the desired response, eventually leads to the originally neutral stimulus becoming a conditioned stimulus which is capable of producing the desired response. For example, Pavlov paired a bell (neutral stimulus) with meat powder (unconditioned stimulus) when eliciting saliva from his dogs (desired response). Eventually the bell (now conditioned stimulus) elicited salivation, even in the absence of meat powder.

Staats & Staats (1957) have proposed a theory of attitude acquisition and change that applies the principles of classical conditioning to social psychology. Staats & Staats assume that after a neutral stimulus, such as a word, becomes able to elicit some response, it can be paired with other neutral words in a process of higher order conditioning to yield some response from a word that has never been associated with the original eliciting stimulus. For example, suppose ice cream (eliciting stimulus) has repeatedly been paired with the word *good*. The word *good* will come to elicit the same delight as ice cream. At some point *good* may be paired with some other word, such as *Republican*. The new word, *Republican*, will come to elicit the same delight as ice cream, even though it has never been directly paired with ice cream. Through this higher-order condition-ing, the subject in our experiment has, through a fondness for ice cream, become a Republican. Unlike the theorists in the previous chapter, who relied heavily on cognition, thought, and mental processes in explaining attitude acquisition and change, the conditioning theorist assumes that the process does not even involve the awareness of the subject or person acquiring the attitude. "The meaning of stimuli may be learned without awareness – without cognition" (Staats & Staats, 1957, p. 76). Presumably attitudes are acquired through physiological processes centered lower in the brain stem than cognitive psycho-logists would believe.

Research Example

In one study designed to clarify the physiological nature of attitude acquisi-tion, Staats, Minke, Martin, & Higa (1972) asked subjects either to skip breakfast and lunch or to eat a good meal just prior to an experiment. Subjects were assigned to one of these two conditions randomly but knew about the nature of the condition that they would not occupy as well as the one they would occupy. During the experiment subjects saw originally neutral nonsense syllables (like *qug*) paired with food words (like ice cream) on 75% of the trials and paired with other neutral words (like book) on the other 25% of the trials. Their hypo-thesis from classical conditioning theory – that hungry subjects would rate the nonsense words pleasant while food-satiated subjects would not – was supported by their data.

Evaluation

The empirical phenomenon identified by Staats *et al.* and by many others is widely accepted. That is, many researchers in the attitude field agree that pairing "good" words with neutral words or "good" things with neutral things will lead to more favorable opinions of the neutral things. Considerable contro-versy, however, surrounds the interpretation of the findings. Many cognitive psychologists believe that experimental demand characteristics (Orne, 1962) transform the experiment into a problem-solving study in which subjects figure out that they should like the nonsense syllables and cooperatively comply with the experimenter's perceived expectation (e.g. Page, 1969). For example, Page & Kahle (1976) were able to replicate the Staats *et al.* study with sophisticated subjects, who presumably understood classical conditioning, but not with intro-ductory psychology students, who had not yet learned about classical condition-ing in their classes. (Staats *et al.* used subjects from "various undergraduate psychology courses.") This finding is more consistent with the demand charac-teristics interpretation than with the classical conditioning interpretation be-cause an unconscious process should not require understanding to function. Kahle & Page (1976) further undermined the physiological explanation by in-viting only well-fed, sophisticated subjects to their lab and then asking half of these subjects to pretend to be hungry. Those subjects pretending to be hungry did indeed display "conditioning", while the full subjects who were not feigning hunger rated the originally neutral words as still neutral after the conditioning phase. Thus, manipulating the demand characteristics while holding the physiology constant produced the supposedly physiological effect. In both studies "conditioning" was manifested only by subjects who could articulate the conditioning hypothesis postexperimentally.

A good deal of other evidence undermines the empirical evidence cited to support classical conditioning theory applied to attitude change (e.g. Page, 1969, 1974). For example, the attitude conditioning studies with children generally fail to show attitude conditioning (e.g. O'Donnell & Brown, 1973). Brewer (1974) recently completed a comprehensive review of classical conditioning of normal human adult attitudes and concluded that no convincing evidence for noncognitive classical conditioning of these people's attitudes can be found in the literature, although a few researchers may still question this conclusion (Zanna, Kiesler, & Pilkonis, 1970).

Operant Conditioning

Theory Summary

Operant, instrumental, or Skinnerian conditioning is more free-form than classical conditioning. In operant conditioning the experimenter waits until a targeted response is freely or randomly emitted by the subject and then either reinforces the response, if an increase in response frequency is desired, or punishes the behavior, if a decrease in response frequency is desired. The subject's behavior is eventually shaped to the point that the subject learns to behave appropriately. Some doubt whether the shaping even involves attitudes, properly defined.

Research Example

One typical verbal conditioning study of "attitudes" involves the Taffel (1955) task. In this task the subject is shown a series of cards, each with a verb and six pronouns. The subject is told to make up a sentence with any one of the pronouns. After establishing a baseline, the experimenter unannounced begins to reinforce with praise the use of a certain pronoun. For example, every time the experimenter hears the subject use "I" in a sentence, the subject is told, "Good". Nearly all of the large number of studies following this paradigm have found that the subjects in the experiment will on average increase the frequency of producing the reinforced pronoun.

Evaluation

As in classical conditioning, the empirical phenomenon is not at issue, but the interpretation of it clearly has generated a long-term controversy. Once again, the awareness problem raises questions about attributing change to reinforcement and punishment rather than to the cognitions about reinforcement and punishment. A fairly strong data base once again is consistent with the cognitive rather than the learning interpretation of the data (Brewer, 1974; Dulany, 1961; Goldstein, Rosnow, Goodstat, & Suls, 1972; Page, 1970a; Spielberger, 1962). Subjects figure out how to make the experimenter reinforce them and then do just that.

Several research examples should suffice to illustrate the awareness problem in operant conditioning of adult humans who are normal. Page (1970a) showed that by saying the word "reinforcement" rather than "good" after one pronoun, students taking their second psychology course, but not students taking their first psychology course, produced the "reinforced" pronoun more frequently in an unusually small number of trials. Only subjects who described the experiment in problem-solving terms did this, however. The implication is that the problem solving nature of the task was hidden from the naive subjects by using the jargon word "reinforcement" rather than the "good" used both in research and in popular psychology. In another experiment Page (1972) told "conditioned" subjects to make him stop saying "good". Nearly all subjects were able to do that immediately. Of the 52 subjects who did not reach the criterion of conditioning (13 successive reinforcements on 15 trials), 32 were able to reach the criterion immediately after being asked by the experimenter to, "Make me say 'good' on every trial". These subjects apparently were aware of the contingency but not initially cooperating with it, perhaps because they viewed the experiment as a study of conformity rather than as a study of problem solving.

It is important to note that the distinction between calling these studies investigations of "conditioning" or of "problem solving" does not deal merely with the question of a research method artifact, as some have suggested, or with some other methodological triviality. On the contrary, the issue is one of the most fundamental and profound in science and philosophy. The behaviorist assumes that behavior is the fundamental fact of psychology, whereas the cognitivist assumes that thought is the fundamental fact of psychology. The implication of the "demand characteristics" studies in both classical and operant conditioning is that the behaviorist philosphy is not compatible with the research evidence.

Another major theoretical problem, which operant psychology does not share with classical conditioning, is the undefinability of *reinforcement*. Even though reinforcement is a key and central concept in the highly parsimonious system of operant psychology, it defies definition. What is a reinforcer? Something that increases the probability of a particular response being emitted. How do we find out whether something is a reinforcer? We try it and observe whether the frequency of the behavior increased. As can be seen here, the definition is circular. The circularity of this definition makes behaviorism, like cognitive dissonance theory, untestable and unfalsifiable. If a particular thing that is thought to be a reinforcer fails to increase the probability of a particular behavior being emitted, one concludes that the "reinforcer" is not a reinforcer, not that operant conditioning is wrong (see Greenwald, 1975).

One version of operant psychology has attempted to circumvent the problem of human thought by proposing "social learning theory". Social learning theory actually is a number of different theories from a number of different theorists. Many of the theorists are inconsistent with themselves, once denying cognition and later praising it, for example. Other than unification in the attempt to salvage discredited learning theory, to preserve the concept of reinforcement in spite of its problems, and to perpetuate a dying metaphor, the theorists probably have very little in common with each other.

Although one wonders why the mental gymnastics to preserve the learning theory jargon are necessary, some of the most recent writings on social learning theory have been quite sophisticated. For example, a number of noteworthy studies by Bandura and his colleagues have underscored the contribution of modeling to attitude change. In one such study, Bandura, Blanchard, & Ritter (1969) showed that modeling affectionate behavior towards reptiles increased pro-reptile attitudes and behaviors in originally snake-phobic subjects.

Self-perception Theory

Theory Summary

Bem's (1965, 1967, 1972b) self-perception theory takes some relatively old ideas (Cooley, 1922; James, 1884) and applies them to a more contemporary problem. Bem assumes that *"Individuals come to 'know' their own attitudes, emotions, and other internal states partially by inferring them from observations of their own behavior"* (Bem, 1972b, p. 2). At first blush one might think that Bem's theory should be classified as a person-oriented theory rather than as a situation-oriented theory, given words like *know* and *inferring* in such a key theoretical statement. But closer examination makes clear that the emphasis of this theory is situational. (Bem has more recently articulated theories on different topics that clearly embrace interactionism (e.g. Bem, 1979); however, contemporary interactionism was not yet a fashionable concept when Bem first conceived of self-perception theory and may have at that time escaped his theoretical considerations.) For one thing, *know* is in quotation marks, implying that it is a concept in this context not to be taken seriously. More importantly, since this chapter deals with theories of attitude *change*, we must consider how attitudes change in his theory to understand their nature. Clearly, attitudes do not change through modifying inferences; they change through modifying situationally-determined behavior. To understand Bem's view of attitudes, we must first understand his view of behavior since attitudes result from, not cause, behavior in self-perception theory.

What causes behavior in self-perception theory? As a "sometimes radical [Skinnerian] behaviorist", Bem endorses the concept of operant conditioning as pivotal in his view of the nature of behavior. Bem enters the world of attitudes through the door of Skinner's theory of language acquisition. We learn language through adult socialization, Skinner and Bem suggest. When a child uses the right word, parents reinforce that usage. Wrong words are punished. Since the vocabulary of emotion must be taught to us, we also learn it through conditioning. Our parents or socializing agents teach us when to use happiness, when sadness, when frustration, when anger in describing our inner emotions. But they have no more access to our "true" inner feelings than the man in the moon. They examine the external situation and determine from situational cues what our emotional state must be. This phenomenon is known to film editors, who can make the least talented actors and actresses look like brilliant conveyors of emotion through simply splicing the right situations into the right places.

Bem would not have created nearly the controversy he did if he had ended self-perception theory with a simple agreement with Skinner's theory that children are taught language. But Bem took this analysis one step beyond and used it to reinterpret dissonance phenomena. He argued that dissonance research could be reinterpreted within a behavioristic perspective by adding the concept of self-perception. We acquire our attitudes through observing our behavior. If you observe yourself eating brown bread, an event in fact caused by situationally determined conditioning contingencies in Bem's view, you will infer that your behavior must have come from an attitude favorable toward brown bread. You infer your attitude by observing your own behavior, just as you might infer the attitude of someone else by observing his or her behavior.

Research Example

Bem's reinterpretation of the Festinger & Carlsmith (1959) experiment assumes that the results were obtained through an inference about behaviors on the part of the subjects. Subjects in that study, self-perception theory maintains, observed their own behaviors and sought to infer what their attitudes must be. They inferred a new attitude (the boring tasks were fun) when paid $1 but not $20 because $20 is an amount they would be paid for 5 minutes work only if their behavior were dishonest. The $20 payment for so little work signaled that a lie was being told ($20 in the late 1950s bought more than it does today), and the subjects therefore did not believe themselves. The $1 payment, on the other hand, signified honest and fair behavior and compensation. When only paid $1, subjects inferred honesty in their own behavior.

Bem (1965) sought to show this effect more directly in his laboratory. Because the monetary honesty signals are confounded with other symbolism in real life, Bem had to "raise the stimuli from birth in the laboratory". He first asked subjects to rate cartoons in terms of funniness. Then he trained subjects, with completely different stimuli, to lie or speak the truth, depending upon whether a green or amber light flashed in front of them. Subjects learned in this way that they were honest and trustworthy only in front of the amber light. Finally, subjects were asked to say that some cartoons, previously rated as not funny, actually were funny. When they did this, sometimes the "lie light" was on, sometimes the "truth light" was on for what they thought were random reasons. The result? "Seven of the eight subjects were persuaded to a greater extent by comments made in the presence of the truth light than by comments made in the presence of the lie light" (Bem, 1965, p. 215).

This inference may be questioned, however. Two of the seven did not change a statistically significant amount, if alpha = 0.05. One subject changed only 1 millimeter in the mean markings on the 100 millimeter scale, a difference that may be attributable to pencil sharpness or some other variable more trivial than self-perception. And yet a fourth member of the seven had his data selectively revised because he made "two incorrect overt statements," a comment not elaborated. Thus only three of the eight subjects, fewer than half, showed the self-perception effect unambiguously. Thus, although this study superbly illustrates the logic of the self-perception alternative to dissonance theory, its empirical status is more ambiguous. Maslach (1971) and Kiesler & Munson (1975) report several failures to replicate it, which may or may not imply invalidity.

Evaluation

As befits an enormously provocative and heuristic theory such as self-perception, this theory has generated a wide variety of criticisms. It has also generated a large number of studies in areas other than attitude change, suggesting at least a continuing heuristic utility.

The two criticisms most damaging to self-perception theory are quite different. The first is conceptual. Greenwald (1975) showed that self-perception theory, like dissonance theory, can account for almost any empirical outcome observed. This fact was driven home in dramatic and embarrassing fashion when the two most highly-regarded journals in social psychology almost simultaneously published articles, each by well-respected experts on attitude change, that formulated opposite interpretations of the two theories (Ross & Schulman, 1973; Snyder & Ebbesen, 1972).

The second criticism of self-perception theory that seems damaging in spite of the impossibility of truly disconfirming the theory because the theory only applies "to the extent that internal cues are weak or ambiguous", is the accumulation of evidence that the "behaviors cause attitudes" hypothesis is not viable when dealing with certain circumstances. Although many laboratory studies dealing with trivial topics have shown behaviors leading to attitudes, Taylor (1975) has shown that self-perception theory does not apply when the attitudes involved are important. This conclusion has been corroborated in several survey studies using the more sophisticated new technology for interpreting survey results that often allows researchers to make "causal" inferences. It has now been shown that for attitudes on topics such as self-concept, outgoingness, political preferences, religion, and alcohol and drug use, attitudes rather consistently "cause" behaviors (Andrews & Kandel, 1979; Bentler & Speckart, 1981; Jessor & Jessor, 1977; Kahle & Berman, 1979; Kahle, Klingel, & Kulka, 1981; Kahle, Kulka, & Klingel, 1980). This basic empirical phenomenon has been shown with different subject populations, by different researchers, in journals of different disciplines, with alternatively worded questions, over different and multiple time lags, and with different statistical techniques; hence, it appears to be fairly replicable and robust.

Attribution Theory

Theory Summary

In many respects attribution theory is not really one theory but rather a loose confederation of many different theories, many of which have very little to do with one another. Most theories of attribution begin with an interest in how the lay psychologist understands and explains behavior in daily life, particularly when these understandings are not "normatively correct". Nothing inherent in attribution as a concept dictates that it should be situation-oriented rather than person-oriented or interactive. Some work in attribution theory, for example, does indeed examine the person's contributions to attributions (e.g. Kelley, 1967). Most of the aspects of attribution theory that have attracted the attention of persuasion researchers, however, deal with situational influences on attributions. Some authors have institutionalized the focus on situations by purporting that the "fundamental attribution error" is the overestimation of the role of people in determining behavior and the underestimating of the importance of the situation (L. Ross, 1977). When applied to self-attributions, the logic of this brand of attribution theory suggests that situationally supplied attributions will change one's self-concept and consequently one's related attitudes. This view is, of course, hardly different from self-perception theory, which is itself one type of attribution theory. Yet another type of attribution theory concerned with persuasion deals with the attributions that an audience might make to a communicator and how those attributions would influence persuasion. For example, if a communicator apparently defends a vested interest, then the audience may experience more skepticism and respond less favorably to the communication's appeal. If Mobil Oil advocates an end to all taxation on the oil industry an audience might see less sincerity in the message and therefore be less influenced by it than if the message originated in the research of an advocate of consumer rights.

Research Examples

Two separate examples will be given of attribution research, one from the self-attribution literature and one from the other-attribution literature, because the types of experiments tend to differ considerably and because some controversy exists over the question of whether self-attributions and other-attributions are fundamentally the same, as Bem (1972) maintains, or are fundamentally different.

Self-attribution. Miller, Brickman, & Bolen (1975) illustrated the basic theory of self-attribution perhaps more clearly than the lie-light research, since their research goals were not distracted by any attempt to show the relationship between their own work and cognitive dissonance theory. They used three fifth-grade classrooms from Chicago as their three research conditions: attribution, persuasion, and control. The attribution group heard repeatedly over the course of a week that it was not litter-prone, although in fact on a pretest the littering behavior of it did not differ from the other two groups. For example, the class bulletin board displayed a large poster of a Peanuts cartoon character proclaiming, "We are Anderson's Litter-Conscious Class". And the teacher commended the class for not throwing candy wrappers on the floor of the auditorium. In the persuasion condition, the class heard of the evils of litterbugs. The teacher explained how auditorium litter could attract flies, endanger health and contribute to pollution. And a Peanuts poster in the class advised, "Don't litter". After eight days of this kind of divergent treatment, the three classes all received candy in a wrapper. Significantly more wrappers were placed in the classroom wastebasket by children in the attribution condition than by children in either the persuasion or the control condition. Two weeks later when children received wrapped puzzles as Christmas presents, the same results again occurred; more wrappers were properly disposed in the attribution class than in either the control or persuasion class, even though no attributions about littering had been offered in any of the classes during the intervening weeks. These results were interpreted as providing evidence that attributions are effective persuasion tools precisely because the persuasive intent of attribution is hidden.

Other Attributions. Eagly, Wood, & Chaiken (1978) discussed two types of bias, knowledge bias and reporting bias. In their experiment an example of a knowledge bias, which is the perception that a person's information is non-veridical, was an industrial attorney speaking on industrial waste disposal. The assumption would be that the attorney would not favor an environmentalist position. The flip side of the knowledge bias manipulation was an attorney who had volunteered to work for preserving forested land and for improved garbage disposal. The reporting bias, which refers to the speaker's willingness or lack of it to convey accurate information based on such factors as audience composition, was manipulated by describing the audience as comprised of members of "citizens for industrial growth" or "citizens for the environment". Supposedly industrial growth advocates would not favor environmentalism. Based on attribution theory, Eagly *et al.* proposed that an advocate of any position contrary to the anticipated bias would more effectively persuade the audience than an advocate of a position confirming the perceived bias. Their prediction was confirmed in the case of each type of bias. Situations with speakers advocating a position that might be perceived as counterattitudinal or as counteraudience tended to have a greater impact than situations dominated by proponents of the expected bias.

Evaluation

Many of the comments above directed at self-perception theory also apply to attribution theory in general, especially attribution theory dealing with self attributions. In addition, Kiesler & Munson (1975) have criticized attribution research as failing to generate studies contrasting attribution predictions with other attitude theory. Many attribution researchers are content to produce only demonstration models of research, proceeding on an intuitive basis to generate catchy but theoretically sparse studies, in contrast to the two studies we cited as examples of attribution theory, which apparently formulated *a priori* hypotheses implied by the theoretical orientation. In spite of the obvious heuristic value of attribution theory, many of its ostensibly main assumptions remain untested, especially as applied to attitude change (Oskamp, 1977).

Although neither of the studies cited as examples of attribution theory claim the extreme situationist position popularized by other attributionists, the dogma of situational autonomy in the determination of behavior persists in spite of the scant empirical evidence. When L. Ross (1977) claims to give "the evidence" he presents only 22 references to counteract 50 years of personality research and the thousands of studies. Of the 22 he calls 4 counter-theoretical, some are clearly only modestly germane, and many do not contain any data. Many of the studies cited to provide evidence of the unimportance of person factors have in fact only demonstrated that situation factors are important, not that person factors are unimportant. Nisbett & Wilson (1977) have shown that people often overlook the importance of ordinality in self-descriptions of the causes of behavior. Proving that ordinality is important, however, does not refute the significance of other factors. For example, proving that flame is necessary for fire does not refute that additionally oxygen is necessary for fire.

Certain methodologies may tend to obscure the significance of person factors relative to situation factors. Kahle (1980), for example, demonstrated that people often select situations based on the type of person they are. If in a true experiment people are randomly assigned to a situation, they may behave consistently with the demands of that situation rather than with the demands of their personality style; however, the inference that situations have more impact than personality on behavior would not be an externally valid inference from that experiment if the person would have avoided that situation unless forced to go to it by an experimenter.

Impression Management Theory

Theory Summary

Impression management theory (Tedeschi, Schlenker, & Bonoma, 1971) has been proposed as an alternative to dissonance theory (Festinger, 1957). It does apparently lead to empirical predictions that differ from dissonance predictions, and it cannot be readily subsumed by any restatements of dissonance theory. Impression management theory maintains that:

(1) subjects in typical dissonance experiments change their self-reports of attitudes in order to appear consistent and mentally healthy to the experimenter and that

(2) "behaviors intended to restore impressions of consistency will be emitted only when the individual believes the *observer* has perceived two actions as tacted and, further, as contradictory in their attribu-tional implications" (Tedeschi *et al.*, 1971, p. 690, italics as in original).

Contrary to the "intrapsychic" process of attitude change postulated by disso-nance theory, impression management asserts that creating the appearance of attitude change and cognitive consistency is an interpersonal tactic determined by social roles and norms. This focus on the interpersonal also differentiates impression management theory from self perception theory since self-perception theory's concern is with whether an actor's or actress's [role theory jargon terms] own behavior is tacted [not coerced], whereas impression management theory concerns itself with whether an actor or actress believes that an observer perceives that the actor's or actress's behavior is tacted.

Research Example

Several experiments have provided evidence consistent with impression management theory. Joseph, Gaes, & Tedeschi (1975) manipulated women's perceptions of the experimenter's attitude toward their counterattitudinal essays under conditions that would be expected to arouse dissonance. When subjects perceived that the experimenter agreed with their counterattitudinal essays or when they received no feedback concerning the experimenter's attitude, they changed their attitudes more in the direction of the counterattitudinal essays than when they perceived that the experimenter disagreed with their essays. In another study Schlenker (1975a) manipulated experimenter attractiveness and subjects' perceptions of the experimenter's attitude toward an unattractive group that they were to join following an initiation. As dissonance theory and impression management theory would predict, the women in this experiment liked the group they were to join more when an unattractive experimenter ex-pressed an unfavorable opinion toward the group than when an attractive experi-menter did the same thing; however, the opposite relationship held, which is only derivable from impression management theory, when the experimenter expressed a favorable opinion toward the group that the subjects were about to join. Both of these experiments suggest that tactics to enhance one's social image overrule restoration of cognitive consistency after counterattitudinal behavior.

Evaluation

Much of the research on impression management theory to date has isolated instances in which impression management theory ventures predictions that one cannot derive from dissonance theory or self-perception theory (Joseph, Gaes, & Tedeschi, 1975; Schlenker, 1974, 1975a, 1975b; Schlenker & Schlenker, 1975). Dissonance theory has also yielded accurate predictions which one could not derive from impression management theory. If dissonance-like experimental results were purely a "public spectacle", then one would not predict that on some occasions anonymous counterattitudinal acts would lead to attitude change (see Collins & Hoyt, 1972). One would not expect that a dissonance manipulation would influenece behavior in response to a mail solicitation un-associated with the experimenter several months after an experiment (Rokeach, 1973). Nor would one expect a dissonance manipulation to decrease alpha wave production (McMillen & Geiselman, 1974).

The study (Kahle, 1978) mentioned in the previous chapter showing that justification and self-esteem interact in a typical dissoance study also tested the impression management hypothesis that the attitude of the experimenter would influence attitude change. In that experiment the experimenter let slip his own attitude toward smoking after the counterattitudinal essay but before the post-test measurement of the dependent variable, the subject's attitude toward smoking. Confirming one prediction of impression management theory, the experimenter's attitude did influence the subject's self-reported attitude change as predicted by impression management theory. Subjects indicated a more favorable attitude toward smoking when the experimenter upheld the virtues of smoking ("The evidence that smoking causes cancer is just correlational and would only impress a second-rate scientist like a medical doctor, not a true scientist like a psychologist") than when the experimenter opposed smoking ("Everyone, even smokers, dislikes smoking").

A closer examination of this study, however, shows that impression management theory suffered damage at the hands of the study because the confirmation of the dissonance hypothesis and the confirmation of the impression management hypothesis were completely orthogonal. That is, both appeared but they did not interact with each other. If the impression management hypothesis that dissonance-like experimental results are obtained only when impression management tactics are evoked is correct, then the self-esteem by justification interaction should have been replaced by an experimenter attitude by justification interaction or by an experimenter attitude by justification by self-concept interaction. Neither effect was found.

A purely interpersonal theory of attitude change is hard pressed to explain the importance of self-concept in attitude change. Tedeschi *et al.* (1971) do not deny the possibility that personality variables may influence impression management, but they prefer to focus on individual differences that have clear interpersonal implications (e.g. Machiavellianism). Schlenker (1975a) failed to find a relationship between impression management and several interpersonal personality variables. Schlenker, Soraci, & Schlenker (1974) further speculated that, independent of self-esteem, all people will seek to advance positive self-presentations. The attitudinal mercenaries in the Kahle (1978) study, who changed their attitudes more when the pay increased, sacrificed their self-presentations at the expense of impression management theory.

Life Position Theory

Theory Summary

Although not often articulated in the social psychological literature, a theory of life position (e.g. geographic region of the country) as the source of attitudes frequently is implicit in the writings of demographers and other social scientists. For example, Duverger (1972) stated, "Women are generally more conservative than men" (p. 47). One national news magazine in the United States during the 1980 presidential election noted that "inexplicably" more women than men opposed Ronald Reagan. The author observed that women are more conservative and more enthralled with movie stars as evidence that they should support Reagan over Carter. Frequently something about a person's life position is given as an explanation for an attitude or an attitude change.

Research Example

A large number of reports of surveys of the public include implicit references to this type of theory. For example, Maykovitch (1975) points out three correlates of racial prejudice in the United States: age, education, and geographic region.

Evaluation

The idea that a person's life position is related to attitudes is beyond question. Age, sex, income, education, religion, geographic region, etc., have all reliably been shown to correlate with some attitudes. Until recently, however, the dictim that "correlation is not causation" has undermined the assertion that life position causes attitudes. Researchers have been unable to assign people to life situations randomly for the purposes of causal inference; hence, belief in the causal import of life situation variables has been a matter of faith. Now that many researchers accept the new methodology that enfranchizes nonlaboratory studies with the possibility of causal inference, the question of the significance of these variables can be addressed empirically. To know that life situation "causes" an attitude, however, only establishes the first step toward scientific understanding of the attitude. To argue that women oppose Reagan only initiates the investigation into the source of the attitude; the question of why still persists. Do women oppose Reagan because he opposes the Equal Rights Amendment, which would give women a constitutional basis for equality with men? Do women oppose Reagan because his militaristic views may lead to the death of their children? Do women oppose Reagan because he failed as an actor to become a star? Or do women oppose Reagan only in contrast to men, implying that the significant question is not why women oppose Reagan but why men support him. What is it about gender that would lead to divergent political views? Likewise, on other issues we may advance the proposition that identifying a life-situation correlate of attitudes only inaugurates the line of inquiry, it does not complete it. On the flip side we may question whether the fact that a background characteristic influences attitudes alters the psychological significance of that attitude (Allport, 1966).

Conclusion

All of the theories reviewed in the past two chapters have at least some supporting empirical evidence. Likewise, all of the theories have at least some shortcomings when evaluated. None of the theories, then, can be called completely "true" or "false". McGuire has procided an excellent evaluation of the state of theory in attitude research:

> [Attitude change theories] seem to have a rather peculiar career. Each has an appreciable *a priori* plausibility; each has given rise to intriguing predictions; each has provoked admirable research. In short, each deserves to be true. Unfortunately, none seems to have any great deal of empirical validity. Nevertheless, it seems to us that, in an area to which one of these theoretical approaches has been applied with persistence, the result of interaction between them and the data has been a clarification of the problem and an advance of the question. (McGuire, 1968, p. 271).

Given that neither person-oriented nor situation-oriented theories capture the entirety of attitude change processes, the Kahle (1978) study is especially important in that it illustrates how both a person-oriented theory, dissonance, and a situation-oriented theory, impression management, can significantly account for unrelated variance in the same study. Justification interacted with the self-esteem, as dissonance would predict, and the attitudes of the experimenter exerted a direct influence on the attitudes of the respondents, as impression management theory would predict. But the two processes were independent. This implies that both person-oriented and situation-oriented theories can make contributions to understanding attitudes and attitude change. Unlike the approach of trying to "prove" that one type of theory is right and the other wrong, the implication of the Kahle (1978) study would seem to be that we need to understand when and why one theory may do a better or worse job of predicting attitude change. It should not be assumed that all theories are inherently contradictory if they base predictions about the same event on entirely different information. If one researcher has a theory that flame causes fire and another proposes that oxygen is necessary for fire, the immediate reaction should not necessarily be that one of the theories is right, the other wrong. Most of the theories reviewed in these two chapters probably are partially right, probably capture part, but not all, of how attitudes change. Assuming that attitude change is complicated and multiply-determined seems highly justified at this point in time. Assuming that both person variables and situation variables influence attitudes appears to be almost an inevitable conclusion from the available research literature. Just as personality researchers through their dialectic have come to recognize that person influences and situation influences interact in the determination of behavior, it would seem reasonable to assume that attitudes depend upon interactive processes.

An illustrative study of interaction in the attitude literature may be helpful at this point. Warner & DeFleur (1969) obtained a general measure of attitudes toward blacks from a sample of college students. As a manipulation of the situation, they sent out to each subject one of eight different forms of a letter. These letters requested that the subjects agree or refuse to perform some subsequent behavior toward blacks, and this agreeing or refusing was the dependent variable. The letters varied in terms of social distance (e.g. dating a black versus donating 25c to a scholarship program for black students) and in terms of social constraint (assurance of anonymity versus promise of disclosure to the campus newspaper). As any good interactionist might expect, pre-existing attitudes played an important role in the determination of the outcome of the study. The relationship between attitudes and behaviors depended upon which subjects were responding and upon the situation. Under conditions of high social constraint in which social distance could be maintained, there was a significant correspondence between attitudes and behavior for the least prejudiced subjects. Under conditions of high social constraint in which social distance was reduced, there was a significant correspondence between attitudes and behavior for the most prejudiced subjects.

It thus appears that an adequate theory of attitude change must account both for person influences and for situational influences on attitudes and attitude change. Interaction has been displayed in several attitude change studies; hence, forcing the false dichotomy of person-oriented theory versus situation-oriented theory may be less useful than striving for a new dialectic of interactive theory that can simultaneously incorporate person and situation variables.

CHAPTER 4

An interactive theory of attitude change

WE now know that attitudes can change both as a function of the social situation (e.g. Lamm & Meyers, 1978) and as a function of purely personal activity (e.g. Tesser, 1978). We have learned that both societal demands (e.g. Tedeschi *et al.*, 1971) and cognitive activity (e.g. Wicklund & Brehm, 1976) play important roles in attitude change, yet no one theory adequately integrates both the internal and the external aspects of attitude change into a unified framework. This shortcoming is particularly ironic in light of the emphasis on person-situation interactions in the personality half of personality and social psychology, both in the historic, wide-range theories (Lewin, 1935, 1936) and in more recent, empirically-derived theories (e.g. Argyle & Little, 1972; Endler, 1975). Only recently has the interaction concept from personality crept into attitude theory explicitly (e.g. Romer, 1981). In this chapter a person-situation interactive theory of attitude change will be proposed, although the theory must be viewed as tentative and preliminary since many of its implications have yet to be researched.

One of the most sophisticated interactive theories in psychology, as well as one of the most sophisticated cognitive theories, is that of Jean Piaget (1976). Although this Swiss psychologist's theory deals with disciplines as wide-ranging as mathematics, philosophy, and biology, his primary identification and his greatest impact have been in developmental psychology. Except for moral development (Piaget, 1932), he bestowed scant attention on areas of social psychology, although several of his followers have studied social development (Shantz, 1975); furthermore, except for an occasional well-rounded scholar (e.g. Kelley, 1973), few social psychologists have examined his theory. Both of these omissions are unfortunate, since the implications of Piaget's theory, especially the nondevelopmental aspects of it such as the equilibration model, are enormous for social psychology. In this chapter we will explore some implications of Piagetian theory for the social psychology of attitudes.

Change Conditions and Functions of Attitudes

Piaget's theory is, of course, somewhat different from other interactive theories in social psychology. Interaction is more dynamic, complex, ongoing, and rapid than in many other theories. Its functions and mechanisms are more clearly described. Furthermore, the structures necessary for interaction have clearer definition. These differences will become evident as we explore the basic theory in this chapter and again in the final chapter, when we review the concept of interaction.

Adaptation

Equilibration model and the person. The primary function of attitudes and other social cognitions is adaptation. Piaget's theory has most articulately expressed the significance of adaptation in cognition. As noted in Chapter 1, in Piaget's view a function of cognition is to facilitate the process of adaptation to one's environment. "There is adaptation when the organism is transformed by the environment and when this variation results in an increase in the interchanges between the environment and itself which are favorable to preservation" (Piaget, 1952, p. 5). An organism is not adapting when those interchanges interfere with normal functioning. This transformation consists of equilibration with the environment via ongoing assimilation of new information into existing mental structures and via complementary ongoing accommodation of existing mental structures to incorporate new, discrepant information. Usually the two are held in balance, with neither the naive realism of extreme accommodation nor the autism of extreme assimilation dominating (Flavell, 1963). A complementary function of external adaptation is internal organization, which is the tendency to systematize processes into coherent, coordinated systems (see Flavell, 1963; Tomlinson-Keasey, Eisert, Kahle, Hardy-Brown, & Keasey, 1979). Adaptation and organization are the two functional invariants. A person absorbs external information and transforms both the information and himself or herself in such a way as to promote adaptation. For example, if I observe a "conservative" friend wearing a loud tie, I would need to accommodate my concept of conservatives or of my friend, perhaps viewing him as sometimes liberal.

Several key terms of this theory warrant definition. *Assimilation* is the process by which we seek "to transform perceptions to the point of rendering them identical to the appropriate thought, i.e. to previous schemes. To assimilate is thus to conserve and in a certain sense to identify" (Piaget, 1928, p. 142). It is the "fusion of a new object to an already existing schema" (Piaget, 1928, p. 143). The inevitable partner of assimilation is *accommodation*, which is the environment acting on the organism. If the schema is neither applied (assimilated) nor ignored, it is modified — accommodated. Assimilation and accommodation are the two components of *adaptation. Equilibration* is the key change mechanism in Piagetian theory and the process through which assimilation and accommodation are brought into a coordinated or equilibrated state. Note how this view of adaptation as passing from less to more stable equilibrium between the organism and the environment differs from the genetic hereditary view of environment yet is similar to it. In genetic heredity we inherit fixed structures (e.g. organs like the heart), whereas in cognition we develop structures; yet both have the function of adaptation.

Keeping straight the relationships among content, function, and structure fosters understanding of Piagetian theory. *Content* is the raw, uninterpreted data. The *functions* of cognition are adaptation and organization. Functions do not vary. The *structures* do vary throughout life with experience and with age. They are the "organizational properties of intelligence, organizations created through functioning and inferable from the behavioral contents whose nature they determine" (Flavell, 1963, p. 17).

Selye (1956) has provided an unusually poetic statement of the importance of social adaptation for life in general (pp. vii–viii, 127):

> Life is largely a process of adaptation to the circumstances in which we exist. A perennial give-and-take has been going on between one living being and another, ever since the dawn of life in the prehistoric oceans.
>
> But there is another type of evolution which takes place in every person during his own lifetime from birth to death: this is adaptation to the stresses and strains of everyday existence. Through the constant interplay between his mental and bodily reactions, man has it in his power to influence this second type of evolution to a considerable extent, especially if he understands its mechanism . . . We are just beginning to see that many common diseases are largely due to errors in our adaptive responses to stress, rather than to direct damage by germs, poisons, or other external agents. In this sense many nervous and emotional disturbances, high blood pressure, gastric and duodenal ulcers, certain types of rheumatic, allergic, cardiovascular, and renal diseases appear to be essentially *diseases of adaptation*. (italics as in original)

Equilibration Model and the Situation

The answer to the question, what is adaptive, depends upon the situation as well as the person. A trait or attitude that is adaptive in one situation may not be at all adaptive in another situation. For a boxer unrestrained physical aggression may be adaptive in the boxing ring but not adaptive at a cocktail party. All evolutionary predictions are applicable only to specific environments (Feinman, 1980). Although actors and actresses can be expected to behave as if they want to enhance their inclusive fitness, the mere fact of one success does not at all imply eternal success and certainly not cross-situational success. An irony of adaptation is that most people interact in many different environments; hence, most people probably deal with some situations more adaptively than others because of their differential skills and because of the cross-situational persistence of some attitudes. To the extent that one believes most traits are highly cross-situational, adaptation is necessarily decreased in some situations. Actors and actresses who succeed may be ones who select situations and roles most carefully to fit their characteristics or who develop high versatility and flexibility.

Equilibration, a process of adaptation, may be likened to steering a boat. The captain steers the boat in an approximate direction, hoping that the vessel will maintain a steady, forward course. Sometimes waves and winds will not interrupt (e.g. they are assimilated to the available schemata), other times they will disrupt or destroy the possibility of moving ahead satisfactorily at all. Likewise, equilibration tends to maintain a steady, forward course in normal conditions of inference but may go awry in unusual situations and not expedite adaptation. A good deal of research in social psychology has of late focused on these conditions in which the storms prevail in guiding cognition to uncharted regions (e.g. Kahneman & Tversky, 1973; Nisbett & Ross, 1980). The important point is that equilibration does imply stable forward progress, as with a moving boat, rather than static stagnation, as with an anchored boat. "Equilibration means a continual search for a better equilibrium rather than only a return to a previous equilibrium following some imbalance" (Inhelder, 1976, p. 5). Nevertheless, whether the final destination is utopia is a question for philosophers to argue.

The "environment" to which one adapts is multi-level. Of course, one adapts to one's culture and nation. One strives to fit in with others with shared systems of securing provisions and protection. One also adapts to more immediate social situations through occupying roles and following role prescriptions. Several discussions of social adaptation exist which address this genre of adaptation more thoroughly (e.g. Campbell, 1975, 1977; Insko et al., 1980); individual psychological adaptation, as well as individual biological adaptation, of course, also occurs. Optimal adaptation coordinates adaptation on all of these levels. Balancing adaptation on the various levels is one of the most difficult tasks people face. If the culture to which one adapts is a "sick" culture, the most successful multi-level adaptation may require some culturally maladaptive responses. People who oppose the cultural status quo may commit a maladaptive act culturally but behave very adaptively on an individual level. Rebels and reformers almost always face the difficult task of balancing the different levels of adaptation against each other.

Another important consideration about the environment concerns whether the environment of interest is the psychologically perceived environment, as some theorists have suggested (e.g. Lewin, 1936), or whether the actual physical environment enters into the interaction predominantly, as others have suggested (Kantor, 1959). Piaget sees this issue as a type of false dichotomy. Both the actual physical environment and the psychological environment are important in both the digestion of food and of ideas. When we eat food, the actual physical properties influence us. If we eat starch, the impact on us will certainly differ from the impact if we eat protein. Therefore, the physical reality of the external world does influence us. Nevertheless, as soon as food or information enters us, we begin to transform it into shapes more useful to us, whether biochemically, as in the case of food, or cognitively, as in the case of information. As ideas are assimilated into existing structures, their new structures may bear no more resemblance to the original ideas than blood or bones do to steak or beans. The psychologically interpreted environment will determine the subsequent behavior of the individual, but the physical environment's differences from the psychological environment may provide feedback if the perceived environment and the real environment differ too greatly or in crucial ways. As Bem philosophized, "The real world will bite back soon enough" (Bem, 1972, p. 25).

Presumably our knowledge tends to reflect the external reality of a psychological situation better as time goes on, but enough shortcomings call into question our perceptions that a completely accurate picture of the physical environment is unlikely. For example, we know from attribution research that many of our processes of social inference are faulty (Nisbett & Ross, 1980). We also know that we have a finite number of ways to perceive, even though far many more ways may in principle exist. For example, we have discovered X-rays and ultra-violet rays by using new perceptual methods. Other perceptual methods will undoubtedly one day be discovered, and these methods may help us to observe things that we have never before observed. Finally, what we perceive is constantly changing. Whenever we interact in a social context, what we do influences both our perception of the environment and the environment itself. "In order to know objects, the subject must act on objects, and therefore transform them." (Piaget, 1976, p. 12).

Attitude change. The concept of attitudes as adaptations provides a particular view of human nature. Humans and their attitudes are not exclusively reactive, although they do in part develop reactively. The active process of equilibration does not replace or deny learning and maturation; rather, these more traditional processes are subsumed into a broader human process that also allows for dynamic growth of an open system. By "open system" it is implied that attitudes continually change through assimilation, accommodation, and organization as new information is obtained and old information is enhanced or clarified. Attitudes and cognitions are not static and fixed but rather are often growing and being adjusted. When we measure an attitude, we are not capturing the exact external position of the attitude, as a picture of a statue might. Rather, the measured attitude is better conceived as a single frame from a motion picture of an active object. As we interact with an attitude object more and more, our attitude becomes more complex. For example, an attitude toward a best friend is more complex than an attitude toward a casual acquaintance. Since attitudes serve the individual and because the adaptation is of the individual, attitudes also develop actively as the individual develops. The individual actively filters societal and cultural demands, refining and redefining attitudes in the process, in order to enhance their adaptive worth. Attitude formation and change, like all of human development, is a life-span task (see Runyan, 1978).

Adaptation can involve both fitting the person to the environment and fitting the environment to the person. When people build houses, for example, they are adapting the environment to fit themselves biologically (Bowers, 1973). Likewise, attitudes may at times involve adapting a social environment to fit the person. For example, a person who likes parties may plan a variety of frequent parties, thus developing a more complex concept of parties and therefore a more complex attitude. The important point is that, in part because the various levels (societal, role, and individual) often imply different adaptive strategies, in part because conflicting attitudes even within one level may dictate opposite solutions, and in part because adaptation may involve assimilation or accommodation of either the person or the situation, adaptation and attitude formation and change cannot ever be solely passive or unidirectional processes. An implication of this view definitely is *not* that the only way to reach equilibrium when an attitude of "dislike a social problem" exists is to change an attitude. Equilibrium can also be restored by correcting the social problem. More typically, adaptation involves changing both the person and the environment. When the person acts on the environment and learns the consequences, both the person and the environment have thus been changed. Descriptions of Piagetian theory as strictly mental (e.g. Sampson, 1981) are simply wrong. It is quite common for people to select or change situations in order to achieve equilibrium. Kahle (1980) found that people with an internal locus of control were more likely to select a situation where they could display skill, and people who selected the skill situation were more likely to cheat once there, creating the appearance of skillfulness.

How, then, can we summarize the process of attitude change? Attitudes are constructed dialectically via assimilation of environmental information and influences into schemata, via accommodation of schemata to environmental information and influences, and via the internal organization of these schemata into unified states of equilibrium. When one state of equilibrium demonstrably fails or seems inadequate to balance all salient information, change to a more complex state of equilibrium is likely. The process is constructivist rather than passive, and it is thoroughly dialectical. Continual thesis-antithesis tensions spiral toward new syntheses of attitudinal information. What are some of these tensions? Assimilation-accommodation, adaptation-organization, structuring-structured, person-situation, and probability-logic are key polarities. The resulting abstractions about adaptation that emerge from these dialectical processes are the structures that have important psychological and behavioral consequences.

Some clarifications. At this point it may be useful to identify one of the major divergences between our contribution and that of another recent book also dealing with adaptation, *Adaptation to Life*. Vaillant (1977) reported on a longitudinal psychiatric study of the lives of several graduates from an Eastern university. The cornucopia of data he summarized led him to several significant inferences about adaptation. The main difference between his book and the present theory has to do with the concept of adaptive development. In his lucid book Vaillant (1977) considers adaptation to be a virtual synonym of defensiveness and of wealth, whereas we define it as equilibration with the environment.

In the present view defensiveness is less central to understanding psychological functioning, and wealth beyond some point may well be nonadaptive in this sense of the word. First, it increases the complexities and some of the worries of life, perhaps leading to diseases like heart attack and ulcers. Second, long-term inequitable distribution of wealth may eventually lead to uprisings against the wealthy, which would be more adaptive for the nonwealthy than the rich. The maladaptive cultural implications may eventually overtake the short-term individual pleasures.

A second recent usage of adaptation from which the present usage should be distinguished is that of sociobiology (Wilson, 1975). Sociobiology is far less concerned with uniquely human behavior than the present theory. Wilson, for example, was only able to conceive of four differences between the social behavior of homo sapiens and other primates, one of which is continuous sexual activity through the menstrual cycle (Wilson, 1975, p. 552). In the present view the differences between human and nonhuman social behavior are sufficiently numerous and important to defer listing them for another book.

A more fundamental difference has to do with the meaning of adaptation. Wilson's social adaptation is literal. For him the purpose of social life is to perpetuate DNA. He intends to convey a literal concept of natural selection of genes in his theory of social behavior. In the present view social adaptation is a metaphor or a heuristic concept, not a literally genetic force. By following the genetic aspects of adaptation literally, Wilson misses the remarkable adaptive flexibility humans attain from intellect, from savvy. He also seems oblivious to the fact that physical environment is no longer the key obstacle to survival for most people. With rising militarism, we may well see more human survival destroyed by attitudes than by physical environment restraints such as bad weather. Most of our genes adapt us particularly well to hunter-gatherer societies, he says, but he missed the full import of the fact that our flexibility and intellect, which are only in an obscure sense genetic, probably contribute more to our adaptation in contemporary society than the hunter-gatherer skills provided by our genes.

Another philosophically consequential point to pursue here is that adaptation never involves actually arriving at the ultimate equilibrium. More to learn always remains. Ultimate adaptation cannot even be defined, let alone assessed or achieved. At some points the state of equilibrium may be more stable, but it eventually will encounter anomalies that necessitate accommodation and equilibration.

One final way to clarify our concept of adaptation may be to contrast it with several of its synonyms. *Adjustment* implies only changing the self to fit the environment, whereas adaptation implies an interactive process of continual changing of both the environment and the self. *Coping* and *survival* usually imply more of a minimal level of achievement, a slight surpassing of the lower threshold. *Adaptation*, on the other hand, implies optimal levels of equilibration under the circumstances.

Abstraction

In addition to adaptation, a second function of cognition, including social cognition, is abstraction. Piaget has noted that "abstraction consists in adding relations to perceptual data and not merely in deducing such relations from them. If we recognize the existence of common properties such as square or round, large or small, 'flat' or three dimensional, etc., it means that we construct schemas which are related to the actions of the subject as well as to the properties of the object . . . In a still more general way the common properties upon which a classification is based are 'common', to the extent that the action of the subject makes them common, as well as to the extent that these objects are suitable to be made common" (Inhelder & Piaget, 1964, p. 247).

Abstraction works in concert with adaptation. Adaptation abstractions emerge continuously from a process of assimilation, accommodation, organization, and integration of environmental information and thought, in order to promote interchanges between the individual and the environment that, from the individual's perspective, are favorable to preservation and optimal functioning. The abstraction in a sense provides a prototype from which behaviors are manufactured. For example, under an attitude "I like ice tea" a person may store a number of abstract statements about what must be done when faced with ice tea. In another sense abstraction probably characterizes attitude change; that is, much change involves movement to a new abstraction.

Self definition

A major way in which we define who we are and what we are about has to do with our attitudes and other social cognitions. And self-concept, in turn, is pivotal in this context from a variety of theoretical perspectives, including social adaptation theory (Aronson, 1969; Block, 1971; Douvan, 1974; Erikson, 1968; Rogers, 1959). The self-concept continues to generate an enormous amount of research in psychology. The fact that Wylie's (1979) most recent book on the topic has over 80 pages in the bibliography alone underscores this assertion. And that book only purports to deal with theory and research (not methodology, which is her speciality) "on selected topics" related to the self-concept. When we formulate our attitudes we give definition to our selves and how it is that we differ from other people.

In one sense self-definition is simply another type of social cognition, of adaptation abstraction. We develop self-concepts to summarize prior dealings with the environment. The self-concept then summarizes strategies for future behavior.

Several studies have shown how these self-defining adaptation abstractions function. Kahle, Kulka, and Klinger (1980) showed that the self-esteem of adolescents leads to styles of interacting successfully or unsuccessfully with others. They found that adolescents with low self-esteem subsequently developed problems interacting with others. This sequence is, of course, the opposite of self-perception theory's prediction. Eisert & Kahle (1982) similarly demonstrated that self-evaluation by adolescents leads to social comparisons. That is, the information-gathering strategies employed reflected the self-evaluation of the adolescent boys in the study rather than the opposite, which other theorists would predict. It is thus clear that abstractions (about how a person can himself or herself adapt) influence social behavior.

In another sense the self-system concept raises the issue of structuralism. The self-system is a type of structure, in the Piagetian sense of the word, within a theory that has been called structuralist. In psychology, contemporary structuralism has primarily been contrasted with atomistic theories that reduce wholes to their prior elements. Many other areas of knowledge besides psychology also have prominent structuralist theories. An example of a structure from mathemathics would be the concept of integers. The existence of integers does not constitute a set of isolated, accidental discoveries of different individual integers that eventually were unified into a whole. Rather than existing apart from one another, the integers are unified and interfunctioning elements that have collective properties and even existence quite apart from the individual elements. Thus integers coalesce into a structure. Piaget has clarified the concept of structure with this preliminary definition:

> A structure is a system of transformations. Inasmuch as it is a system and not a mere collection of elements and their properties, these transformations involve laws: the structure is preserved or enriched by the interplay of its transformation laws, which never yield results external to the system nor employ elements that are external to it. In short, the notion of structure is comprised of three key ideas: the idea of wholeness, the idea of transformation, and the idea of self-regulation. (Piaget, 1968, p. 5).

The self-system and the attitudes that constitute it may thus be considered an integrated self-view that includes strategies of self-maintenance and for self-change through assimilation, accommodation, and organization. The self-system guides both one's operations and one's rhythmic functions toward an ostensibly ever-better level of equilibration.

Evidence Related to Several Hypotheses of Social Adaptation

All good theories imply an infinite number of empirical manifestations, and social adaptation theory likewise implies numerous empirical outcroppings, the discovery of which is limited only by the resourcefulness of the theory's user. A number of specific differences between social adaptation theory and other theory's predictions are, of course, detailed throughout this book. Other people have also gone to great lengths to accentuate strategies for testing adaptation theory and the equilibration model (e.g. Moessinger, 1978). And many researchers have directly and successfully tested both social adaptation theory (e.g. Eisert & Kahle, 1982; Kahle *et al.*, 1980; Kahle *et al.*, 1981) and the equilibration model (e.g. Kuhn, 1972; Silverman, 1979; Tomlinson-Keasey *et al.*, 1979). In this section a sampling of hypotheses will be considered, along with empirical evidence that is relevant. Explicitly excluded will be studies designed specifically to test social adaptation theory or the general equilibration model, which have been and/or will be elaborated elsewhere.

Empirical Evidence Regarding the Person in Social Adaptation

One hypothesis about the person is that *schemata are used to structure information*. Tesser (1978) has authored a fascinating review of the literature related to this hypothesis. A good deal of empirical evidence supports this hypothesis. For example, people tend to distort social information systematically, in order to force it to conform more clearly with prior stereotypes (e.g. Bem & Allen, 1974; Markus, 1977; Passini & Norman, 1966; Schank & Abelson, 1975), as the principle of assimilation would suggest. For example, in the 1968 American presidential election, supporters of Hubert Humphrey perceived their candidate as having a similar view to their own on the war in Vietnam (a major issue in that election) regardless of their view (Granberg & Brent, 1974). Likewise, empirical evidence also suggests that *increasing experience with a social object results in more complete and accurate schemata*, implying that both sides of adaptation, including accommodation, function in social cognitive realms. For example, Sistrunk & McDavid (1971) found greater attitude change for women when masculine topics were presented, whereas men changed more on feminine topics. If we assume that women have more advanced schemata on feminine topics and men on masculine topics, then this suggests that more accommodation occurs when attitudinal schemata are less equilibrated.

Organization has also been demonstrated empirically. Tesser (1978) cites studies demonstrating that within a social schema domain mere thought fosters greater consistency, polarization, and balance (in Heider's sense of the word). For example, Sadler & Tesser (1973) showed that thinking about a liked person increases the liking, and thinking about a disliked person increases disliking. Balance and its empirical support (e.g. Insko, 1981), of course, also bear to a considerable extent on the hypothesized process of equilibration.

Empirical Evidence Regarding the Situation in Social Adaptation

One hypothesis of social adaptation theory is that our attitudes serve to help us adapt to our environment. Lieberman (1965) revealed that the attitudes of factory workers grow with the demands of their jobs. Workers elected to represent the union as shop stewards developed attitudes to serve them in this role, supporting the union more and the management less. On the other hand, workers who became foremen adapted to this situation by developing pro-management attitudes.

One interesting and highly testable hypothesis of social adaptation theory is that *truth-seeking may not always be the foremost goal.* Sometimes adaptation may dictate skirting the truth. Nisbett & Ross (1980) present a thought experiment which illustrates how people may ignore normatively correct information. Imagine that you want to buy a car. You narrow your choices to a Volkswagen and a Ford. After consulting with a reputable consumer magazine you learn that engineers consider the Volkswagen to be superior and that a survey of 50,000 car owners revealed much greater satisfaction with the Volkswagen. The day before you purchase your new car, however, you meet your dear Uncle Harry. When you describe your decision to buy a Volkswagen, Uncle Harry shouts, "Not a Volkswagen! I have one, and it's the worst car imaginable. First the heater didn't work. Then the brakes went out. Then it threw a rod. Everything has gone wrong, it seems. The car has been in the repair shop more than in my driveway. Please, please do *not* buy a Volkswagen." Which car would you buy? Most people say the Ford, but that would not be the rational choice, according to Nisbett and Ross, because 50,000 people made their decisions based on more information than one Uncle Harry. But it is only incorrect if truth is the issue in selecting the better car. If social adaptation is the goal, preventing Uncle Harry from taunting you when the Volkswagen malfunctions may be more adaptive than purchasing a slightly better car mechanically.

A recent review by Hogarth (1981) suggests that many of the examples of normatively incorrect judgments expressed in social information processing fail to distinguish between discrete and continuous events. The experiments involve discrete events, but most of our social judgments rely on feedback and continuous information. Wrong judgments often lead to consequences that modify generalizations, according to the research Hogarth cites.

Empirical Evidence Regarding Interactions in Social Adaptation

A thorough discussion of the concept of interaction will be presented in Chapter 10. Nevertheless, at least one study that clearly illustrates the value of an interactive perspective in attitude change research will be presented here. Romer (1981) constructed a structural equation model to examine the interaction between self-esteem and length of attitude message. He did indeed find a model that fits with an interactionist perspective on attitude change.

Social Adaptation and Other Theories of Attitude Change

At this point perhaps the best mechanism to clarify the nature and implications of social adaptation theory and its view of attitudes as adaptation abstractions would be to compare and contrast it with several other theories of attitude change along certain salient dimensions.

Person-Oriented Theories

The most obvious difference between person-oriented theories and social adaptation theory has to do with the importance of the situation, which is underplayed in person-oriented theories. Admittedly Heider discussed situations extensively, Festinger did experiments that manipulated situations, McGuire has elsewhere at least considered situations (see Chapter 5), and some of the functional theory change conditions appear to invoke situations. However, for all of these theories the situation is seen as a psychological construct rather than external structure existing in the environment with some reality apart from the perceiver or as an interactive structure.

At least dissonance and balance theory begin from a neo-Lewinian Gestalt perspective. Clearly social adaptation theory and Gestalt theory have divergent perspectives on the relationship between perceptual forms and transformations: "In Gestalt psychology, the perceptual forms that are said to have a Gestalt character are, generally speaking, static. But it is unwise to view an intellectual current exclusively in terms of its origin; it should be seen in its flow" (Piaget, 1968, p. 11). Just as our concepts are actively changing and adapting to new "realities", likewise the "realities" are continually becoming new, continually being transformed.

A third difference between social adaptation and a straight person orientation becomes most evident when examining conversion experiences (see Flay, 1978). Most person-oriented theories, except for functional theory, cannot explain radical attitudinal shifts, as when the son of a Baptist minister joins Hare Krishna or when a Grand Cyclops of the Ku Klux Klan suddenly converts to a pro-black, pro-union perspective, as in the case of C.P. Ellis (Terkel, 1980). Notions of balance, harmony, or cognitive response usually imply that a new piece of information or two should fine-tune an attitude, not shift it to a different clef, different instrument, and different key. In social adaptation theory, on the other hand, a catastrophic change in the perception of the most adaptive response or of the situational structure could lead to a commensurately radical reinterpretation of social reality.

A final major difference between person-oriented theories and social adaptation theory has to do with the concept of function. Many person-oriented theories postulate no functions of attitudes or one function of attitudes. Katz (1960) has postulated four functions, making his theory comprehensive but untestable. By postulating one primary function, social adaptation theory limits the possible accounts of outcomes and therefore is indeed testable in that regard.

All in all, the similarities between social adaptation theory and person-oriented theory probably outweigh the differences. Both postulate an active information processor. Both object to atomism. Both believe that the person is important in attitude change processes. Only the special cases mentioned above involve major differences. In many instances, the predictions based on equilibration (Inhelder & Piaget, 1958; Piaget, 1924, 1950) and balance (Heider, 1958) may not differ.

Situation-Oriented Theories

If the obvious difference between person-oriented theories and social adaptation theory has to do with the importance of the situation, then it is equally obvious that the major difference between situation-oriented theory and social adaptation theory has to do with the importance of the person, which is underplayed in situation-oriented theory. Admittedly some aspects of some situation-oriented theories at least consider the possibility of the importance of the person, but by and large the active part a person plays in forming and changing his or her own attitudes is ignored in situation-oriented theory. The compelling evidence that people actively construe and construct their worlds (see Mischel, 1973b; Bowers, 1973) simply does not receive adequate theoretical or empirical attention from situation-oriented theorists.

Conditioning theory. Conditioning theories most explicitly attend to the external features of attitude change and ignore the "black box" of the human mind. The assumption that conditioning always occurs "without awareness, without cognition" is without adequate empirical support. More than just stimuli or contingency pairings influence the form of attitudes. Of course people note reinforcements and of course people develop behavioral patterns that are reflective of previously-observed stimulus-response bondings. But those reinforcements and bondings are filtered through structures that people have when approaching a situation. The meaning and significance of stimuli and reinforcements will alter how they influence behavior.

The social learning approach to attitudes, if it is a unified conditioning approach at all, differs from adaptation theory in the root metaphor it selects to elaborate. It takes an anti-mentalist behaviorism jargon and pretends that inserting cognition into the theory does not alter the integrity of the theory. Behaviorism was founded, however, to eradicate mentalism. A "cognitive behaviorist" is inherently contradictory, like jumbo shrimp or hereditary sterility. One can only claim that a small number of words mean the opposite of what they did a few years ago before one must ask whether an entirely new vocabulary would not be less confusing than a vocabulary in which nothing means what it does.

Self-perception theory. Social adaptation theory is essentially the opposite of self-perception theory. Social adaptation assumes that adaptation abstractions guide behavior, whereas self-perception theory assumes that attitudes are epiphenomenal products of behaving. In at least three direct attempts to assess whether social adaptation theory or self-perception constitutes a more viable explanation of attitude functioning, the evidence seems to support social adaptation theory (Kahle & Berman, 1979a; Kahle et al., 1980; Kahle et al., 1981). Self-perception theory, nevertheless, has some interesting contributions in the field of attribution theory, as will be discussed in the next chapter. In Chapter 8 we will additionally probe the attitude-behavior question more carefully, which is an obvious area of discrepancy between social adaptation theory and self-perception theory.

Impression management theory. The basic metaphor of impression management theory is plausible within social adaptation theory. Certainly people from time to time try to appear consistent, often for quite adaptive reasons. By claiming that always trying to appear consistent is the motive behind all attitude change, however, impression management theory oversteps its plausible areas of application. It is doubtful that creating the appearance of mental health is the fundamental motive behind all attitude change. For example, attitude change can occur even in anonymous situations (Collins & Hoyt, 1972). Even emotions that seem peculiarly social, such as embarrassment, can develop in social isolation (Apsler, 1975). Thus, it would appear that projecting certain images may foster some beneficial adaptation, but attitudes do involve more than just appearances.

Life situations. Life situations cannot account for all of our attitudes, but they do help define the limitations on adaptation. They help to show what attitudes and social systems may or may not be invoked when seeking to adapt; hence, understanding the person's life situation and his or her cognitions about it should generally improve predictions about attitude change.

Additional Attitude Change Theories

Two additional theories of attitude change, which have not yet been discussed here, require some comments because of their ostensible similarity to social adaptation theory.

Social judgment theory. In some respects social judgment theory is quite similar to social adaptation theory. It appears to be an interactive theory, which is why it was not discussed in Chapters 2 or 3. It uses the concept of assimilation. Attitudes are even, in a sense, viewed as abstractions.

The key to understanding attitude change within social judgment theory is understanding what an attitude is. Sherif and Sherif have defined it:

> Operationally, an attitude may be defined as the individual's set of categories for evaluating a stimulus domain, which he has established as he learns about that domain in interaction with other persons and which relate him to various subsets within the domain with varying degrees of positive or negative affect (Sherif & Sherif, 1967, p. 115).

A "set of categories" in social judgment theory is quite similar to an abstraction in social adaptation theory. In social judgment theory an attitude may or may not be changed as a function of a persuasive communication, depending upon which of three classes of categories the communication falls into: latitude of acceptance, latitude of rejection, or latitude of non-commitment. Each of these categories defines the possible responses, relative to prior attitudes, that a person can give to new information.

Change of an attitude in social judgment theory is predicted from a metaphor that is based in psychophysical judgment literature. When two things are quite similar, but not identical, and we are asked to make a physical judgment about their relationship, we tend to judge them to be even more similar than they are. When things are quite different, we tend to judge them as being even more different than they are. Sherif & Sherif predict the same response in judging social information such as attitude change appeals. Appeals that fit into our categories of acceptable or non-committal are assimilated into existing categories. Appeals that are quite different and fall into our rejection categories tend to be contrasted. That is, we tend to view statements that we reject as being even more extreme and less desirable than they in fact are. At least some empirical evidence supports social judgment theory (e.g. Sherif, Sherif, & Nebergall, 1965).

In spite of the obvious similarities between social judgment theory and social adaptation theory a number of salient differences obviously contrast (force the accommodation of?) the two theories. The first has to do with the difference between *contrast* and *accommodation*. A discrepant statement that falls into the latitude of rejection, according to social judgment theory, will create contrast effects that will drive the attitude more toward the initial attitude's direction, drive it away from the position advocated by the communication, or foster misperception of the advocated position. In social adaptation theory, on the other hand, a discrepant communication, to the extent that it is perceived as accurately representing reality, will foster change in the direction of the discrepant communication. The target of the change appeal will try to reform his or her relevant abstractions to account for the new information.

This difference between accommodation and contrast, in spite of the similarity of assimilation in the two theories, implies that in social judgment theory no true communication between involved disputants can ever take place. Once it is established that someone's views on the topic at hand fall within your latitude of rejection, you will cease to listen open-mindedly to that person and will perhaps become more radical in response to more information. In social adaptation theory, on the other hand, miscommunication is not inevitable. Genuine dialogue, and even conversion, is possible in certain circumstances.

Another difference between social judgment and social adaptation is that the basic metaphor is quite different. Social judgment theory, like balance theory, begins with a psychophysical metaphor. Balance theory, however, embraces the common sense of psychophysics, whereas social judgment theory follows the counter-intuitive notions from psychophysics of the illusions from assimilation and contrast. Social adaptation theory, of course, looks to biology for its metaphor.

Finally, *interaction* in social judgment theory means that a person is influenced by and *cognitively* transforms the attitude object. Both of these possibilities also exist in social adaptation theory, but in addition it is recognized that people *physically* change attitudinal objects as well.

Adaptation level theory. Helson (1959, 1964) has proposed yet another theory based on a metaphor (my term, not Helson's) from perception, this one a theory that explicitly uses the concept of adaptation. According to Helson, the adaptation level one is experiencing at a given moment is the weighted geometric mean of all stimuli impinging on one at that given time — the neutral point of all relevant polarities facing one at a given moment. Helson's theory is basically a conformity one, in which the prediction is that people will try to conform with the average attitude in their environment. In this sense, Helson's use of the word is quite different from the present usage of adaptation. Perhaps a phrase like homeostasis-level would have been more appropriate. In addition, as a situation-oriented theory, the perspective underplays the importance of the person, leading to another important difference between social adaptation and adaptation-level theories.

Much of the early research on adaptation-level theory tested inappropriate hypotheses and was not well-conceived (Insko, 1967). More recently a number of clever studies have tested adaptation-level hypotheses with some success (e.g. Dermer, Cohen, Jacobsen, & Anderson, 1979). In one such study Brickman, Coates, & Janoff-Bulman (1978) investigated the effects of winning a lottery on happiness. Conventional American wisdom would suggest that economic success breeds happiness (although one could argue that "money cannot buy happiness"). Lottery winners took significantly less pleasure away from mundane post-lottery events when compared to a control group. Since lottery winners are selected at random, this study represents a shrewd use of a natural experiment. The study was interpreted as providing evidence that an upward shift in the adaptation level of happiness, or a redefinition of average, homeostatic joy results from winning; thus, other events seemed less happy by comparison.

Conclusion

We can thus see that social adaptation theory proposes an interactive theory with many predictions that differ from other theories currently being debated. The theory clearly is testable, but the exciting possibilities for research have only begun to be explored. It clearly redefines some of the important issues in attitude research, and it places other issues in new light. For example, the personality and persuasibility debate seems more important when viewed from interactive theory than when viewed from at least some other perspectives. In the next chapter we will examine research on topics that influence the person side of interactions.

CHAPTER 5

Scope of persons: personality and persuasibility

THE interface between the study of individual differences and the study of susceptibility to social influence has long interested psychologists (McGuire, 1968c). Indeed, Binet (1900) worked in this area prior to his investigation of intelligence. After the Yale Communication and Attitude Change Program published a volume (Hovland & Janis, 1959) of research on the slightly narrower topic of personality and persuasibility, a rash of studies testing various implications of the Yale research program emerged.

Much of this long-standing interest in personality and persuasibility, aside from the intrinsically interesting nature of the topic, stems both from the practical applications that can be derived from the research (e.g. Bettinghaus, 1968; Gordon, 1971) and from the theoretical implications of the research both for theories of personality and for theories of the social psychology of attitude change. A paradox exists, however, in that, in spite of frequent application of personality and persuasibility research to theories about other psychological phenomena, few theorists have had the courage, or audacity, to fit personality and persuasibility research into a comprehensive theory capable of accounting for the often confusing and complicated results of that research. The one notable, contemporary exception to this rule can be found in the theorizing of McGuire (1968a, b, c). Unfortunately, McGuire's interactive theory has received neither the experimental nor the critical attention it warrants, an oversight that this chapter will attempt partially to rectify, at least in the second case.

Personality is a major part of the person component of the person half of person-situation interactions. In a sense the topic of personality and persuasibility deals with a type of person-person interaction that transforms the person-situation interaction into a three way interaction. Whether conceived as a two-way or a three-way interaction, the concept of the individual difference side of interaction will be the focus of attention here.

This chapter divides its exploration of personality and persuasibility research into four sections. First, we will explicitly consider the relationship between social adaptation and personality. Section two briefly summarizes McGuire's interactive theory of personality and persuasibility. The third section will examine various personality variables that have been correlated with persuasibility in an attempt to discover how well social adaptation theory and McGuire's theory can account for the available data on personality and persuasibility. The final section will comment generally on McGuire's formulation as related to social adaptation.

Social Adaptation and Personality

Many theorists (e.g. Mischel, 1968; Nisbett, 1980) have disparaged the area of personality research in recent years, although others have voiced often-convincing defenses, both theoretically (e.g. Alker, 1972; Allport, 1966; Bem, 1979; Bowers, 1973; Wachtel, 1973) and empirically (e.g. Block, 1971, 1977; Costa & McCrae, 1980; Epstein, 1979, 1980; Kahle et al., 1980; Leon, Gillum, Gillum, & Gouse, 1979; Underwood, 1981). The main criticisms seem circumvented by recognizing that personality is interactive. In many ways the same logical forces that lead one to conclude that attitude is an interactive concept also lead one to conclude that personality is an interactive concept. In fact, the order may be the other way around since interactionism has been far more widely discussed in personality publications than in attitude publications in recent years (cf. Endler, 1975). Whichever the direction of influence, it is clear that many personality traits are quite similar to attitudes in their methods of measurement, epistemological status, and psychological functions. Both are abstractions about adaptation. Both are types of social cognition. Both follow the general equilibration model. Both are modified through assimilation, accommodation, and organization. Even many individual differences that ostensibly do not fit the mold of social cognitive variables, such as age and sex, may very well exert their primary behavioral influence as a function of their social cognitive aspects. Kohlberg (1966), for example, has shown how it is possible to interpret sex-role stereotyping as a cognitive-developmental variable. He suggests that children cognitively classify themselves and then seek to understand how to behave as a function of that classification. What determines sex-typed behavior is not the plumbing of the genitals per se, but rather the cognitive classifications and interpretations that follow from the self-observed biology plus the role-mandated consistent behaviors that follow.

At least two types of interactionism in personality may be identified at this time: (1) Mischel (1968, 1969, 1973b) exemplifies neo-Skinnerian interactionism, which may be referred to as social learning interactionism; and (2) Bowers (1973) calls his interactionism biocognitive interactionism. The two types of interactionism differ primarily in terms of what interacts. The biocognitive interactionist claims that traits and situations interact, by which he or she means that innate characteristics, acquired characteristics, and personal constructs (traits) influence and are influenced by environmental variables (situations). The social learning interactionist emphasizes that environmental forces and contingencies of reinforcement (situations) lead to the development of personal constructs and characteristic modes of response (traits), which in turn influence the environment (See Mischel, 1968, Chapter 6). Note that the biocognitive interactionist emphasizes traits, whereas the social learning interactionist emphasizes situations, in terms of the starting point of the causal spiral.

Mischel arrived at interactionism from a situationist position, Bowers from a trait position. Although both pledge allegiance to their new homeland, their ethnic origins and accents are still quite apparent. Most attempts to explicate similarities and differences between the two perspectives have either glossed over the differences between the two types of interactionism or have misconstrued one of the positions. The central issue appears to be whether traits have an origin that is primarily independent of the situation (genetic or intrapsychic) or that is primarily environmentally derived.

Mischel arrived at an interactionist perspective after a critical examination of the concept *trait*. He coined the term "personality coefficient" to describe the correlation characteristic of personality research, which is around .3, accounting for about 10% of the variance. This correlation of low magnitude is not artifactual according to Mischel, but rather "the observed inconsistency so regularly found in studies of noncognitive personality dimensions often reflects the state of nature and not merely the noise of measurement" (Mischel, 1969, p. 1014). "The notion of 'typical' behavior, which is fundamental to trait conceptualization, has led psychometricians and trait theorists to view situational variability as a form of 'error'. The social behavior position [Mischel's], however, construes what the psychometrician considers error to actually be critical determinants of behavior" (Mischel, 1968, p. 296). In one sense Mischel's interactionism is an interaction between experience with previous situations (traits) and present situations. Although Mischel's recent writings (1973b, 1976, 1977) have more heavily emphasized the utility of trait concepts and cognitive determinants of behavior, his status as a situationally-oriented social learning interactionist remains.

Bower's interactionism relies more heavily on genetic psychological dispositions and cognitive factors than Mischel's. He emphasizes that *"situations are as much a function of the person as the person's behavior is a function of the situation . . .* Moreover, there is an obvious sense in which man creates the circumstances that sustain him; after all, most of us live in houses, not in caves" (Bowers, 1973, p. 327, italics as in original). The traits which interact with situations in Bower's conceptualization are much more like the traditional trait concept than in social learning interactionism.

Social adaptation views personality and the situation as dialectically and inextricably interactive. Both the person and the situation continually transform one another through the interactive process of equilibration. Individual differences emerge where different skills, interests, experiences, etc., have fostered the development of divergent schemata regarding situational adaptation. These schemata guide and regulate behavior and cognitive activity. Determining the starting point of the person-situation dialectical spiral is futile. Both are necessarily a dynamic part of the other. Neither exists alone.

Eisert & Kahle (1982) have presented the essentials of the social adaptation perspective on interaction and personality in the context of a discussion of the self-system:

> The basic social-cognitive components of the self-system (e.g. self-esteem, self-concept, and self-evaluation), like Piaget's concept of structure, provide means for analyzing social experience. The self-system both specifies and limits the ways in which the individual can understand social events by providing rules or strategies of relating that have developed through interaction with the environment. The structure of the self-system intervenes between stimulus situations and resulting behavioral acts so that these acts are instigated, modified, and guided by the social-cognitive representation. The self-system provides a range of behavioral strategies of adaptation that the individual tests out in an attempt to find the best cognitive summary of the fit between the relatively stable characteristics of the self and environmental information. This approach implies that the structure of the self-system facilitates understanding of social information through such means as selective attention, information gathering strategies (structures), and social comparison. (Eisert & Kahle, 1982, p. 99).

Eisert and Kahle tested and supported this hypothesis in a cross-lagged panel study that examined aspects of the self-concept and information strategies as they developed in a group of adolescent boys over a one year period. In both the physical (e.g. "how strong are you?") and the role (e.g. student, friend) domains, self-evaluations and self-concept consistently influenced how boys sought out information through social comparison. Contrary to the common sense idea that adolescents develop their self-concepts by comparing themselves to others, in this study the adolescents sought out comparisons to confirm their self-evaluations.

Kahle *et al.* (1980) likewise tested a similar hypothesis over a two year period, looking at the development of interpersonal relationships among adolescent boys. Do unpopular students develop low self-concepts, or do students with low self-concepts become unpopular? The second hypothesis, which is consistent with the social adaptation perspective on personality, was confirmed. The boys with low self-esteem increasingly failed to interact with other boys in a manner that fostered favorable interpersonal relations.

This conception of personality as strategies, unique to the individual and derived from previous experience, circumvents the problem of personality being used as a formal cause, in the Aristotelian system of types of causes, rather than as a more scientifically-acceptable efficient cause. Scientific philosophies of knowledge have generally preferred causal explanations based on events (efficient causes) rather than explanations based on the nature of something (formal causes). Formal causal explanations tend to stop the process of complete understanding before a full and optimally useful description has been developed. To argue that John hit Bob because "that's the way John is" does not help one predict future hitting behaviors of John like an understanding of the events precipitating the hitting. If personality is viewed as a strategy abstracted from previous events in order to foster adaptation, however, the causal explanation returns to the realm of efficient causes and scientific conventions. (In some sense the canons of causal dogma from natural science need not always apply to social science reasoning. For example, a natural scientist should avoid explanations that are "anthropomorphic"; but for the social scientist who theorizes about *anthropos* [human beings], an anthropomorphic explanation may be perfectly valid.)

This perspective is fundamentally different from the social learning view of personality, which is based on self-perception theory:

> Thus while the traditional personality paradigm views traits as the intrapsychic causes of behavioral consistency, the present (social learning theory) position sees them as the *summary terms* (labels, codes, organizing constructs) applied to observed behavior (Mischel, 1973, p. 264, italics from original).

Thus, in social adaptation theory the summary terms both result from prior and guide subsequent behavior, whereas in social learning theory (Mischel, 1973) only the former is true. Furthermore, the meaning of the concept of prior behavior is somewhat different in the two theories, since social learning theory places more emphasis on the reinforcements and punishments *per se*, while social adaptation theory gives more attention to the understanding of the reinforcements and punishments as they relate to adaptation.

Since traits and attitudes are quite similar in social adaptation theory, it should not be surprising that personality and life situation variables are not the only aspect of the person that may influence attitude change. Attitudes also matter. For example, Kahle (1979) has shown how attitudinal entailment may influence resistance to attitude change. Attitudinal entailment may be defined as the extent to which an attitude is related to other attitudes and beliefs that are not part of the specific quasi-logic or psycho-logic governing why a person holds that particular attitude. The greater the number of attitudes and beliefs that effect or are effected by the particular attitude, but result from different syllogistic paths, the greater the attitudinal entailment of that attitude. If, for example, a person has one attitude, "I like blueberries", that has no relationship to any other attitudes but has another attitude, "I like New York", that has a strong influence on a person's definition of favorite sports teams, favorite vacation plans, and favorite politicians, then the second attitude would be said to have greater entailment.

The opposite of attitudinal entailment is cognitive differentiation (cf. Jones & Gerard, 1967), which is the degree to which an attitude results from a linear, clear, and unique series of psychological syllogisms. For example, if some, in response to the question "Why is red your favorite color", says, "I don't know", then that attitude would have poor cognitive differentiation. If, however, in response to the question "Why do you support nuclear power", the person produced a long series of syllogisms, each following from the previous one in the person's mind, then the person's nuclear power attitudes could be called highly differentiated.

Kahle (1979) tested the hypothesis that highly differentiated attitudes are less resistant to change than highly entailed attitudes. This hypothesis is similar to McGuire's (1964) notion of anchoring, which assumes that linking beliefs to other cognitions should induce resistance to persuasion. The results of the Kahle (1979) study supported both the anchoring and the entailment hypotheses. The attitudes that were modified by focusing attention on the entailment aspects survived a change manipulation more readily.

We turn now to McGuire's important theory of personality and persuasibility, which is essentially compatible with social adaptation theory.

McGuire's Theory of Personality and Persuasibility

McGuire's Definitions of the Limits of His Theory Warrant Attention

By *personality* McGuire (1968b) refers to any variable on which people may vary, whether it be a capacity variable, a demographic variable, or a dynamic variable. This definition includes variables that we previously defined as situational. By redefining a life-situation variable to "cognitions about life-situations", it is possible to transform the situation variable into a person variable. McGuire (1968c) uses the term *persuasibility* to denote susceptibility to any type of social influence. Although here we will concentrate on the identification and internalization processes proposed by Kelman (1958), as did Hovland & Janis (1959), the reader should note that McGuire considers compliance, as well as suggestibility, also to be within the scope of his theoretical usage of *persuasibility*.

In the third and most formalized statement of his theory McGuire (1968b) appropriately names his theory an information-processing theory. For any type of persuasion to take place, six successive steps must be passed through for information to be processed, each of which is dependent on the previous step as a necessary but not sufficient condition. (1) There must be some type of communication. (2) A person must attend to and (3) comprehend the message. (4) He or she must yield to and be convinced by the message. (5) The message must be retained, and, finally, (6) there must be behavioral manifestations that persuasion has taken place.

To explain the relationship between personality and persuasibility McGuire states three postulates and two corollaries. McGuire labels the first postulate the

Multiple-Mediation Assumption, he names the second postulate the Compensatory Assumption, and he calls the final postulate the Situational Weighting Assumption. The first postulate, proposed to counter the popular overemphasis on yielding, asserts that any personality characteristic can affect attitude change by having an impact on any one or more of the mediational steps just outlined. The second postulate states that any personality characteristic that has a positive relationship to reception (attention and comprehension) tends to be negatively related to yielding, and vice versa. This postulate has two corollaries. The first corollary suggests that because of the compensatory contributions of these two mediators (reception and yielding), the overall relationship between the personality variable and attitude change will tend to be nonmonotonic with maximum influenceability found at some intermediate level of the personality characteristic. The second corollary claims that an experimental manipulation of an acute (experimentally induced) personality characteristic will have an effect on influenceability that depends upon the person's chronic (not experimentally induced) level on that variable, as well as other chronic variables. The third postulate states that the precise shape and location of the inverted-U relationship between individual difference characteristics and attitude change will vary with specifiable aspects of the communication situation.

Data Relevant to These Theories

One criterion for evaluating a theory is the adequacy with which it can account for the evidence that is relevant to it. Of the many variables that have been studied in personality and persuasibility research, McGuire has concentrated primarily on only two — self-esteem and anxiety. His purpose in limiting the scope of his data reviews has been pragmatic. With such a wide variety of potential variables available to illustrate his theory, a comprehensive review of the literature would probably require a book, and his theoretical expositions have all been monographs. Nevertheless, it may prove to be instructive to attempt a somewhat more inclusive examination of the literature since McGuire may have overlooked important studies and since new studies have been published since he formulated his theory. Here we will begin by examining self-esteem and anxiety and then will move on to look at other variables that McGuire has not directly used to support or illustrate his theory. Self-esteem is especially interesting since social adaptation theory also proposes clear predictions.

Self-esteem

Unarmed with theory, the casual surveyor of the literature on self-esteem and persuasibility might conclude that the empirical knowledge in this area is at least as advanced as the empirical knowledge in the area of extraterrestrial life. It has been demonstrated that as self-esteem increases, attitude change following exposure to persuasive communication increases (Gollob & Dittes, 1965), decreases (Janis, 1954), increases then decreases (Cox & Bauer, 1964), or decreases then increases (Silverman, 1964a); furthermore, to keep us honest, Freedman (1965) found no main effect for self-esteem. Such a state of affairs does not bother Levonian (1970), who claims that all of the self-esteem studies lack sufficient control to deserve serious attention, although Silverman maintains that only the Yale studies (Janis, 1954; Cohen, 1959; Janis & Field, 1959; Janis & Rife, 1959) and one other (Cox & Bauer, 1964) are discredited by Levonian (Silverman, 1970).

If McGuire's advice about situational variables and about the relationship between receptivity and yielding is followed, much of the literature on self-esteem looks somewhat more logical. Gollow & Dittes (1965) found that as self-esteem increases, more complex communications are more persuasive. Likewise, Stone (1969) found that message innoculation is more effective for subjects with high self-esteem than for subjects with low self-esteem. Although Silverman, Fordy & Morganti (1966) found a negative relationship between message complexity and self-esteem for male subjects, they reported the same type of relationship for female subjects as Stone and Gollob and Dittes reported (although the Silverman *et al.* relationship was an inverted-U since they divided their data into more categories than did Stone or Gollob and Dittes). This sex difference may in part explain the difference between Cox & Bauer (1964) and Silverman (1964a) since Cox & Bauer used female subjects and Silverman used male subjects. Stone and Gollob and Dittes apparently used subjects of both genders and did not separate subjects on the basis of sex. The point here for both McGuire's theory and social adaptation theory is that as reception becomes more difficult, it is less insulting to subjects with high self-esteem (and ability) but more insulting to subjects with low self-esteem. This interaction between message and self-esteem level, which is quite consistent with McGuire's theory, appears to account for many of the discrepant results in the self-esteem research. Kahle (1978) found that the nature of the change influence interacts with chronic self-esteem in a dissonance situation such that high self-esteem subjects are likely to experience attitude change when justification is low but low self-esteem subjects like attitudinal mercenaries are prone to experience change when incentives are high.

Another type of interaction that fits in nicely with McGuire's theory is the interaction between the source of the communication and the subject's level of self-esteem. Dabbs (1964) and Stone (1969) have discovered that subjects who identify with the source in terms of level of self-esteem are more readily persuaded by that source than subjects with different levels of self-esteem than the source's. Although both the source and message interactions appear to account for many of the discrepancies, it should be noted that often the reviewer must make inferences from inadequate information about the complexity of the message and the level of self-esteem of the source.

McGuire self-admittedly cannot explain the differences observed in acute as opposed to chronic self-esteem. Gelfand found a main effect for acute, but not chronic, self-esteem (Gelfand, 1962). Nisbett & Gordon (1967) found a main effect for chronic, but not acute, self-esteem. Silverman (1964b) found an inter-action in which only attempts to manipulate acute self-esteem in the direction of chronic self-esteem were effective. Perhaps one way to account for these differ-ences, which are typical throughout the self-esteem literature, is to assume that some experimenters are more skillful manipulators than others. From a social adaptation perspective chronic self-esteem ought to reflect a much more care-fully defined schema than acute self-esteem, leading to a better definition of how to respond to a persuasion attempt.

Anxiety

In order to become totally confused about the relationship between chronic anxiety and persuasibility, one need search no further than the work of Janis. He has found a negative correlation between chronic anxiety and persuasibility (Janis, 1954), a positive correlation (Janis, 1955), and a lack of correlation (Janis & Field, 1959). Steiner & Rogers (1963) suggested that this correlation is negative for males and positive for females, but the Janis study that found a positive correlation between chronic anxiety and persuasibility used male subjects.

The literature on chronic anxiety makes a bit more sense if the definition of persuasibility is allowed to include verbal conditioning. The two correlate posi-tively, it seems, regardless of whether the subjects are male (Sarason, 1958), female (Doherty & Walker, 1966), or of both sexes (Fire, 1957).

Manipulated, or acute, anxiety may correlate negatively (Janis & Feshbach, 1953) or not at all (Moltz & Thistlethwaite, 1955) with persuasibility, but most investigators have found a positive correlation (Berkowitz & Cottingham, 1960; Leventhal & Niles, 1964; Insko, Arkoff, & Insko, 1965; Leventhal, Singer, & Jones, 1965). If anxiety at moderate levels implies greater activation of inform-ation processing abilities, then those finding of a generally positive relationship between experimentally-allowed (by an ethics committee) anxiety and change fit well with adaptation theory. Accommodation ought to be greatest when anxiety is aroused, at least up to some point.

Certainly these results support McGuire's notions about the complexity of the relationship between personality and persuasibility, but not one study has found the nonmonotonic relationship McGuire predicts, unless nonmonotonicity and nonsignificance are used synonymously (a topic to be discussed later). McGuire hypothesizes that the relationship between anxiety and persuasibility would be an inverted-*U* since the insecurity associated with anxiety should en-hance yielding but the introversion associated with anxiety should diminish receptivity. Although he implies that the anxiety research generally supports his theory, he fails to account for the universal linearity of the correlations be-tween anxiety and persuasibility. The best account of these findings within his theoretical framework would invoke the situational weighting assumption and suggest that the positive relationships were discovered when the sample of subjects came from a point to the left of the inflection point of the inverted-U and that when a negative relationship was uncovered, it was because the subject pool came from the right of the inflection point. Very little information about the subject samples would suggest that such an account of these findings is viable.

One of McGuire's students, Susan Millman, carried out one of the few experiments designed specifically to test McGuire's theory (reported in McGuire, 1968b). She found no relationship between chronic anxiety and receptivity or yielding. Although she also did not find a relationship between acute anxiety and yielding, one of her two issues revealed that high acute anxiety enhances receptivity. These results can hardly be interpreted as supporting the main premise of the compensatory assumption. She did find solid support, however, for its corollary regarding the relationship between chronic and acute personality variables. Her results indicated that subjects chronically low in anxiety showed more attitude change under induced high anxiety than under low acute anxiety but that those subjects who were chronically high in anxiety showed only minimal opinion change when they were exposed to a large threat.

Locus of Control

Since Strickland (1977) superbly reviewed the literature on locus of control and its influence recently, it is not necessary to belabor the topic here. She concluded: "Internals are more likely to maintain their own individual judgment in the face of contrasting evidence from external sources that call their perceptions and/or behaviors into question . . . Moreover, internals not only appear to resist influence but react more strongly than externals to the loss of personal freedom . . . Internals appear to want to 'keep the reins in their own hands', behaving in ways which facilitate independence and negate the other's influence." (Strickland, 1977, p. 232). Thus, it appears that internals are both more resistant to reception and to change, contrary to McGuire's theory. If locus of control is viewed in social adaptation theory as a consistent strategy of self-reliance, then these results are not contrary to it.

Intelligence

McGuire belabors his predictions about the relationship between intelligence and persuasibility since one can easily and intuitively grasp his point regarding this relationship. The intelligent person has more information at his or her disposal and greater critical capacities, which minimize his or her yielding potential; but the intelligent person also tends to be more interested in the outside world and thus attentive to what is going on around, increasing receptive capacities. The inverted-U prediction stands firm regarding intelligence. Unfortunately, the few published studies that have probed the relationship between intelligence and persuasibility (Janis & Field, 1959; Janis & Rife, 1959; King, 1959; Linton &

Graham, 1959) have almost all failed to find any significant relationship between these variables. The one exception (Eagly & Warren, 1976) found that verbal intelligence correlates positively with comprehension and agreement with a complex message. As with anxiety, unless McGuire uses nonmonotonicity and nonsignificance synonymously, his frequently stated and intuitively plausible hypothesis is still awaiting a pattern of research providing confirmatory evidence.

Machiavellianism

Although Machiavellianism does not correlate with intelligence (Christie & Geis, 1968), one might expect that, following McGuire's theory, a manipulative person would behave much like an intelligent person in a situation of persuasion. The Machiavellian would be highly receptive but would not be too yielding. The two studies done on Machiavellianism and persuasibility do follow McGuire-type predictions. Epstein (1969) showed that Machiavellians are more prone to change their minds on the basis of the strengths of an argument, as opposed to low Machiavellians, whereas low Machiavellians, as opposed to high Machiavellians, are more likely to change their attitudes after counterattitudinal role playing. Burgoon, Miller, & Tubbs (1973) assert that high Machiavellians are more likely to be persuaded when the potential gain is high, whereas low Machiavellians are more likely to alter positions in dissonance-producing circumstances. Aside from the important implications for the debate between dissonance theory and reinforcement theory that this piece of research has, it seems to support and follow the predictions of all three postulates of McGuire's theory quite neatly.

Age

Social adaptation theory. Adult human behavior, including attitude-relevant behavior, does not leap onto the scene without developmental antecedents. Virtually no research, with a few very recent exceptions (e.g. Meyer, DeChenne, & Albano, 1981), has examined developmental precursors of attitudes. Fortunately, the development of attributions has been investigated. As noted in Chapter 1, attributions are the building blocks of attitudes. Attributions coalesce into beliefs, which become attitudes when linked with evaluations; hence, one should look at the development of attributions in order to comprehend the ontogeny of attitudes. Certainly the first step in attitude formation constitutes a logical focus for any attempt to understand the first step in attitude development.

Many developmental researchers in the area of social cognitive development (e.g. Livesley & Bromley, 1973) have found that a cognitive developmental perspective (e.g. Piaget & Inhelder, 1969) is useful in understanding attribution development, particularly Piaget's work on language and thought (1926), conceptions of the world (1929), physical causality (1930), moral development (1932), and especially logical operations (Inhelder & Piaget, 1958). The sequence of developmental stages proposed by Piaget (1970) to describe the acquisition of logical operations (i.e. sensorimotor, preoperational, concrete operational, formal operational) is widely known by social cognitive development researchers, as is the description of change mechanisms in his equilibration model (e.g. adaptation through assimilation and accommodation). Piaget & Inhelder's (1975) important work on probability development, however, has been generally overlooked.

The central argument of Piaget & Inhelder's report on the development of change concepts is that adaptive reasoning about probability and chance requires the ability to identify non-chance events. Understanding the idea of randomness requires the ability to perceive order and lawfulness, an ability that emerges as a function of the capacity to perform logical operations.

On the basis of their research and thinking in the area, Piaget & Inhelder (1975) argue for a three-stage model of the development of probability and chance. During the first stage, the realms of chance and nonchance are undifferentiated. The preoperational child lacks the intellectual equipment required to articulate the realm of order and lawfulness and as a consequence is also unable to understand the realm of randomness. During the concrete operational period, logical operations and probabilistic thinking gradually begin to differentiate, enabling the child to discriminate the random from the deducible. Yet, the child during this period is unable to integrate deduction with probabilistic thinking. Thus, although chance events may be recognized as such, they cannot be adequately managed (Flavell, 1963). The ability to deal with probabilistic events is dependent upon the ability to think in terms of combinations and proportions, an ability that develops during the formal operational period. At this level logical operations and chance concepts become integrated, enabling the child both to recognize and deal with probabilistic events.

Adult-like attributions involve the integration of both logical structures probability structures in the evaluation of behavior, according to social adaptation theory. The ability to use both logic and probability simultaneously, probabilogical theory of attitudes (McGuire, 1980) has identified as important, develops through a dialectical process roughly comparable to the transitions in thought about the physical world from preoperational to concrete operational to formal operational stages. Much of the research points to three distinct stages in the development of social attributions (Eisert & Kahle, 1982). Each social adaptation stage will be identified below with two terms, the first referring to the level of logical structures and the second to the level of probability structures. It should be noted that theories of adult attribution have focused on adult use of logic (e.g. Kelley, 1967) or probability (e.g. Fishbein & Ajzen, 1975; Suppes, 1970).

I. *Preoperational subjective*:   The child lacks the logical skills necessary to differentiate chance and nonchance events. The child has some logical skills, but makes errors in determining when to use them; however, an intuitive grasp of probability exerts a primary influence on the child's attributions.

II. *Operational objective*:   At this stage, the emphasis is on the newly acquired capacity for logical operations. Logic, however, is frequently used at the expense of probability structures, which are relatively dormant early in the stage. Advanced logical skills make the child better able to recognize psychological and motivational constructs (e.g. internal states) as possible causes of behavior; however, the dormant probability structures render him insensitive to temporal and situational influences on behavior. As a result, attributions are often in the form of stable but stereotyped traits that have the flavor of unchanging, historical truths.

III. *Operational subjectivism*:   At this stage, individuals acquire the ability to make attributions on the basis of logical and probability structures simultaneously. Attributions are more organized, more complex, and coherent. Individuals are able to consider simultaneously the temporal and situational influences on behavior. They can integrate apparently discrepant information into complex coherent explanations. Finally, by virtue of abstract reasoning ability, they can consider causes not immediately present.

Research results.   The availability of college students for use as experimental subjects has greatly diminished the potential generalizations one could make about age and its relationship to persuasibility. Of the studies cited in this chapter, fewer than ten have used subjects who were neither high school nor college students. Furthermore, two (Whittaker & Meade, 1967; Singh, 1970) of the three studies that specifically considered age as a persuasibility variable made the generalizations about age from evidence obtained from college samples.

Marple (1933) found that high school and college students are more susceptible to social influence than average adults. Whittaker and Meade (1967) observed that in several different countries persuasibility tends to decline with age, and Singh (1970) detected the same trend in India.

This evidence is hardly sufficient to support any theory. Nevertheless, from a social adaptation perspective, it seems likely that younger subjects at the ages employed have probably failed to temper logical arguments with probability information. The operational objective person's attitude is nearly the same regardless of the attributional base of it, whereas the probabilistic nature of the attributional base will influence the operational subjective person. For example, "I like Bob because he was nice to me once" and "I like Bob because he was nice to me 30 times" should imply equally strong attitudes for the operational objective person but a much weaker attitude in the first case for the operational subjective person. The older people in these studies of age and persuasibility may have tempered the small amount of information in a typical attitude change study more than the younger ones; hence, the older people showed less change.

McGuire would probably maintain that all three of these studies used subjects who were very close to or to the right of the inflection point of the inverted-*U*. Infants would lack receptivity, and senility would inhibit yielding. If such is the case, none of these three studies are contradictory to McGuire's theory, but more evidence is necessary before any type of judgment can be made about the relationship between age and persuasibility. The relationship could be a bi-modal inverted-U, or senility could inhibit both receptivity and yielding.

Dogmatism

Rokeach's (1960) trait of dogmatism appears to be unrelated to changes in values (Cochrane & Kelly, 1971; Rokeach, 1973), but it does relate to attitude change. Three studies have found a strong and positive correlation between dogmatism and persuasibility (Noris, 1965; Kleck & Weaton, 1967; Cronkhite & Goetz, 1971). Cronkhite & Goetz (1971) have severely criticized the one study (Miller, 1965) that found a negative relationship between dogmatism and persuasibility for using unconventional alpha levels (.1, with one-tailed tests) and for an unusual method of grouping data. Miller divided his subjects into three groups: high on dogmatism and involvement, low on dogmatism and involvement, and high on one of the two variables and low on the other. This strange method eliminates the possibility of finding any interaction between the two variables and of discovering whether only one of the variables or whether both of the variables are contributing to the main effect(s). For the purposes of Cronkhite and Goetz these criticisms are probably well founded, for within the context of previous research it would seem that only involvement is contributing to the negative correlation which Miller found. For our purposes here, however, Miller's results are interesting since they point out how with only one additional variable the entire outcome of an experiment can switch completely around, just as McGuire's third postulate would predict.

Powell (1962) discovered that dogmatic people tend to wed source and message, whereas open-minded, or less dogmatic, people can separate attitudes between source and message more adequately. His study implies that dogmatism inhibits receptivity. Since the studies mentioned in the previous paragraph generally found that dogmatism enhances yielding, it appears that dogmatism research tentatively confirm McGuire's compensatory assumption, although the lack of any inverted-U relationships slightly detracts from this tentative confirmation.

Dogmatism and authoritarianism are closely related. Indeed, Rokeach (1960), who initiated contemporary psychological inquiry into dogmatism, called authoritarianism right wing dogmatism; therefore, a more comprehensive examination of the implications of the findings of studies on dogmatism will be deferred until after looking at the more extensive research on the relationship between persuasibility and authoritarianism.

Authoritarianism

Although two studies failed to find a significant relationship between authoritarianism and persuasibility (Linton & Graham, 1959; Cochrane & Kelly, 1971), most studies have found a positive relationship between the two variables. Centers, Shomer, & Rodrigues (1970), using 1275 adults representative of Los Angeles as subjects, found a positive correlation between authoritarianism and attitude change. The sampling method of this study makes it especially note-worthy. Stone (1969) found that authoritarians were both more persuasible and more inoculable. In studies of conformity, authoritarians have been found to follow the group more consistently than people who score low on the California F Scale in both Asch-type conformity situations (Nadler, 1959; Steiner & Johnson, 1964) and in Sherif-type autokinetic-illusion conformity situations (Canning & Baker, 1959). One study (Katz, McClintock, & Sarnoff, 1957) reported a McGuire-type inverted-U relationship between authoritarianism and attitude change. Unlike most of the research in personality and persuasibility, very little contraction has emerged in the studies on the relationship between authoritarianism and persuasibility.

Interaction studies in authoritarianism have likewise resulted in few contradictory findings. It seems that changes in the content of the message have a greater impact on non-authoritarians than on authoritarians (Wagman, 1955; Harvey & Beverly, 1961), that changes in the source have a greater influence on authoritarians than on nonauthoritarians (Johnson, Torcivia, & Poprick, 1968), and that the authoritativeness of the source correlates positively with authoritarian change (Wagman, 1955), although several authors have added stipulations to this last finding. Berkowitz and Lundy (1957) maintain that authoritative sources have a positive impact only on high authoritarians who are also high on interpersonal confidence, and Wright and Harvey (1965) conclude that source status is positively correlated with authoritarian attitude change when the issue is of low involvement for the authoritarian and that source status is negatively correlated with authoritarian attitude change when the issue is of low involvement for the authoritarian and that source status is negatively correlated with authoritarian attitude change when the target issue is of high involvement for the authoritarian. This finding of Wright and Harvey might help to account for the Miller (1965) study which did not fit in with the majority of studies on dogmatism mentioned in the last section. One other interaction study which deserves to be mentioned (Harvey & Beverly, 1961) discovered that role playing creates greater attitude change for high authoritarians while persuasive communication creates greater attitude change for low authoritarians.

At this point a note of skepticism is in order. It seems that no research problem is too grave for certain researchers blatantly to ignore. In a scathing critique of the development of the California F Scale, the instrument used to measure authoritarianism, Hyman & Sheatsley (1954) raised some very serious questions about the validity of the F Scale; nevertheless, researchers still employ the F Scale, or a slightly modified version of it. Furthermore, although Hyman & Sheatsley only attacked the F Scale, there is reason to believe that the instruments used to measure some of the other personality characteristics mentioned in this chapter have less-than-optimal validity. Although an extensive discussion of personality assessment is not within the scope of this chapter, the reader will do well to maintain a healthy skepticism, although not a cynicism, toward the findings of some of the studies reported in this chapter.

We might speculate based on social adaptation theory that dogmatics and authoritarians are developmentally less advanced and therefore are likely to integrate probabilistic information less adequately than nondogmatics and non-authoritarians. Authoritarians may be like the operational objective person who adjusts attitudes excessive to new information, failing to consider the probabilistic worth of new information and alternatives not present.

Returning to McGuire's theory, how would the results of the studies on authoritarianism be explained? Although authoritarianism has been described in many ways since it first entered the personality literature (Adorno, Frenkel-Brunswik, Levinson, & Sanford, 1950), the most recent articles have stressed that authoritarianism is merely simple-mindedness (e.g. Peabody, 1966). As such, it would be expected that the relationship between receptivity and yielding for the high authoritarian would be the inverse of the relationship postulated for the intelligent, who would be complex-minded, and for the Machiavellian, who possesses skill in complex role performance. As with the dogmatic person described by Powell (1962), the authoritarian probably lacks receptivity but has high yielding potential. Since the pattern of outcomes for authoritarians and for dogmatics is about the same, it is safe to conclude that Rokeach's (1960) statement about the relationship between authoritarianism and dogmatism has some validity and that the two characteristics would react to persuasive communication in the same manner. Almost all of the studies that examined dogmatism and authoritarianism in isolation did find that these two traits are positively related to yielding. Furthermore, the interaction studies, when taken in the context of what we discovered about receptivity and self-esteem, conform to the receptivity half of this hypothesis (i.e. Wagman, 1955; Harvey & Beverly, 1961; Powell, 1962; Wright & Harvey, 1965) with one inexplicable exception (Berkowitz & Lundy, 1957). If role playing is interpreted as beneficial to receptivity, both the authoritarian role players and the Machiavellian role players fit within McGuire's predictions since Burgoon, Miller, & Tubbs (1973) found that role playing diminishes Machiavellian persuasibility but Harvey & Beverly (1961) showed that it enhances authoritarian persuasability. When the Katz, McClintock, & Sarnoff (1957) confirmation of the second postulate's first corollary is added to this already impressive list of support for McGuire in authoritarianism and dogmatism research, it appears that, more than any other personality variable that has received extensive research attention as it relates to persuasibility, this area of research supports McGuire's theory quite well. It is unfortunate that all of the studies of authoritarianism and dogmatism have dealt with this trait in its chronic state, for only the second corollary of the second postulate has failed to receive support in this literature.

Abstractness

Using the This I Believe Scale, Harvey (1965) showed that concrete-thinking subjects changed their opinions more readily than abstract thinkers in counter-attitudinal advocacy (role playing) situations, a finding that is consistent with what McGuire and social adaptation theory would probably say, assuming that this dimension is somewhat related to authoritarianism. Another finding of this study that is consistent with, although not necessarily predictable from, the situational weighting assumption was that public advocacy produced more lasting change for concrete thinkers, whereas private advocacy led to greater attitude change for subjects high on abstractness.

Sex

Hovland & Janis (1959) summarized the literature on sex and persuasibility by stating that women are more susceptible to social influence than men, but personality measures correlate with behavioral measures more strongly for men. McGuire (1968c) agrees, as do most other authors (e.g. Janis & Field, 1959; Whittaker, 1965; Singh, 1970), although at least one study failed to detect a main effect for sex (Stone, 1969). A few authors claim that sex interacts with other variables but that personality variables are no less detectable for women than for men (Steiner & Rogers, 1963; Silverman, Ford, & Morganti, 1966). Other authors have found personality-persuasibility correlates when using exclusively female populations (Katz, McClintock & Sarnoff, 1957; Cox & Bauer, 1964; Doherty & Walker, 1966) or have found women to be less persuasible (Kahle, 1978).

Although McGuire (1968c) does not disagree with the data description of Hovland & Janis, he does disagree with their interpretation of sex differences as being a culturally dictated artifact. There are two ways McGuire's theory could account for sex differences. One way, sex as an interactive variable, simply cannot handle the sex-personality interactions that have been reported. The other way, invoking the situational weighting assumption, McGuire avoids. The danger of excessive use of the situational weighting assumption without more carefully considering the nature of situations (although McGuire fails to mention this factor) is that it could easily become the Great Protector from accepting null hypotheses. Since it is, of course, quite impossible for a dichotomous variable such as a sex to display nonmonotonicity without the use of interaction, McGuire can only account for sex differences by means of extra-theoretical factors, which he does. After a long and atypically rambling discussion of sex in persuasibility, he concludes that a plausible explanation might involve genetics. He cites (1968c) a dissertation by Rosenberg which failed to find any culture, culture x sex, or culture x sex x age main effects, from which he builds his genetic hypothesis. Whittaker & Meade (1967) report on one study that calls even this hypothesis into question. After studying sex and age variables in relation to persuasibility in the United States, Rhodesia, Lebanon, Peru, Brazil, and Hong Kong, they conclude that sex differences in persuasibility are determined culturally by roles. One could, of course, counter the Whittaker & Meade study by showing that different cultures also have different gene pools. Furthermore, the persuasibility sex difference is unrelated to masculinity and femininity, at least as measured by the MMPI M—F Scale (Whittaker, 1965).

Fortunately, an excellent and recent meta-analysis has examined the relationship between gender and the slightly broader topic, when compared with persuasibility, of influenceability (Eagly & Carli, 1981). Two hypotheses received special attention, one concerning the nature of materials typically used as stimuli and one concerning the researcher's gender. Both hypotheses obviously, in terms of McGuire's theory, relate to situational weighting. The meta-analysis failed to support the hypothesis that masculine stimulus materials have been over-represented in such a manner as to bias the outcome of influence studies. It did support the other hypothesis, however. "The most striking aspect of the present findings is the relationship obtained between the sex of the researchers and the outcomes of their experiments: Male authors were more likely to obtain female influenceability than were female authors" (Eagly & Carli, 1981, p. 16). This would suggest that as more women become researchers, the trend may change.

Omnibus Studies

Most of the experiments cited thus far have looked at one or several personality variables; tried to change an opinion, attitude, or behavior; and then related the two findings in some way. Several studies, however, have tried to find relationship between the Janis & Field (1956) test of general persuasibility and a large number of personality variables. Most of these studies have found either no relationship or only chance relationships between the trait of persuasibility and the many personality variables (Janis & Field, 1959; Appley & Moeller, 1963; Cochrane & Kelly, 1971), although Linton & Graham (1959) found a large number of traits, mostly centered around weakness and passiveness, that correlated positively with persuasibility.

Most of these studies have been carried out in quest of evidence for a general trait of persuasibility. Hovland & Janis (1959), as well as McGuire (1968c), find that there is some weak evidence for such a trait. Although one might detect an emerging controversy over the evidence by superficially scanning research, in fact the dispute is more over how to interpret a correlation of .4. Cronkhite & Goetz (1971), armed with no correlation coefficient larger than .4, seem to consider persuasibility an important characteristic, whereas Touhey (1973) claims that the fact that attitude change in one situation correlates with attitude change in another situation at only .47 is not very reliable evidence for a general trait of persuasibility, even though this correlation is significant beyond the .01 level. Thus, it seems reasonable to assume with McGuire and Hovland and Janis that there is some evidence for a general trait of persuasibility, in excess of Mischel's (1968) .3 "personality coefficient."

General Comments on McGuire's Theory and Social Adaptation

The multiple-mediational assumption, McGuire's first postulate, asserts that any personality characteristic can affect attitude change by having an impact on any one or more of the mediational sets proposed by McGuire (and others — e.g. Bem (1970) and Hovland & Janis (1959) mentioned similar steps). This assertion, while superficially obvious, has often been overlooked by many researchers in the area of personality and persuasibility. By emphasizing such a logical and supported point, McGuire has, in principle, opened up a box full of hypotheses about where to look for the relationship between personality and persuasibility and about why many of the studies in personality and persuasibility may have so consistently found inconsistencies. In fact, very few researchers have studied the many implications of this postulate.

The compensatory assumption, postulate number two, suggests that any personality characteristic that has a positive relationship to reception tends to relate negatively to yielding, and vice versa. Although for the most part this assumption seems logical, it is possible to speculate about exceptions. For example, in the discussion about age it was mentioned that senility may be negatively related to both yielding and reception. Likewise, autism may inhibit both reception and yielding. When considering high levels of yielding, it may be necessary to discriminate between yielding and unreliability. For example, when a subject with asymptotically low intelligence yields to persuasive communication as measured by a rating scale, will that change last and have behavioral ramifications? Such questions and speculations must await testing and empirical evidence. As with the multiple-mediational assumption, the compensatory assumption has generated disappointingly few specific tests of its proposals.

The first corollary of the second postulate states that the overall relationship between a personality variable and attitude change will tend to be nonmonotonic with maximum influenceability found at some intermediate level of the personality characteristic. If one grants the logic of the postulate, the logic of this corollary follows. Although the U-shaped functions mentioned in this paper were few and far between, they generally did take the inverted-U shape that McGuire predicts. Again, the research that this corollary has generated is minimal.

One confusion with this corollary centers around McGuire's use of the term *nonmonotonic*. Hays says that ". . . a function that plots as a parabola is nonmonotone. . .   In general, any functional relation with a plot showing one or more district 'peaks' or 'valleys' is nonmonotone" (1973, p. 787). If by the term *nonmonotonic* McGuire means "the lack of monotonicity", then this corollary has very little utility but one cannot quibble with McGuire's use of the term. If, however, McGuire means by the term what Hays defined as nonmonotone, then certain questions arise. It appears that the second proposition is the case (that McGuire followed the Hays definition) since McGuire often appears to use the words *nonmonotonic* and *curvilinear* (as opposed to *nonmonotonic* and *non-significant*) as synonyms. Yet almost all of the examples of "nonmonotonicity" that McGuire cites (especially in McGuire, 1968c) were in fact examples of non-significance. In instances where authors used Pearson product-moment correlations or other statistics that are only capable of detecting linear relationships between variables, this oversight might be justifiable, although dubious may be a better word; but McGuire also cites references that failed to detect significant relationships between variables when using statistics that should be capable of detecting nonmonotonicity. For example, he says:

> One illustrative study by Appley and Moeller (1963) illustrates the ubiquity of non-monotonic relationships between personality characteristics and influenceability . . . On only 5 of the 38 variables was a monotonic relation found. On 33 of the 38, the high and low subgroups lay on the same side of the middle personality group as regards conformity. These results do not, of course, constitute 38 independent tests, since the personality characteristics measured by these standardized inventories are far from orthogonal (Peterson, 1965). However, the results are impressive when we consider the overwhelming ratio of nonmonotonic effects despite the homogeneity of the sample (McGuire, 1968c, p. 1147).

And later:

> The actual occurrence of this case is quite widespread. We saw in the Appley and Moeller study, for example, that 33 of their 38 variables showed a nonmonotonic relation to conformity. We suspect this situation obtains fairly generally between personality characteristics and many other dependent variables besides influenceability (McGuire, 1968c, p. 1171).

In fact, this Appley & Moeller (1963) study, around which McGuire builds his case for nonmonotonicity, did find only 5 of 38 "linear" relationships; but only one of the 38 Spearman rank-order correlations met the authors' alpha level (.1, apparently one-tailed) and only one of the 38 analyses of variance was beyond the authors' alpha level, in both cases fewer statistically significant relationships than one would expect by chance alone. Although the correlations were tests of linearity and therefore not necessarily contrary to McGuire's predictions, the ANOVAs should have been able to detect nonmonotonicity, given the way in which they were set up. Furthermore, of the 33 "nonmonotonic" variables, 17 were U-shaped and only 16 were of the inverted-U type that McGuire predicts, a fact that McGuire conveniently ignores; hence, it seems that unless one invokes the situational weighting assumption, this corollary is at best weak and provides minimal help accounting for most of the available data.

The second corollary states that an experimental manipulation of an acute personality variable will have an effect on influenceability that depends upon the person's chronic level on that variable, as well as any other chronic variable. This corollary could have just as easily been derived from the third postulate as from the seond postulate. Although its deductive logic is a bit unclear, its empirical logic is obvious. There seems to be very little relationship between the influence of chronic variables on persuasibility and the impact of their acute counterparts. The hard-line experimentalists who attack correlational studies (studies of chronic variables) may in fact not be studying the personality variables that they claim to be in their experiments (studies of acute variables). Although one may not be able to generalize about causation from many types of correlational studies, this corollary and its empirical support seem to suggest that one may not even be able to generalize to chronic personality relationships from experimental studies. Experimental studies may in fact not be studying personality at all, but instead they may only be looking at various types of social influence. Social influence is, of course, an important research topic, however, one should be careful to represent what one is studying accurately.

To summarize, we have seen that McGuire's ambitious theory has both strengths and weaknesses. In some cases it can account for what has been found logically and can lead to interesting predictions. In other instances it has trouble explaining what research has uncovered and in making predictions. In a few cases it is simply untestable. Perhaps this last factor is why few experiments have been designed to test some of the more specific predictions of the theory (cf. Cialdini, Brauer & Lewis, 1974). At any rate, it is both the best and the worst theory in the area that it is trying to cover. It contributes to social adaptation theory by focusing attention in specific places, and in some instances social adaptation theory expands it by clarifying predictions.

Many of the suggestions that McGuire makes about the proper design for future research in personality and persuasibility should be heeded by psychologists whom personality and persuasibility interest. For example, experimental designs capable of detecting higher order interactions and the use of statistics such as analysis of variance, for detecting interactions, and *eta*, for detecting "nonmonotonicity" in simpler experiments (as opposed to the exclusive use of linear correlational techniques), would probably enhance the current status of knowledge about the relationship between personality and persuasibility. More exploitation of new correlational techniques would also be useful (cf. Kenny, 1979). Indeed, much of the difficulty in decoding the contradictory findings in personality and persuasibility research is the result of the great variability in experimental design. Many people do not recognize that research methodology contributes greatly to person-situation interactions on the situation side, a topic we will discuss in the following chapter. More careful replications and similarly-designed experiments could only help matters. As J.S. Mill pointed out (quoted in Eysenck, 1953):

If there are some subjects on which the results obtained have finally received the unanimous assent of all who have attended to the proof, and others on which mankind have not yet been equally successful; on which the most sagacious minds have occupied themselves from the earliest date, and have never succeeded in establishing any considerable body of truths, so as to be beyond denial or doubt; it is by generalizing the methods successfully followed in the former enquiries, and adapting them to the latter, that we may hope to remove this blot on the face of science.

With this in mind, let us now move to a consideration of methodology.

CHAPTER 6

Methodology in attitude research

WE TURN now to an examination of the situation side of the person-situation tension. First, the pervasive situational domain of methodology will be examined. Then, in Chapter 7, we will turn to other aspects of situations.

Many researchers do not recognize what a dramatic situational influence on their research results is determined by methodological decisions when they plan how to do a study. Methodological decisions are usually made for theoretical, philosophical, and practical reasons that have little to do with the anticipated nature of the results. Few researchers would explicitly begin a research project by thinking, "I sure hope my research supports person-oriented theories rather than situation-oriented theories; therefore, I had better design a survey, not an experiment". Yet, the nature of the methodology selected may often lead to the exact results as much as any other aspect of the study. Kulka (1982) has shown, from a series of interviews with the authors of some of the most well-known studies in the history of social science, that often researchers make methodological decisions for totally arbitrary reasons or for reasons that few reputable scientists would admit publicly. For example, many methodological decisions are based on biases of professors the researcher knew as a graduate student or on biases of a journal to which the researcher wants to submit the eventual research results. Quite often availability of money severely restricts decisions about research design and sampling. Other times misunderstanding of the methodological issues related to alternative methodologies restrict a researcher's degrees of decisional freedom. All too often, researchers fail to think clearly through the relationship between the methodology and the research question, in order to detect any possible biasing that might emerge from failure to employ an appropriate methodology. The process of methodology decision making, relative to its importance, remains one of the least explored or understood aspects of social science research.

In spite of this arbitrariness of methodology selection, the results of many studies are not interpreted arbitrarily. In many areas of attitude research, for example, one research tradition may rather consistently support one theoretical perspective and another research tradition may rather consistently support another research tradition. Yet researchers continue to interpret results of such studies as if they yielded more information about theories than about methodology. For example, in laboratory studies self-perception theory is often supported, but in survey studies it rarely is supported.

Bowers (1973) has shown how laboratory methodology has often been misleadingly cited as providing support for the situationist or stimulus-response school of psychology. In the typical laboratory design the stimulus (independent variable) is manipulated, and then the response (dependent variable) is measured. If the study provides significant results, it is often interpreted as supporting stimulus-response theory, even though by definition the results have either to support that theory or to be nonsignificant. If the results are nonsignificant, of course, the researcher throws out the study (You cannot prove the null hypothesis. Maybe the manipulation was too weak or the experimenter unskilled). Thus, within laboratory experimental research methodology, stimulus-response theory is unfalsifiable, which should be an attribute of no adequate scientific theory (Rychlak, 1973). Many careful and capable laboratory researchers, however, have not understood this point and have continued to interpret laboratory studies as if they were probative regarding the veracity of stimulus-response theory.

It may be that the person-situation controversy is as much a function of failure to understand how methodology dictates results as any other factor.

The two types of methodologies used in most attitude research are the laboratory experiment and the survey. Both have assets and liabilities which we will now consider.

Survey and Polls in Attitude Research

Presser (1981) has shown how the frequency of survey data usage in most social sciences has increased from 1950 to 1980. The percentage of survey studies has jumped in sociology from 24% to 56%, in economics from 6% to 29%, in political science from 3% to 35%, and in interdisciplinary attitude research, as operationalized by articles in *Public Opinion Quarterly*, from 43% to 91%. Only psychological social psychologists have resisted this trend, although even that may be changing. As we shall see, however, the public opinion poll is also far from flawless.

Public opinion polls and surveys measure aggregated attitudes of individuals. Different individuals usually have different abstractions about adaptation, but when sufficiently many people have overlapping attitudes about important social questions, the aggregation of attitudes may lead to noteworthy consequences. When discussing public opinion, however, it is important to remember that the concept of public opinion is itself a type of abstraction about many individuals' abstractions about adaptation. All of the problems, complexities and concerns

about individual attitudes are multiplied when we move to attitudes of aggregated individuals.

Several writers have listed empirical and logical fallacies that are used in poll
interpretation. Let us look at a few of those writers' notions.

Floyd Allport was one of the first critics of public opinion poll abuse (in
Katz *et al.*, 1954, p. 51 ff.), yet his criticisms remain valid regarding public
opinion poll abuse today. Allport lists eight "fictions and blind alleys" pertain-
ing to public opinion: 1.) The personification of public opinion. Public opinion
is not a soul or conscience that decides important issues. 2.) The personification
of the public. Not only is the public opinion process not a super being, neither is
the public. The public is comprised of many individuals. Minority opinion is
often important in public opinion polling, perhaps as important as majority
opinion. In 1964, seven percent of American adults believed Hitler was "wholly
or partly" right to try to kill all the Jews. Knowing about this misguided seven
percent (which projected to eight million people) of society who advocated or
condoned genocide may be more important, because of the implications for
civilization, than knowing that most Americans in 1964 thought that Hitler was
wrong in trying to kill all Jews. 3.) The group fallacy. Even when it is acknow-
ledged that the public is a conglomerate of individuals, "public actions" are
often described. The public does not do anything. Only certain members of the
public can do something. 4.) The fallacy of partial inclusion in the use of the
term public. Opinions are not held by the subgroups of the public, for subgroups
are also made up of individuals. An example of this fallacy is found in the statement: "Blacks opposed Reagan".   5.) The fiction of an ideational entity.
Opinion is not an essence like a Platonic Idea. Opinions are held by individuals
for various adaptive reasons and with various intensity. One frequently hears
politicians violate this fallacy when they claim that the majority that elected
them gave a mandate to implement an entire philosophy of ideas. In fact many
voters may have voted for candidates in spite of, not because of, a particular
philosophy.   6.) The group-product or "emergent" theory. Public opinion in
contemporary Western democracies is unlike Golden Age Athenian public
opinion, where the entire population gathered together to discuss issues and
arrive at some sort of a conclusion. 7.) The eulogistic theory. This fallacy often
is a byproduct of the group-product theory. Public opinion is not necessarily
superior to individual opinion. What is reported in public opinion polls is not the
result of a group discussion in which several talents combine forces to produce a
hybrid opinion. Bogart (1972) reports that when 80 percent of the students at a
Japanese university failed an exam, some protested that their answers, not the
key's answers, were correct because they were in the majority. The instructor
remained unconvinced. In 1954, Gallup reported that 62 percent of America
favored using atomic artillery shells on Red China. In retrospect implementing
that policy would have been disastrous less than superiorly. 8.) The confusion
of public opinion with the public presentation of opinion, or the journalistic

fallacy. Allport classifies non-statistical opinion here. Editorials and journalistic hunches do not constitute public opinion.

Another critic of polls is Blumer (Katz *et al.*, 1954, pp. 70 ff). He proposes a more functional approach to the study of public opinion. Opinions of individuals are formed by many diverse factors. Certain key figures and groups have greater influence in forming opinions (cf. Kahle & Sales, 1978, 1980; Kahle, Sales, & Nagel, 1980). Rather than asking randomly selected people what their opinions are, Blumer suggests that we study how key people, key associations, and key social organizations influence public opinion and then tap what can be obtained from the sources of opinion. Certainly a good deal of evidence supports the hypothesis that the opinions of leaders are quite important (e.g. R. Kahle, 1977). Although such surveys can never lead to representation of the entire population, they may be extremely helpful in understanding and predicting trends.

Bogart (1972) cites some provocative statistics that support Blumer's contention that the "man in the street" may not know what he is doing when he gives a pollster an opinion. In 1948, regarding the Metallic Metals Act controversy, 59 percent of the sample agreed that "it would be a good thing but should be left to the individual states", 16 percent considered it to be "all right for foreign countries but should not be required here", and 30 percent had no opinion. Unfortunately, there was no such controversy as the "Metallic Metals Act", nor was there even a "Metallic Metals Act". If 70 percent of the people are willing to take a stand on the basis of no information, one must suspect that many people could easily have such attitudes changed by an opinion pace-setter with comprehensive information. In general one gains little by measuring attitudes based on nonexistent or crude abstractions.

Laboratory Experiments in Attitude Research

During the Golden Age of Cognitive Dissonance research in the 1960s and early 1970s, laboratory experiments on attitudes were considered by many to be the ultimate methodology for theoretical advancement in attitude psychology. It is difficult today to imagine the naive optimism that swept social psychology during that period in its innocent love affair with that femme fatale, the laboratory deception experiment. For example, by way of introduction to a list of problems with laboratory deception experiments, hardly more than a decade ago, Kiesler, Collins, and Miller clarified that the problems were not to be taken too seriously by giving the punch line before the joke: "It is almost inevitable, then, that a book concerned with theory should concentrate on data from experimental studies. The experiment is unsurpassed as a source of causal and theory-testing data" (Kiesler, Collins, & Miller, 1969, p. 45). Today few attitude researchers share the infinite forgivingness toward the devastating wrongs of the experiment expressed during the 1960s, in spite of its continuing superficial but stunning beauty. Indeed, many of the experiment's former leading advocates have seen virtue in other methodologies recently (e.g. Aronson, Blaney, Stephan, Sikes, & Snapp, 1978; McGuire, 1973; Zajonc, 1980). The criticisms are for the most part not especially new, but the content of the criticisms now often is taken more seriously. More researchers today recognize the virtue of multiple methodological approaches, of diversity. Let us examine some of the criticisms of the laboratory experiment as a situation, to see why the love affair of the 1960s has gone awry, in spite of the persistence of inherent beauty of randomly assigning people to conditions as a way to eliminate alternative explanations.

Experimenter Bias

Sometimes experimenters may unintentionally, or even intentionally, bias the results of their experiments (Rosenthal, 1966). Although some of the research often cited to support this hypothesis has been criticized (Barber & Silver, 1968), it is probably true that some unknown quantity, perhaps a small quantity, of research results in attitude experiments reflect the intentional or unintentional results of experimenter bias, whether it be based on callous disregard for the truth, carelessness, or incompetence.

Subject Bias

Weber and Cook (1972) identified at least three artifactual roles that subjects may adopt during the course of an experiment, above and beyond the "faithful" role that researchers hope will be followed. Each type of role warrants some consideration.

The Good Subject Role. Subjects often seek to make themselves look good to the experimenter through complying with the experimenter's implicit demands (Kahle & Page, 1976; Orne, 1962; Page & Kahle, 1976). For example, we saw in the discussion of the classical conditioning of attitudes how the subjects complied with the implicit demands of the setting by manifesting "conditioning" after solving the riddle of the purpose of the experiment. Many laboratory attitude studies potentially create demand characteristics within the context of the attitude manipulation. In addition to conditioning studies, for example, communicator credibility studies often provide unambiguous cues to research subjects about what the experimenter expects of them (Page, 1970b). Researchers in all attitude change studies should routinely probe postexperimentally for the cognitions that subjects experienced when completing the dependent measures, if researchers want to make certain that attitudes rather than role compliances are crucial in the research results (cf. Page & Kahle, 1976).

The Negativistic Subject Role. Masling (1966) identified the negativistic subject role, more frequently called (in the technical scientific jargon of social psychology) the "screw you" subject. Sometimes research participants feel hostile toward researchers, especially when the researchers make the subject look foolish or feel like an object. Sometimes college subjects simply resent their research participation requirements. Other times they are hostile because they previously have been deceived by researchers (Silverman, Shulman, & Weisenthal, 1970) or view psychologists as intrusive. Whatever the reason, some subjects seek to show that they are not objects by performing in the opposite manner from what they perceive to be the experimenter's hypothesis. In attitude change experiments this often means that the subject will respond in the opposite way from the advocated message of the persuasive attempt. Although this role probably occurs less frequently than the good subject role, it often clusters in manners that are especially devastating. For example, I once had a group of subjects waiting for an experiment when one of them vehemently and loudly denounced psychology, psychologists, and research on "human introductory psychology students". The session generated data entirely contrary to the hypothesis being tested and the results of all previous similar sessions. It rendered the study useless. Often "screw you" subjects will cluster in one or two cells of a design, confusing any subsequent interpretation of the data.

The Apprehensive Subject Role.   Probably more apprehensive subjects show up to participate in attitude change experiments than any other type of "unfaithful" subject. Hardly any subject wants to look stupid. If the test requires memorizing 20 nonsense syllables that the subject as a student would refuse to learn, the subject as a subject may nevertheless willingly learn the words to prove to the experimenter his or her ability (Rosenberg, 1965, 1969). Rosenberg (1965) has shown how evaluation apprehension, the fear of being negatively appraised, can alter the results of an attitude change experiment. Many researchers in attitude change have probably encountered the subject who post-experimentally asks, "Did I do well?", even though most attitude studies are not designed to test ability.

To the extent that subjects assume any of these three roles, an extent that almost certainly varies from study to study, the data from an attitude change experiment may reflect role-related behavior rather than the nature of what the direct impact of the experimental manipulation *per se* would be if that manipulation were conducted outside the laboratory.

The Volunteer Subject.   Many psychology studies of attitude change rely on volunteers for research. Ethically, this is usually necessary. Scientifically, it is not always desirable. For example, volunteers, when contrasted with non-volunteers, tend to be more intelligent, better educated, higher in need for approval, more sociable, more arousal-seeking, less conventional, less authoritarian, and more responsive to experimenters' purposes (Silverman, 1977). We know from Chapter Six that individual differences such as these will influence the results of attitude change research. And we know that theoretically good research should begin with sampling and sampling theory (Kish, 1965), preferably by drawing a probability sample from some well-defined population to which a researcher wishes to generalize; finding volunteers will by definition be a bad sampling strategy.

Design Bias

Often times the very design will bias the nature of the study and its likely results. Most often this type of bias can only be identified on an *ad hoc* basis, since it usually interacts with the specific hypothesis and procedures being utilized in a particular study. Several types, however, have more universal status.

Ethics and Deception. Stricker (1967) reported that 72% of balance and dissonance studies involve deception of the subjects. Some psychologists are beginning to question the wisdom of such habitual dishonesty (Baumrind, 1964; Kelman, 1968, 1972). Most researchers are also professors, whose job it is to impart accurate information and to serve as role models for students. When such calloused disregard for truth is conveyed by the researcher-professor and in social psychology texts and journals, it is possible to expect that some unintended and unfortunate side effects and lessons are learned from deception psychology. Students may develop a lower regard for honesty, subjects may develop a suspiciousness toward research that alters their behavior, the public may develop a lower regard for psychologists and the funding of psychological research, and the psychologist's ability to promote human dignity may be impaired. The second point is especially important vis-a-vis biasing research results. The climate of mistrust undermines honest responding by the subject. Why should a subject want to be honest to someone who is lying? All researchers should ask themselves before each study whether any planned deception can be avoided or reduced, and the profession as a whole should continually seek ways to minimize and counteract any necessary deception. Nevertheless, some form of deception does at times seem necessary for research to proceed, and it would be unfortunate to advance any universal ban on deception research without a case by case consideration of the worth of the research.

Relevance. Often laboratory studies research trivial topics because trivial attitudes are far more easily changed than deeply held attitudes. Most fifteen minute studies, for example, will not convert a person from an atheist to a Baptist, or vice versa. And if they did, the ethical implications for such research would be even more profound than they already are. There is nothing *per se* wrong with research on trivial topics (cf. Taylor & Fiske, 1979), except that good evidence is available showing that trivial topics differ fundamentally in terms of attitude change processes from phenomenologically important topics (Taylor, 1975). But presumably some researchers are interested in studying important attitudes (cf. Sherif, Sherif, & Nebergall, 1965). The researcher often has a dilemma, then, if he or she is an experimentalist, of selecting careful research on trivial topics or sloppy research on meaningful topics. Ring (1967) further interjected into this debate the motion of "fun and games" social psychology. Some studies seem purposefully to seek to display dramatic but meaningless effects. This issue has at least contributed to the decline of total faith in the experimental method of social research (cf. Rosnow, 1981) and thereby also trivializes the research.

Generalizability. Many critics have attacked experimental methodology for its frequent lack of generalizability or external validity, which is closely akin to the issue of relevance. The criticism essentially maintains that many aspects of laboratory research have such a small degree of relevance that they hardly represent anything likely to be found in the world beyond the laboratory. Subject behavior may be contrived and ungeneralizable. For example, studies of juror attitudes have often asked college sophomores, who are unlikely to be jurors, to read a couple of paragraphs and then describe their new attitude, as if it were an attitude based on visiting an actual trial. These attitudes, however, almost certainly do not represent what attitudes real jurors would espouse, who base their attitudes on far more complex information and who realize the serious consequences of their attitudes (cf. Diamond & Zeisel, 1974). On the other hand, some paradigms, such as the Prisoner's Dilemma Game, which appears to be artificial, may indeed have good external validity (Bem & Lord, 1979).

Variance Components. The analysis of variance approach to studying attitudes is one of the most widely used and most respected ways of studying attitudes. Typically, researchers measure or manipulate some attitude variable, assign subjects to various situations, and then measure some dependent variable. Inasmuch as these types of studies are used to make inferences about components of variance attributable to situations, attitudes, or interactions, they are subject to design criticisms. By manipulating the types of attitudes and situations it is quite easy to alter what will lead to the largest component of variance. For example, if one wanted to demonstrate that attitudes or other person-variables can account for more variance than situations, it would only be necessary to select heterogeneous attitudes while selecting homogeneous situations. With the person-variable of ethnicity, for example, it would be easy to show that American college freshmen score higher on an English language intelligence test than aborigines, regardless of whether the situation is a blue or green testing room. Likewise, one would expect that the person-variable of height would not account for nearly as much variance in joke-telling behavior among a group of American college freshmen as would the situations of a concentration camp versus an ice cream store. Sarason, Smith, and Diener (1975) reviewed several hundred studies and found that neither person-variables, situations, nor their interactions consistently accounted for large amounts of variance, implying that in the final analysis this abuse may not be too consequential.

Nevertheless, many researchers fail to recognize that "amount of variance accounted for" is a game to play, not a serious scientific question. For example, Mischel (1968) has suggested that person-variables ought to be called into question because they often do not account for large amounts of variance, when correlated with behavior. Yet without a more detailed examination of the specific design involved and the politics of publication (Studies that make "obvious" findings are harder to publish than studies that report "subtle but counterintuitive" effects), such an observation is irrelevant, within the context of statistically significant relationships.

An additional criticism of ANOVA designs like these is they make no effort to select independent variables randomly. Authors are typically not interested in making random-effects analysis of variance inferences (inferences to all possible levels of the independent variable), being satisfied rather with writing only about the specific independent variable levels in their experiments. When others use original data for making components of variance inferences, however, these others must incorrectly assume that the original design was a random-effects analysis of variance design.

Causal Inferences. Although often analyzed with analyses of variance, many designs are not truly experimental analysis of variance designs since the personal factor — the trait or the attitude — has been measured only and subjects have not been randomly assigned to traits or attitudes. (In cases where subjects are randomly assigned to trait or attitudes, the experiments are often trivial for the reasons mentioned earlier and because the manipulated trait or attitude often interacts with the subject's true trait or attitude (McGuire, 1968c).) But just as this design is not a pure experimental design, neither is it a pure correlational design since situations are usually assigned randomly; hence, this type of design is subject to both the criticisms of correlational studies and the criticisms of true experiments with analysis of variance mentioned above. And it is not legitimate to interpret causation for anything except the situation (manipulated variable) main effect if the data are examined only with ANOVA.

Stimulus Condition Self-selection. According to social adaptation theory, the human is actively involved in determining what situations he or she will allow to determine subsequent behaviors. This assertion contradicts the conception of the human research participant popularized by situationism, which often views the human's response to situations as functionally equivalent to the white rat's response. Yet most experimental research designs do not allow for stimulus condition self-selection.

Researchers have generally preferred to assign subjects to stimulus conditions randomly because random assignment is an assumption of true experiments with analysis of variance, which used to lead to stronger inferences than traditional correlational designs. If one assumes that all human behavior is completely and situationally determined, then assigning subjects to stimulus conditions does not violate any ontological assumptions. If, however, one assumes it is possible that people may on occasion select and/or modify their stimulus conditions, then random assignment to stimulus conditions may distort inferences about the relative importance of situations.

Failure to consider stimulus condition self-selection fully has created unnecessary pessimism about the predictive utility of trait and attitude measures. Consider the following example: A researcher wants to study whether gambling and religious attitudes predict behavior. He or she identifies a population of priests who are indifferent to gambling and a population of gamblers who are indifferent to religion. Representatives of each population are randomly assigned to a cathedral or to a bingo-for-cash game. The researcher discovers that, independent of attitude, subjects at the cathedral behave reverently and subjects in the bingo game bet. Our researcher infers, therefore, that attitudes and behavior are unrelated and that situations have more predictive utility in the realms of religion and gambling than do attitudes. If our researcher had allowed the priests and gamblers to select their own stimulus conditions, however, the inferences may have been different. Priests would head for the cathedral while gamblers would place their bets with the gaming room. But our researcher would not allow such events to occur because the independent variables would have been correlational and the inferences therefore weakened.

Some empirical evidence for stimulus condition self-selection as a determinant of behavior comes from the research generated by dissonance theory (Festinger, 1957) on selective exposure to information. Although the early research on this topic did not provide strong support for the hypothesis that people seek out information consonant with their attitudes (Freedman & Sears, 1965), more recent research has been more consistent with the original hypothesis. Brock and Balloun (1967), for example, showed that subjects would push a button to eliminate static more to hear consonant than dissonant information about smoking and religion. Barlett, Drew, Fahle, & Watts (1974) mailed envelopes with "Voters for Nixon" or "Voters for McGovern" in the return address position to families with all voters registered in the same political party. The enclosed letter claimed no association with either Republican Nixon or Democrat McGovern and asked subjects to return the enclosed postcard for a study on bulk mail. More Democrats than Republicans returned the postcards when the envelope was from "Voters for McGovern", and more Republicans than Democrats returned the postcard when the envelope was from "Voters for Nixon". They interpret these results as supporting the hypothesis that voters attend to consonant information more than to dissonant information.

The general lack of research on stimulus condition self-selection may in part be due to the difficulty of conceptualizing stimuli as dependent variables in analysis of variance research. In a recent ingenious experiment, Brickman and D'Amato (1975) recognized this same problem in the mere exposure controversy (Stang, 1974; Zajonc, 1968). By allowing subjects to select auditory stimuli from a jukebox, they were able to integrate several previously perplexing hypotheses about mere exposure. In order truly to test the hypothesis of stimulus condition self-selection it is necessary for stimulus conditions to function both as independent and as dependent variables.

Kahle and Berman (1979b) showed the hypothesized relationship between attitudes, stimulus condition self-selections, and behaviors, at least in the realm of politics, when they used a cross-lagged panel correlation design to demonstrate that attitudes lead to stimulus condition self-selections, which in turn lead to behaviors.

Kahle (1980) demonstrated the hypothesized sequence in a laboratory setting with locus of control as the person-factor. He provided evidence that internals are more likely to select a situation in which they can demonstrate skill and externals are more likely to select a situation ruled by chance. This pattern conforms to the questionnaire data of Schneider (1968, 1972). It also conforms to data others have collected in other arenas (Fyans & Maehr, 1979; Holland, 1966; Kelley & Stahelski, 1970; Snyder, 1981). Thus, some evidence undermines the viability of random assignment to situations as an element of a research design proposed to assess the importance of situations. In this Kahle study, once people entered the skill-versus-chance situation, their cheating on an examination reflected the person-situation interaction expectation.

Summary

We can thus see that the laboratory attitude change experiment has sufficient problems that it hardly deserves the unqualified confidence expressed by many attitude researchers in the 1960s. Experimenter bias, subject bias, and design bias can all alter the results from laboratory studies and thus lead to mistaken inferences. At the same time that the utility of the experiment has been declining, the utility of the survey and poll has been increasing. But the two types of studies each have areas of special prowess.

Polls Versus Experiments

Hovland (1959) discusses the role of the experiment in public opinion measurement. An apparent contradiction between survey findings and experimental findings stimulated Hovland's exploration of the two techniques. Experiments usually find much larger effects for change manipulations. Hovland suggested that one major difference between the survey and the experiment is that in experiments the experimenter selects what the subjects will be exposed to, whereas in non-experimental settings, subjects themselves select what they will allow to influence their opinions. In personality research this has been called stimulus condition self-selection (Kahle, 1980), and it almost by definition implies that the abstractions formed will differ such that greater accommodation takes place in the laboratory. Other differences also exist. Pollsters usually try to obtain representative samples, whereas experiments usually study college sophomores. Pollsters are more likely to study phenomenologically important attitudes than are experimenters, which we saw in the self-perception literature leads to different processes of attitude change (Taylor, 1975). Experimenters usually study newly-formed attitudes, which have had too little time to filter through subjects' cognitive structures (Liska, 1974; McGuire, 1960). Counterpersuasion occurs more often in the field during the lag between manipulation and measurement, in part because the interviewing time is usually longer in the field. Finally, experimenters typically provide more structure and more control to the interview situation.

This last point implies that the basic difference between laboratory and field studies may be yet another aspect of the person-situation dichotomy. By its very nature the laboratory tends to emphasize the situation, whereas the field study tends to emphasize the person. Laboratory studies impose structure on situations, in part because manipulation, a requirement of true experiments, is more easily done to situations than to persons. Surveys question persons. Here the person-situation dialectic would seem to invite an increase in the new methodologies that integrate the two.

The Dialectic Between Laboratory and Survey Research

Since it is obvious that both laboratory studies of attitudes and surveys or polls of attitudes are flawed, it is equally obvious that to debate about which methodology should be used to study attitudes is to debate a misleading question. A more appropriate question would be: What have we learned from the debate between laboratory and survey proponents? Has the dialectical tension created a new synthesis that advances our knowledge? The answers to these questions fall into at least two categories: 1) What we have learned about the metatheory of methodology, about the principles one should bring to research, and   2) What we have developed in methodologies capable of overcoming at least some of the shortcomings of earlier methodologies.

On the level of metatheory of methodology, one principle is that no one methodology should ever be the exclusive workhorse for an entire area of research. Each methodology obscures some important ideas and phenomena, and each methodology flaunts some phenomena that are trivial. A second principle is that truly adequate research ought to allow for, not obscure, the full complexity of human behavior. Over the lifespan humans occupy multiple roles with multiple other humans in multiple environments and contexts. All of the multiple elements potentially interact in reciprocal, interdependent ways with one another, continuously changing one another (Bronfenbrenner, 1977). Methodologies that limit investigation to a single frame will remove much of the excitement and action of person-situation interactions.

Several new developments in methodology seem particularly promising within the context of the previous methodological problems and the above principles. First we will consider several advances in the consideration of independent variables, and then we will turn to dependent variables. This distinction is, of course, not always a useful one when "dependent variables" are influencing "independent variables".

Independent Variables

Correlation and Causation. One historic reason psychological social psychologists have opted for the laboratory study more often than for the survey has been the superior quality of inferences available from the former. That is, random assignment of research participants to experimental conditions made possible "causal" inferences not available in other types of research. Steady progress in inferential techniques within the field of survey research, however, is beginning to change that (e.g. Kenny, 1979). Researchers now are developing techniques known as structural equation models, borrowed primarily from econometrics, that in some circumstances enable researchers to venture causal inferences from survey and correlational data. Cross lagged panel analysis (Kahle & Berman, 1979b; Kenny, 1975) and path analysis are two subspecies of structural equation methodology. The methods are complicated and require some difficult assumptions, but the promise of circumventing the ethical and logistical problems of manipulation vault these structural equation methodologies to the top of the dialectical spiral for the moment.

To argue that variable A "causes" variable B implies three things about the relationship between A and B; according to Kenny (1979): 1) A must precede B temporally. 2) A and B must be related. If A changes, that fact must provide some sort of information about probable changes in B, in the statistical sense. 3) The relationship between A and B must be nonspurious (Suppes, 1970). It cannot result from some other factor, such as C.

Cause does not mean definitive. Rather, the current trend in social science views causes probabilistically (Suppes, 1970). Each statistical inference is assigned a probability level (e.g. $p < .05$). Researchers who make "causal" inferences from correlational data use the word *cause*, not to imply new philosophical advances, but rather to underscore the fact that the Humean argument that "correlation does not imply causation" sometimes is irrelevant to certain types of correlational inferences, in the sense *cause* has been defined here. To the extent that experimental researchers who assign subjects to conditions randomly are bothered by using the word *cause* to describe their research (although they rarely object to calling their results *effects*), all correlational researchers should also be bothered by their own use of the term *cause*. Experimentalists do, however, have a more standardized understanding of the nature of their inferences.

One type of methodology useful for "causal" inference is cross-lagged panel correlation. Cross-sectional polls avoid repeated measuring of the same individual because such repetition may lead to biased results. The panel technique, on the other hand, seeks to interview the same person repeatedly and intensively. Ostensibly, this technique would appear to do a more thorough job of demonstrating public opinion since the information obtained is more detailed and the measurer has a greater opportunity to learn about the complexity of the person, the whims to which the person is subject, and the deeper psychological factors that have an impact on the person. Individual growth and longitudinal change have been hopelessly underemphasized in adult social psychology. Furthermore, the interviewer need not seek out the basic demographic data about the panel respondent for each new issue that is measured. The major problem with the panel technique, aside from the cost and attrition factors, is that panel members know that they will be studied and hence may become overinformed relative to a naive random sample. Panel members tend to read the newspaper more carefully and to watch television more carefully since they know that they will be quizzed on issues. Lazarsfeld (in Berelson & Janowitz, 1966, pp. 645 ff.) suggests that panels by themselves may not be excessively useful, but when used in conjunction with other techniques such as cross-sectional polling, they contribute to a deeper understanding of how individuals form opinions. Panel studies do foster superior statistical opportunities (Kenny, 1975; Kahle & Berman, 1979b), and this reason alone justifies more attention to and use of panels.

The cross-lagged panel correlation (CLPC) technique is based on the assumption that "causes" precede "effects". If variable A causes variable B, then A ought to have more impact (a stronger correlation with) on subsequent measures of B than on prior measures of B, given certain assumptions. Kenny (1973) has provided the mathematical proof that if the correlation between A at time 1 and B at time 2 (r_{A1B2}) is identical in absolute value with the correlation of B at time 1 with A at time 2 (r_{A2B1}), then the relationship is spurious (non causal). If, however, the null hypothesis is not true $(r_{A1B2} \neq r_{A2B1})$ and certain assumptions have been satisfied, then nonspuriousness can be inferred. The most important assumptions are the following three, a relatively short list as statistics go: 1) *Synchronicity* means that the processes measured within a given time (e.g. A1 & B1) reflect the same time frame. Retrospective questions, for example, are not allowed. 2) *Stationarity* means that the causal structure does not shift during the study. Equality of synchronous correlation $(r_{A1B1} = r_{A2B2})$ is consistent with stationarity. 3) *Stability* is an assumption which, if violated, could make the variable with the larger autocorrelation $(r_{A1A2}$ or $r_{B1B2})$ incorrectly appear to be an effect. Equality of autocorrelations $(r_{A1A2} = r_{B1B2})$ is consistent with stability. Although these assumptions sound stringent, in practice they can often be satisfied.

This third assumption of stability is an addition to the list proposed by Kenny (1975). Some recent critics (e.g. Rogosa, 1980) have shown why this assumption is necessary. Many of the critics, however, have overestimated the extent to which instability undermines inferences in CLPC. Instability only is one more problem to consider, *not* an unsolvable problem that obliterates the methodology's utility. In cases where the autocorrelations are equal or where the "causal" variable has the larger autocorrelation, CLPC is still valid. Furthermore, the utility of CLPC as a test for spuriousness (as opposed to causation) is in no way undermined by recent criticism. Therefore, the method ought still to be used, but it ought to be used with care. It remains preferable in several respects to some of the alternatives to it.

Kulka, Kahle, & Klingel (1982) present several new criteria for making inferences with CLPC. The larger cross-lagged correlation should be greater than 0 and greater than the absolute value of the smaller cross-lagged correlation. And the larger cross-lagged correlation should have the same sign (+ or −) as both synchronous correlations. These criteria protect against cases in which small, randomly fluctuating correlations might appear to be different, based on the Pearson—Filon test for differences between correlated correlations, in spite of the trivial amount of variance they cover.

Other structural equation models (path models) have different assumptions and do other feats especially well. Although some authors try to argue that one approach or another is especially good, the specific goals of an author really determine what assumptions and techniques are applicable to a particular research project. All of these techniques potentially expand our methodological capacity to study person-situation interactions.

Field, natural, and quasi experiments.   Many researchers advocate experimentation outside of the laboratory (cf. Campbell & Stanley, 1963; Cook & Campbell, 1979). Sherif, Harvey, Hoyt, Hood, & Sherif (1961), for example, infiltrated the power structure of a summer camp and manipulated interpersonal attitudes without the boys in the camp ever realizing the nature of the study. Although this type of research might today violate the ethical principle of informed consent, the concept of an experiment in the "real world" certainly does not violate that ethical standard for *a priori* reasons. Naturalistic studies may be natural in terms of the behavior, setting, or treatment (Tunnell, 1977). In terms of the dialectical tension between laboratory and field studies of attitudes, these studies try to capture the phenomenological significance of surveys while preserving the rigor and, to some extent, the control of the laboratory. These studies certainly accrue additional difficulties and complexities not a part of either the survey or the laboratory study, but the benefits from a well-conceived and executed study justify the extra difficulty involved. They usually require thoughtful, careful consideration of alternative explanations if they are to be useful.

Several quasi-experimental designs have been explored in great detail by Donald Campbell and his associates (Campbell & Stanley, 1963; Cook & Campbell, 1979). In addition to the correlational techniques identified above, they have given considerable attention to the regression-discontinuity techniques, the interrupted time series technique, and nonequivalent control-group designs. The first two techniques are quite similar in that they look for breaks in patterns that might be predicted from some intervention. Regression-discontinuity makes a large number of observations of different persons, units, or groups, one per group, whereas the interrupted time-series designs utilize a large number of observations of the same persons, units, or groups. Nonequivalent control groups create frequent problems of interpretation because of possible pre-existing differences between the groups. Detailed analysis of alternative explanations can sometimes reveal certain types of implausibility.

Idiographic Approaches.   Idiographic approaches to the study of behavior, which may involve independent or dependent variables, focus more on the individual and less on the group in general than other, nomothetic techniques. Several interactionist researchers in the personality literature have recently revived the intense study of the individual (Bem & Allen, 1974; Kenrick & Stringfield, 1981; Tunnell, 1980). Advocates of the idiographic approach to the assessment of attitudes have been around at least since the days of Carl Hovland, and frequently authors note that identical scale points for two subjects on one attitude item may mean something quite different to different subjects (Ostrom & Upshaw, 1968). Nevertheless, careful attention to the individual occurs altogether too rarely.

Q-Methodology.   Stephenson's (1953) Q-technique has been around for over two decades, but it is just now beginning to find its way into personality and public opinion measurement (cf. Bem, 1979; Bem & Funder, 1978). This method isolates intra-individual trait factors using small sample sizes. It is suited particularly well to interactive research because persons and situations can be measured commensurately. It may ultimately replace or supplement other techniques of interviews, but its use has been too limited thus far for any generalizations about its widespread utility or applicability to public opinion to be ventured. Nevertheless, it is a method especially useful in person-situation interaction studies (Bem, 1979).

Observation.   Doob (1948) discusses systematic and participant observation as methods for measuring public opinion. These methods represent another way to obtain detailed information about public opinion, but they are more closely tied up with observer competence than any·other method that has been mentioned. The risk of obtaining biased information is enormous, as is the risk of being guilty of Allport's journalistic fallacy. Nevertheless, understanding interactions may hinge on obtaining the rich detail available from observational studies. Rebirth of this research by psychologists would be appropriate.

Dependent Variables

Just as different types of independent variables will lead to different types of research results for extra-theoretical reasons, likewise the results may vary as a function of the type of dependent variables researchers use. The ubiquitous "Likert-type" scale dominates attitude research like corn dominates Nebraska. The scales are called "Likert-type" because, although they do use numeric options (rate your attitude on a scale of one to five), they do not follow the rigor that Likert advocated fifty years ago, opting instead for the simplest possible scaling. Little empirical evidence justifies this sloppiness and laziness, but both survey and laboratory researchers usually do it. Likert intended that researchers would use multiple items, selected with logical and statistical care, to measure both an attitude and its internal consistency. Most researchers elect to ask only one question, even if the question has unknown method error associated with it. Kahle, Kulka, & Klingel (1980) compared single item dependent variables with composite dependent variables and found that the causal pattern emerged consistently only when composites were used. About half the time single items obscured what composites revealed.

One single item may often tap some idiosyncratic source of variance and thereby deceive the researcher who relies on it. For example, in one study of adolescents the researchers wanted to measure adolescent heterosexual contact with the question, "How often in the last month have you dated a member of the opposite sex?" When the results showed that the best predictors of "dating behaviors" were dishonesty and desire to impress adults, the researchers asked the participants in the study about their responses to that item. The adolescents explained that only "old people" date. No adolescent in vogue would ever describe heterosexual contact as "dating", the respondents explained to the ancient, unstylish researchers. If the researchers had used multiple "Likert-type" measures of heterosexual contact, the "archaic" language would probably not have misled them. On the other hand, social desirability often confounds studies of adolescent sexual behavior. Longitudinal research often discovers "born again" virgins who report prior sexual intercourse at an early point in the study but later claim none.

Each kind of dependent variable in attitude research implies a variety of often ignored assumptions about attitudes. For example, Jaccard (1979) has pointed out how different types of attitude scales imply different relationships between attitudes and behaviors. True Likert scales, which sum multiple items measuring the same concept, imply that the higher the score on the scale, the greater the probability of engaging in target behaviors. Guttman scales, which assume that a respondent will endorse every item up to a point and none of the items beyond it, imply that behavior is an all-or-none function of attitudes. Thurstone scales imply yet a different relationship, a kind of rising and falling of behaviors with given attitudes. Researchers are obliged to consider what implications their measurement techniques might have for different inferences.

Because it is impossible to imagine all of the assumptions and potential pitfalls of any given dependent variable, researchers ought to explore a variety of dependent variables, just as they ought to explore a variety of independent variables. Webb, Campbell, Schwartz, & Sechrest (1966) have proposed quite a diverse array of attitude measures and other dependent variables for social science research. Whiskey bottles in the garbage imply an attitude about consuming alcoholic beverages. Worn out tiles on the floor of a museum suggest an attitude of patrons toward the closest exhibit. Dirty pages in an encyclopedia hint at what topics interest people. Oriental jade dealers apparently believe that dilated pupils in response to exposure to a gem indicate strong fascination. The location of noseprints on the window of a candy store may signal the tastes of youthful consumers. When people respond to the question, "Was the weekly American wage in 1945, $37 or $57 [it was in fact $47]?", they imply whether they remember 1945 as a good or a bad time. And the list goes on. Researchers must learn that attitudes need not always be measured on a scale of one to five (or seven or nine). Diversity and variety of measurement would improve understanding.

Use of appropriate dependent variables is even more crucial. The ways of social adaptation vary widely, and a single measure may often entirely miss the point of some manipulation. The story has been told of the telephone company implementing a service charge for every call to information, in order to discourage use of this expensive customer service. The fee had its desired effect, few customers called information. If only one dependent variable had been measured, the story would end here with a happy telephone company. However, the telephone company also measured requests for free telephone books. In the case of that dependent variable, the small fee on calls to information apparently greatly boosted requests for telephone books, which the company distributed for free. The final result was that the company spent more on books than it saved from a reduced number of requests for information. If only one dependent variable had been measured, the telephone company might not have realized the error in its ways.

Conclusion

The methodological dialectic in the area of attitudes has lagged behind the theoretical dialectic. Methodological progress is urgently needed. Until methods capture the movie of attitudes rather than the snapshot of attitudes and until attitude measures reveal the complexities of how attitudes interact with the situation and with other aspects of the person, we will have to hope that our theories are not distorted too much by the available measurement technique and methodology. In the interim, skepticism has its place. Likewise, creative designs that combine advantages of surveys and experiments ought to be explored and encouraged, since both surveys and experiments have significant disadvantages.

Aspects of the situation that modify attitudes extend beyond methodology. In the next chapter, we turn to these more general situational aspects of attitudes and attitude change. These situational factors are an unignorable part of the dialectical tension between the person and the situation.

CHAPTER 7

Scope of situations

SITUATIONS are discussed far more frequently than they are carefully defined or elaborated. One of the great missing elements in understanding person-situation interactions in attitude research has been the lack of a comprehensive description of the types of situations one might encounter that have clear relevance for persuasion. The area of interactionism in personality has also faced the same problem and repeatedly heard unanswered appeals for the development of a psychology of social situations. From time to time one scholar or another issues the plea for more careful analyses of situations (e.g. Frederiksen, 1972; Gibson, 1960; Jessor & Jessor, 1973; Pervin, 1978). Recently three very import-ant books in the personality literature have focused additional attention on this concern and moved the field forward considerably (Argyle, Furnham, & Graham, 1981; Furnham & Argyle, 1981; Magnusson, 1981). Considerable progress is still needed in the field of attitudes, however. Especially important is the establish-ment of the link between situations and social adaptation.

Cody (1978) and others have noted the variety of reasons why an adequate taxonomy of situations for understanding the important dimensions of attitude change situations is needed. Such a taxonomy would have heuristic value, stimulating research on a variety of new questions. A taxonomy could simplify assessment by focusing attention on certain key aspects of a question. Tax-onomies often help clarify generalizations and generalizability. They aid in the identification of appropriate strategies, both for research and for adaptation. They integrate and underline the relationships among the various aspects of knowledge about a certain topic. Biologists and chemists have reaped consider-able benefit from their access to carefully constructed taxonomies, for example.

One paradox of the low level of situational analysis within attitude psycho-logy is that it implies a low level of advancement of our science, in contrast to the frequent posing of more advanced questions. Piaget has argued that sciences solve various types of problems in approximately the same sequence as children develop cognitive skills as they age. Later skills build on earlier skills. The de-velopment of ability with hierarchical classification skill is an early skill, fre-quently mastered by the time children start school. It would therefore seem that attitude psychology should proceed along this front quickly, in spite of frequent appeals for the resolution of more advanced problems, in order that we first master the necessary skills and groundwork for more advanced problems.

Situational Dimensions in Other Areas of Social Science

Many social scientists have identified dimensions along which situations vary within the context of various types of social influence. Many of these lists are more advanced than anything in the attitude literature. An examination of a smattering of these situations, in order to place later classification systems into context, will be helpful at this point, before progressing to look more carefully at situations relevant to attitudes. Cody (1978) and Ekehammar (1974) have also provided interesting discussions on this topic.

Systems of Classifying Situations

From a social adaptation perspective individuals bring to a situation their relevant schemata about goals, interacting others, themselves and their abilities. The situation holds certain expectations for individuals entering it, and the situation will be developed and transformed through the individual's interactions with it.

Hunt (1981) has suggested that situations may be at one of three levels of difficulty in Piagetian theory. The first is an overlearned situation, which demands virtually nothing of a person except the application of a well-developed schema. Highly routinized aspects of some jobs illustrate this type of situation. Behavior in this type of situation is predictable but may also bore the performer. A second type of situation is one in which no available schema can be applied. For example, first-time prisoner of war in a strange country with a strange language and strange customs may very well not know anything about the new situation. Frustration and misconstrual characterize these highly unexpected situations. A great deal of change may take place in this type of situation, but it may be inefficient of ineffective change. Like the seven year old faced with an advanced geometry problem, a solution may be found to the problem at hand, but it will probably not be the optimal solution. The *alimental* situation is one that challenges the individual by demanding slightly more of the individual than he or she has available at a certain time. The alimental situation creates disequilibrium that the individual seeks to rectify through accommodation and assimilation of the situation. This alimental situation, which necessitates a manageable amount of adaptation, maximizes optimal change and is experienced as the most interesting.

Researchers uninvolved with social adaptation theory have also proposed classification systems.

Krause (1970) has listed seven types of social situations in a frequently cited collection of ideas. Although these situations deal with general social behavior, they may relate to attitudes as well: (1) joint working, involving rewards and mutual goals, (2) trading, involving a compromise of conflict by exchange, (3) fight, in which conflict resolution does not rely upon compromise, (4) sponsored teaching, involving modification of a learner's behavior, (5) serving, which involves one participant servicing the needs of another for compensation, (6) self-disclosure, in which one's opinions are made known to another, and (7) playing, which involves non-serious engagements of socializing and activities which bring pleasure to participants. Certainly these situations all invoke implicit change mechanisms, perhaps for attitudes as well as other social behavior. Miller & Steinberg (1975) similarly classify situations according to a 2 x 2 system, in which relationships may or may not be inter-personal and may or may not imply commitment to future interaction. Pervin (1976) suggests that situations may be classified according to the roles associated with them — home, work, or friends. People would seem to hold different attitudes relevant to each of these roles.

Other researchers have classified situations for very specific purposes. Wish, Deutsch, & Kaplan (1976), for example, utilized INDSCALE to construct a taxonomy of dimensions along which communication episodes, such as attitude change attempts, may vary. Their findings implied at least four distinct dimensions of communication situations: (1) competitive and hostile versus cooperative and friendly, (2) equal power versus unequal power among those people communicating, (3) intense versus superficial interaction, and (4) socio-emotional and informal versus task-oriented and formal.

Health adaptation and situations have long been considered important. Kiritz & Moos (1974) investigated the physiological effects of social environments and discovered that a number of important dimensions along which social situations vary have important consequences for physiological well-being. Support, cohesion, and affiliation tended to foster enhanced physiological adaptation, whereas rapid social change, heavy responsibility, and work pressure tended to lead to opposite physiological states. The same kind of adaptation, this time defined as anxiety, was considered by Ekehammar, Magnusson, & Ricklander (1974). In their system three aspects of the situation influence anxiety: threat of punishment, threat of fear or its anticipation, and inanimate fear.

One researcher (Forgas, 1976), in the true spirit of interactionism, found that the type of social situation that influences social behavior depends upon the type of person involved. For example, among housewives perceived intimacy and subjective self confidence are considered important dimensions, whereas for students involvement; pleasantness, and salience of norms influence situation classification. Wish et al. (1976) also suggest that their dimensions most apply to person-situation interactions.

Finally, some critics have questioned the utility of any attempt to dimensionalize situations, emphasizing the discrete structure of goals in a situation associated with the multiple people, roles, and task demands present in the situation (e.g. Graham, Argyle, & Furnham, 1980).

Kelley & Thibaut (1978) have elaborated on a similar perspective of the goal structure of dyadic interactions in their interdependence (not exchange, a term they reject) theory. Unlike Argyle and his collaborators, Kelley & Thibaut concentrate on the dyad and consider only one motive per person in a given situation. However, their system of describing goals is quite sophisticated nevertheless.

Kelley & Thibaut have identified several continua along which interdependent goals may vary. Outcomes for self and other, of course, may vary. In some cases correspondence of outcomes may be greater than others. That is, cooperation may help both members of the dyad succeed more sometimes than others. Likewise, sometimes people may attain greater control over one another than at other times. Likewise concordance of outcomes may vary. Within this framework, then, at least 9 types of dyadic relationship goals might be manifested: minimizing own, joint, or other's outcomes, maximizing own, joint, or other's outcomes, maximizing own or other's relative outcome, and equality.

Systems of Classifying Systems of Classifying Situations

In some sense the above-listed dimensions for classifying situations represent a sample of what has been accomplished through the examination of situation taxonomies. Perhaps, however, more has been written about where to look for classifications of situations than has been written actually applying the acquired meta-knowledge. Let us briefly examine some of these metasystems.

Cody (1978) found three types of categories of situation classifications when he set out to understand the situations of persuasion. Some systems attend to the type of relationship overtly involved (e.g. interaction with strangers versus close friends, power equality, intimacy, formality), some focus on the type of behavior or feeling (passiveness, loneliness, confidence, pleasantness, hostility, intensity, familiarity, etc.), and some focus on the goal of interaction or consequences of the event that is anticipated.

Attitude theorists Sherif & Sherif (1969) considered at least four classes of situation attributes important within the context of understanding social behavior: (1) attributes of participating individuals and groups, (2) the objective or task of participation, (3) the location, arrangements, settings, etc., and (4) relationships and relevance of the above three categories.

Ekehammar (1974) proposed at least five ways to approach situations. (1) One can consider *a priori* variables of physical and social character, (2) Need concepts generate many hypotheses about characteristics of situations. (3) Often one single reaction elicited by a situation dictates importance. (4) Other times only patterns of reactions elicited by situations justify classificatory attention. (5) Cognitions about and resulting from situations sometimes constitute the dimension that invites study.

Several authors (e.g. Fredericksen, 1972; Jessor & Jessor, 1973) have advocated careful attention to the old distal-proximal distinction in the causation of
behavior. For example, economic conditions may often be situational causes
of consumer attitudes, but they rarely are the immediate cause for attitudes toward at least smaller consumer items. Since most behaviors have multiple causes
and are overdetermined, the ability to think on multiple levels about different
sources of influence is an advantage.

Magnusson & Endler (1977) have proposed a process sequence way of classification of situations. They suggest that situations may be classified by examining
inputs, mediational or motivational aspects, or reactions generated by situations.
Magnusson (1981) has expanded this list in a number of ways. One place he
suggests that classification systems for situations may focus on either the objective environment dimensions of variability (e.g. complexity, clarity, strength,
promotion versus restriction, tasks, rules, roles, physical settings, or other
persons) or on person-bound properties of environment perception (e.g. goals,
perceived control, expectancies, needs and motivations, or emotions). This
same list could be reclassified according to structure (complexity, clarity,
strength, promotion versus restriction) versus content (tasks, rules, roles,
expectancies, motivations). This structural approach is especially important
in social adaptation.

One of the most careful reviews of the literature on situations (Furnham &
Argyle, 1981) and the classification of classifications implies that six basic
strategies characterize the current areas of situational analysis. In this view
research strategy is all-important in uncovering dimensions. (1) In the dimensional approach or perceptual approach, the researcher seeks to list the perceptual categories of subjective interpretation of social situations. (2) The
componential or structural approach emphasizes the uncovering of the components or structure of everyday events by first discovering the component and
then examining the structural relationships. among them. (3) The progress
approach seeks to understand one particular situation, usually for some practical
reason. (4) Environmental psychologists study the physical environment. (5)
Ecological psychologists try to understand complex social settings. Mechanisms
of particular importance in ecological analysis include affective behavior, gross
motor activity, manipulation, talking, and thinking,. (6) Ethogenic or roles—
rules analyses, which emerge from ethnomethodology and symbolic interactionism, examine social episodes, "which are defined as structured groups of
action-sequence clusters that are necessary for the performance of social acts
which collectively constitute a continuing and unfolding social life" (Furnham
& Argyle, 1981, p. xxxv).

The diversity of approaches to the study of situations hardly provides one
with any clear guidance toward the relevant dimensions for understanding the
situations of attitudes and attitude change. Perhaps the specific purpose a
particular scholar has in mind in constructing any particular taxonomy, more

than other factors, should lead toward the selection of the relevant dimensions and questions for a particular project. This factor would seem to be most useful in selecting a set of dimensions along which to evaluate attitudes and their situations.

Situational Dimensions in the Attitude Change Literature

At least a few authors have attempted, for one reason or another, to specify the dimensions of importance in attitude research. Each has generated the list in a different fashion. McGuire ha⁻ reflected on the nature of the available literature, Cody developed his list empirically, and the Yale group relied purely on logic.

McGuire

One sophisticated analysis of the attitude change literature has been provided in McGuire's well-known chapter in the second edition of the *Handbook of Social Psychology*. McGuire's goal in generating this list was to simplify the literature on attitudes somewhat. He said, "The scope of this research and the difficulties of generalizing the findings from one type of study to another will be clarified if we review briefly some of the more widely used social-influence situations" (McGuire, 1968a, p. 175). He listed six types of attitude change situations: (1) Suggestion situations are best illustrated by hypnosis. Generally this type of situation is shaped by the repeated assertion of a point of view without any logical evidence given in support of adopting the advocated position. (2) Conformity situations may involve compliance, imitation, or social contagion. Usually some authority figure or similar other advocates a position divergent from the subject's, leading to change. Many famous studies in social psychology, such as Sherif's autokinetic illusion research, Asch's study on the perception of line length, and Milgram's studies on obedience, would be considered examples of studies related to conformity. (3) Group discussion studies stimulated much of the early theoretical work by Lewin, Bales, and others during the early stages of scientific social psychology. This type of situation is noteworthy because much research has converged around the hypothesis that other people frequently exert an important influence on participants in persuasion situations. (4) Persuasive messages characterize more studies of attitude change, outside of the forced compliance paradigm, than any other category. Common sense dictates that when one wants to influence others, nothing works like a message that presents all of the relevant ideas. People assume that others are reasonable people who, if they knew all of the facts, would see the light. Unfortunately for researchers, simple studies with persuasive messages often contain excessive demand characteristics. (5) Intense indoctrination differs from all other methods in that it includes all of the others. Whether child rearing, brain washing, or psychotherapy, this method uses all of the other methods, and perhaps additional ones, to optimize impact.

McGuire's list seems basically to focus on intensity of attempt to create change as the underlying dimension. Certainly for some types of examinations of the situations of attitude change, this dimension will be quite useful. It is probable that the underlying process of attitude change does indeed vary as a function of the situation, in McGuire's sense, in which the attempt takes place. Unfortunately, McGuire's list is neither hierarchical nor comprehensive. For example, it is unclear where forced compliance research (e.g. Festinger & Carlsmith, 1959) would fit into this paradigm of situations.

In another sense McGuire's situations could be viewed as a catalogue of research traditions in social science. Indeed, McGuire refers to these situations as types of *social influence* rather than simply the narrower *attitude change*. This choice of words underscores the fact that in a sense all laboratory social psychology studies are examples of situations related to attitude change.

Perhaps the most serious weakness of this system, as with social psychology in general, is that the person is missing. In no way does this system suggest how the person and the situation might interact in the determination of behavior. McGuire has, of course, addressed this issue in a different manner (see Chapter 5).

Cody

In his dissertation Cody attempted perhaps the most comprehensive one-study empirical effort to date at classifying the situations of attitude change. Cody obtained descriptions from subjects to document their self-reports of dimensions used to classify persuasion situations. He exploited a variety of advanced statistical techniques to test the hypothesized situational dimensions of Miller & Steinberg (1975) — whether the situation is interpersonal and whether the situation is implicated in future interaction. Although he found little impressive evidence to confirm the utility of the Miller & Steinberg classification system, he did find other interesting and significant dimensions along which respondents perceive attitude change situations to vary. The most noteworthy findings of Cody may be summarized as follows:

> In sum, few of the respondents mentioned any task oriented or productivity type of distinction in their perceptions of situations. Generally, the main distinctions mentioned by the respondents dealt with familiarity with the other interactant (parents, close friends, etc.), rights vs. favors, who benefited from the situation, and, to some degree, whether the situation was formal or informal (Cody, 1978, p. 80).

Cody reports in addition three basic replicable dimensions within the persuasion context: whether the interaction is superficial or intimate, whether the task of persuasion is easy or difficult, and the degree of emotional intensity involved. The distribution of benefits from any successful persuasion may also be relevant.

Although Cody does not discuss his results in these terms, it seems that the common theme throughout all of his findings is one of social contract. We all have a large number of social contracts, which we are expected to observe. Any attempt to force someone to change is a type of violation or infringement of a social contract not to interfere with others. All of the common techniques of persuasion seek to justify the violation of one social contract while maintaining good social credit by invoking or appealing to an even more important social contract to overpower the other violation. Leaders often invoke an abstract social contract (e.g. "we all must work to preserve the defense of our country" or "government should not interfere with us any more than is absolutely necessary") when seeking to advance an otherwise unpopular specific violation of another social contract (e.g. raising taxes or abolition of civil rights legislation). The degree to which a situation involves gross violation of social contracts characterizes the different types of situations of attitude change. Cody's list of categories all imply nature of the social contract to be invoked by the source in the change attempt: specific or general violation of rights, requests for a favor, failure to uphold an implicit agreement, requests for special favors, situation formality, appeals for help, and nature of future personal benefit. It may well be that investigating the various social contract violations and restorations in attitude change attempts would be a useful place to continue developing a taxonomy of attitude change situations.

The Yale Approach

The Yale Attitude Change and Communication Research Projects (e.g. Hovland & Janis, 1959) produced a number of monographs on various aspects of attitude and attitude change situations and related phenomena. In spite of the fact that much of this research is today viewed as flawed, the situational dimensions they mentioned provide useful insight yet today.

Message. Perhaps the most obvious way in which an attitude change attempt differs situationally is in terms of the content of the message. Cody selected one set of message factors, or dimensions along which messages vary, for his investigation. Communication researchers tend to be quite advanced in studying the situational importance of different types of messages.

Examples of message factors that have been investigated include primacy versus recency, whether repetition of arguments is beneficial, whether conclusions should be implicit or explicit, degree of discrepancy between initial audience attitude and position advocated in the communication, level of fear in the communication, and whether metaphors or literal conclusions are preferable. McGuire has proposed a list of three categories of message — ethos, pathos, and logos. Messages of ethos appeal to the source, pathos messages appeal to the emotions, and logos messages concentrate on reasoning.

Source. In McGuire's trichotomy of message factors, the source was included as an aspect of the message. Frequently, however, the source is considered as a separate factor within the attitude change context. Effective sources may be attractive, expert, intelligent, entertaining, objective, similar to the audience, familiar, credible, and/or likable. They also may, on the other hand, lack many of these or other characteristics.

Channel. Research in this area often concentrates on the type of medium used in presenting a persuasive message. Messages are sometimes presented in writing, sometimes on television, sometimes on audio or video tape, sometimes within large or small groups, and sometimes on billboards. Likewise, within one channel variability exists. Television may be network or cable. Small group, in person communication may be through hypnosis, through wispering, or through shouting. Organizations may also be considered a type of channel, since it has often been demonstrated that organizations profoundly influence attitudes.

Evaluation. In spite of widespread interest in situational variability as a factor in attitude change, no comprehensive theory exists to account for what we know about attitudes and situations. Many factors have been postulated, but the variability in the quality of research has been quite large, making it difficult to assess the conclusions from the research in general, from the earliest Yale studies right through to today. Many of the studies that are well done simply document common sense. Many lack quality.

Studies in the area of communicator credibility, for example, have shown that a credible communicator is more effective at creating attitude change than a noncredible communicator. This finding hardly revolutionizes common sense. Yet if the study is intensively examined, it most often shows that the quality of research was insufficient even to generalize about the accuracy of common sense. In a typical communicator credibility study, the highly credible communicator may be called quite qualified to speak on health matters as the "President of the New England Society of Medicine and the recipient of 87 distinguished scientific awards." The low or non-credible communicator is described as a "free-lance reporter for gossip tabloids who recently completed a six month jail term for marketing 'snake oil' as a cure for cancer." The subjects in this study, even if they only see one level of the manipulation, know immediately whether they are supposed to believe the communicator. After the study they can report that they knew the hypothesis and complied with it — the classic example of demand characteristics operating in the laboratory. This phenomenon has been demonstrated often enough that it casts a shadow of doubt about this entire area of research (cf. Page, 1970b). Even studies that appear to be well executed (e.g. Eagly, Wood, & Chaiken, 1978) become difficult to interpret because other literature cannot be compared to them.

Several reviews of the situation literature surrounding message, source, and channel factors do exist (McGuire, 1968a; Petty & Cacioppo, 1981; Rajecki, 1982; Reardon, 1981) for the interested reader, but none of these reviews expand the research into a larger theoretical framework or integrate it with other areas of attitude change research, most notably the research on personality and persuasibility. This area is over ripe for theoretical and methodological advancement.

Recommendations for Future Efforts from a Social

Adaptation Perspective

In the context of these perspectives on situations in social psychology and particularly in attitude psychology, several recommendations concerning future theorizing and research within the context of attitude change seem justified. Especially since this topic area desperately needs progress, these recommendations are proposed in the hope that they will stimulate new efforts.

Theoretical Issues

Research and thought at this point should probably defer attempts to develop a hierarchical classification system and concentrate on understanding the situational issues within one domain, preferably a specific domain. In the long run,, of course, a hierarchical classification system is desired, but for now only the most basic matters should occupy our attention. No wideranging classification system is any better than its specific level classifications; hence, we should build classification systems from the foundation up. Careful observation of relevant detail will for now be the key.

More attention needs to be given to the purpose behind constructing any given taxonomy of attitude change situations. A taxonomy in only useful within the context of some specific purpose. A taxonomy may apply to one behavior but not to another, for example. As we discovered in the section on meta-theory and taxonomy construction, a very wide range of purposes for taxonomy construction exists.

One purpose of taxonomy construction that would seem especially valuable within the context of social adaptation theory would be to consider the adaptive significance of a particular situation within the context of the relevant attitude. Certainly different types of situations have different types of adaptive import. This task could be viewed as one of applying the functional approach to situations advocated by Argyle *et al.* (1981).

A social-adaptation example of a specific-purpose classification of situations can be found in the discussion by Kahle, Klingel & Kulka (1981) of assimilatory versus accommodative situations. Assimilatory situations are ones in which the adaptive implications have previously been abstracted and therefore high attitude-behavior consistency can be expected, whereas accommodative situations are ones in which novelty is the rule, abstractions for guidance are absent, and attitude-behavior consistency can not be expected. This distinction between assimilatory versus accommodative situations also has implications for attitude change. Change can be expected more readily in accommodative situations.

Work on situations should never forget the person, as has been true of almost all situational work in the area of attitude change. The danger here is that the study of situations will become what the study of personality was, only with the narrowmindedness coming from the opposite direction.

One important dimension along which situations vary is the nature of the people who are in the situation. A number of people have suggested that one could characterize situations in terms of the people in them (e.g. Bem, 1979; Snyder, 1981). Snyder, for example, gives the vivid example of describing a bar as the type of place Archie Bunker would frequent. That personal description conveys an enormous amount of information to any follower or fan of Archie Bunker.

People do not just arrive at situations arbitrarily. As discussed in more detail in the chapter on methodology, people often select their situations or are attracted to situations based on the type of personality. Kahle (1980), for example, showed that internals and externals are attracted to different types of situations as a function of their different levels of locus of control.

In regard to the Kahle (1980) study it is worth noting that the relevant dimensions of a situation may well vary as a function of the person-dimension of interest. He found that the situation dimension that varied as a function of locus of control was one of the degree to which the task required skill. One could easily predict that this skill-chance dimension would be important in the context of locus of control. On the other hand, that situation dimension may not be at all relevant to research about introversion-extraversion or other personality traits. Likewise, some dimensions, such as degree to which other people are present, may have more important consequences for introversion-extraversion than for locus of control.

Methodological Issues

Fancy methodology alone will probably not ultimately solve very many of the important issues surrounding the clarification and classification of situations. First of all, the old cliché about "garbage in, garbage out" certainly applies to all taxonomy construction methodologies. Naive or brute empiricism will not magically reveal the "true" nature of situations. Only with careful sampling and selection of input observations can any structure-detecting methodology, such as factor analysis or multidimensional scaling, yield usable information.

Probably the best studies to date with fancy methodology have been two-staged designs in which one group of subjects first gives detailed descriptions of situations relevant to a phenomenon of interest and then these "nominated situations" are further rated and categorized by another group of respondents or subjects. But even this type of methodology has its limits. First of all, if a non-representative sample of respondents is used, the resulting dimensions will also be nonrepresentative (This problem is pervasive and pervasively ignored throughout the attitude literature). Forgas (1976) has demonstrated that the situations of importance are different for different groups of people. Secondly, fancy data analysis techniques only operate on quantitative input and make no attempt to provide logical precision to the input. For example, Mischel (1968) reports on a factor analysis in which the dimensions of books (height, width, and thickness) were measured and submitted to computation. The resulting factors were not exactly the ones that had been used for input but rather were something like size, obesity, and squareness. Method must never become more than a tool, lest we confuse our numbers for reality. Third, some researchers have suggested that subjects often attend to the wrong aspects of the situation when making their judgments (Pervin, 1981). This factor, too, suggests that improved theory, not improved methodology, ought to be the first step toward advancing the understanding of situations in persuasion.

Conclusion

Social adaptation theory clearly points to the importance of the situation and implies that much attention should be given to attempts to understand the situation within the parameters of all interactive theories. Several social adaptation dimensions of situations have been identified. Situations may be familiar, alimental, or novel. They may be assimilatory or accommodative. Others have also provided useful insight into the nature of situations, but mostly the study of the attitudes of situations is a universe awaiting its Copernicus.

CHAPTER 8

Attitudes and behaviors

ONE of the areas in which the benefits of an interactive perspective of attitudes are most clear is in the age-old (see James, 1884) question of attitude-behavior consistency. Unlike what we found in the theories of attitude change, in the area of attitude-behavior consistency the major theories (Fishbein & Ajzen, 1975; Triandis, 1971, 1977) are indeed interactive. The question of how attitudes relate to behaviors continues to be one of the most controversial in attitude research, in part because it is one of the most important. An essential underlying assumption of most attitude change research is that attitudes do indeed influence behaviors. If attitudes have no relationship whatsoever with behaviors except for occasionally sharing something trivial like method variance (see Deutscher, 1966, 1973; Wicker, 1969), then it is almost pointless to attempt to understand attitudes. The basic rationale for understanding attitudes hinges on the notion that attitudes will reveal something about probable behavior. Since behaviors are difficult to predict and to measure, the assumption has been that attitudes would provide a shortcut to understanding behaviors. The practitioner wants to know whether attitudes do indeed predict subsequent behavior. The scientist is furthermore interested in knowing whether attitudes have a causal relationship with behaviors. We will begin our discussion of this issue by considering three classic studies in social psychology that cast doubt on the common sense notion that attitudes and behaviors are related.

Classic Studies of Attitude-Behavior Consistency

LaPiere

Perhaps the best-known early study to cast doubt on the assumption that attitudes predict behaviors resulted from a trip a sociologist made across the country with two Oriental friends (LaPiere, 1934). During the course of the trip, LaPiere and his companions visited around 250 restaurants, motels, and camps. Only once did anyone refuse to serve them. Six months after returning home, LaPiere wrote to the places that had served him during the cross-country trip, in order to inquire about whether the establishments had a policy concerning service to Chinese. Only half of the establishments even bothered to respond, but over 90% of the respondents indicated a policy of discrimination against Orientals governed their decisions. Thus, 45% of the original sample claimed a policy of discrimination in spite of practicing nondiscrimination when visited by LaPiere. The same virtually unanimous results were obtained from responses to letters mailed to establishments not visited by LaPiere and his friends although we do not know the response rate for this part of his study. LaPiere concluded that self-reports of many types of attitudes will not reflect behaviors.

Kutner, Wilkens, & Yarrow

The empirical accuracy of the LaPiere study is bolstered by the results of another study published by Kutner, Wilkens, & Yarrow (1952). These researchers conceptually replicated LaPiere with black rather than Oriental people and exclusively in New York restaurants, rather than at a variety of tourist industry outlets across the United States. Their conclusions agreed with LaPiere's. The restaurants often refused to take reservations for racially-integrated parties but nearly always seated them.

Minard

Minard (1952) studied race relations in the Pocahontas coal field. He found that approximately one-fifth of the whites behaved kindly towards blacks both in the coal fields and in the town. Another 20% behaved inhospitably in both places. The remaining three-fifths of the population acted friendly toward blacks only within the coal field. This majority of the respondents who behaved differently depending upon the situation has often been cited as providing evidence of attitude-behavior inconsistency.

Comments on Classic Studies

These three studies are frequently cited by textbook sources within the debate on attitude-behavior consistency, sometimes exclusively cited, to define the attitude concept as one with a marginal relationship to behavior. Why these three studies so frequently find their ways into the literature from among the seemingly infinite number of possible studies would make an interesting topic of investigation for a sociologist of science. Most of the comprehensive reviews have fortunately found hundreds of other relevant studies to include, regardless of whether the reviews have been positive (e.g. Ajzen & Fishbein, 1977; Calder & Ross, 1973; Fishbein & Ajzen, 1975; Liska, 1974; McGuire, 1976; Schuman & Johnson, 1976) or negative (Deutscher, 1973), although Wicker's negative review narrowed its focus. If all of the studies related to attitude-behavior consistency in all of the social sciences (e.g. communications, economics, political science, psychology, sociology) from the past 50 years were known and listed, including studies that do not purport to test attitude-behavior consistency, but nevertheless bear on the topic because of the other questions being asked, the list of studies may approach the tens of thousands.

Dillehay (1973) has shown that all three of these studies have questionable relevance to the issue of individual attitude-behavior consistency. In both the LaPiere and Kutner *et al.* studies, for example, it is highly probable that the person who responded to the letter or answered the reservation request was different from the person who provided the service when the research team arrived. It is unlikely that the motel desk clerks in LaPiere's study, for example, also handled the official correspondence for the entire establishment. With the organization rather than the individual as the sampling unit, the psychological significance of inconsistency vanishes. These results more appropriately should be cited in discussions of organizational policy implementation than in discussions of attitude-behavior consistency. Furthermore, one may classify the studies as dealing with behavior-behavior inconsistencies based on an inferred attitude rather than a directly measured attitude. This argument applies even more clearly to the Minard study. At no point in the study does Minard report measuring the relevant attitudes. In fact, he does not even claim that his study provides evidence of attitude-behavior inconsistency.

Campbell (1963) has detailed an additional alternative explanation to the Minard study, based on the notion of a mid-range attitude. That is, the fifth of the respondents who always or never behaved favorably toward blacks were consistent with an extreme attitude. The three-fifths who behaved in a friendly manner in the work place but not in the town may be viewed as consistent with a mid-range attitude. This explanation is particularly compelling from a social adaptation perspective. Subjects had much to loose through uncooperative interracial behavior within the mine, but ignoring blacks outside of the dangerous, compact work quarters had fewer adaptive implications. From this mid-range view, it becomes apparent that no one necessarily behaved inconsistently from the assumed attitudes, although even this inference is questionable since the attitudes were not directly measured.

The Theory of Fishbein & Ajzen

The one theory, more than any other, that has received widespread attention in the area of attitude-behavior consistency is the Theory of Reasoned Action (Fishbein & Ajzen, 1975; Fishbein, 1979; Ajzen & Fishbein, 1980). These names, of course, are already familiar, since they provided the definitions of belief, normative belief, and subjective norm in Chapter 1 and the probability theory of adult attribution in Chapter 5. Obviously, then, their perspective in many respects overlaps with social adaptation theory and provides a foundation upon which social adaptation can be built.

In reasoned action theory two basic lines of influence on behavior come together to form intentions, and intentions lead to behavior. The first line of
influence starts with the multiplicative product of beliefs times evaluation. After
summing the product of these two for all relevant beliefs, what remains from
this abstracting process is an attitude as it is in social adaptation theory. Unlike
social adaptation theory, reasoned action theory concerns itself only with attitudes towards acts, not both attitudes toward acts and attitudes toward objects.
The second line of influence results from the product of normative beliefs,
which are an individual's construction of the expectations of referents. The sum
of products of normative beliefs and the motivations to comply with them
results in the subjective norm. Subjective norms and attitudes toward acts, each
weighted for importance, come together to form intentions. Intentions, then,
are the only direct antecedent of behavior. Clearly, intentions in the theory of
reasoned action result from a person-situation interaction in which a psycho-
logically-perceived social situation combines with a type of attitude to result in
action, after being filtered through intention.

The Triandis (1977) model is quite similar to the theory of reasoned action.
Ajzen & Fishbein (1980) note that in many respects the theory of Triandis is
"quite similar to our own, but as Triandis (1977, pp. 231–2) noted himself, it
makes no attempt to be parsimoneous" (Ajzen & Fishbein, 1980, p. 247).
Triandis basically adds several variables Fishbein & Ajzen omit. Several spirited
researchers have contrasted these two theories (e.g. Brinberg, 1979; Jaccard &
Davidson, 1975).

The theory of reasoned action is quite similar to social adaptation theory,
too, in many obvious respects; nevertheless, certain differences do exist, most
notably in terms of scope. Social adaptation theory is an attempt to integrate a
much broader set of phenomena. Therefore, social adaptation explicitly includes a theory of attitude change. It includes attitudes toward both objects
and acts. The concept of situation is not just psychological nor just social. And
habit and ability are seen as important antecedents of behavior in addition to
intention.

Social Adaptation Perspective on Attitude-Behavior Consistency

One implication of social adaptation theory is that to the extent that what is
adaptive attitudinally (i.e. the abstraction) corresponds to what is perceived by
the subject to be adaptive behaviorally (i.e. a particular instance or set of instances), attitudes and behaviors will tend to be consistent, with attitudes
antecedent to behaviors. That is, the strategy implied by the abstraction
(attitude) will be applied (behavior).

A good deal of empirical evidence is compatible with aspects of this hypothesis. One type of evidence has to do with the importance of establishing com-
parability in attitude and behavior research. When attitudes and behaviors are

measured at a comparable level of specificity, adaptation is also more likely to be comparable between the two; hence, achieving a comparable degree of specificity enhances attitude-behavior consistency (Weigel & Newman, 1976; Weigel, Vernon, & Tognacci, 1974). Ajzen & Fishbein (1977) suggest that an attitudinal predictor corresponds to a behavioral criterion to the extent that the attitudinal entity is identical in four elements (action, target, context, and time) with the behavioral entity or instance. Davidson & Jaccard (1979) agree. The more clearly relevant and comparable the abstraction is to the instance, the more likely it will be applied.

Research on reference groups provides another type of evidence about this hypothesis. Knowledge of the attitudes held by a person's reference group generally improves predictions of behavior from that individual's attitudes (Fishbein & Ajzen, 1975; Schuman & Johnson, 1976). This finding may be a function of the added information about the social environment to which a person seeks to adapt that one gains from knowledge of reference group attitudes. That reference group attitudes alone do not predict everything an individual attitude measure predicts (Andrews & Kandel, 1979; Schuman & Johnson, 1976), however, implies that something else above and beyond impression management (i.e. Tedeschi, Schlenker, & Bonoma, 1971), such as organizing cognitive processes, operates here. That is, the goal of adaptation promotes both the impression management necessary to get along in a temporary social context and the long-term organization and integration of consistent principles necessary for social life (Kahle, 1978; Rokeach, 1973), although different people clearly will emphasize one or the other more (Snyder, 1979, in press). Attitudes that are better integrated and organized within an individual's entire system of adaptation abstractions will more likely be consistent with behavior in spite of social pressure because of the added information they synthesize about instances of behavior (Brannon, Cyphers, Hesse, Hesselbart, Keane, Schuman, Viccaro, & Wright, 1973; Kahle, 1979).

Evidence consistent with the converse side of this hypothesis also exists. For example, contrary to Zunich's original claim, one would expect the adaptive implications of a maternal attitude of "encouraging verbalization" to be relatively independent of a behavior such as "observing attentively", and indeed this particular attitude-behavior pair does not correlate (Zunich, 1962). Similarly, we have seen that Dillehay (1973) has shown how some of the other classic studies cited as evidence of the lack of relationship between attitudes and behaviors (Kutner, Wilkens, & Yarrow, 1952; LaPiere, 1934; Minard, 1952) in fact involve attitude and behavior measures with contradictory adaptive implications. For example, in LaPiere's classic study a desk clerk at a motel or hotel, confronted with a pleasant-looking oriental couple and their already-welcome traveling companion, may find serving them more adaptive than expelling them, whereas a manager answering an inquiry about organizational policy toward accepting oriental guests may find nonresponse, or even a negative response in order to prevent an in-person confrontation with potentially trouble-making oriental guests, to be more adaptive and less disruptive.

An important theoretical question is when, in the present view, attitudes will not show causal predominance over behaviors. Although inconsistency may be manifested for many reasons, one set of reasons is of particular theoretical interest. Especially in adaptively ambiguous or unfamiliar contexts, during the formative stages of adaptation abstractions, in situations with no ostensible adaptive significance, or in periods of transformations of what is adaptive, behaviors and attitudes may be expressed rather tentatively while the adaptive implications of each are assessed and abstracted. Behaviors may be used to test hypotheses about adaptations during abstraction. During these phases behaviors may appear to lead attitudes at times. At these times the causal relationship between attitudes and behaviors will reflect the assimilation, accommodation, and organization of the outcomes, as well as the consistency, expected in more stable circumstances. In these less stable or less clear circumstances, or when measurement has been inadequate, either attitudes or behaviors may appear to be predominant over the other, or the two may appear not to be related (Kahle, Klingel, & Kulka, 1981).

Some empirical evidence bears on this issue also. Schuman & Johnson (1976), in their excellent review of the attitude-behavior literature, conclude that most studies designed to test whether attitudes and behaviors are consistent "yield positive results" and that the exceptions "reveal something special about social life — e.g. that the behavior in question is performed with little awareness or informed anticipation or that social constraints on behavior are of exceptional power" (p. 199). That is, inconsistency may result from unknown or altered adaptiveness. For others the conclusions appear to be the same. Fazio & Zanna (1978) found: "Direct experience produces a well-defined and certain attitude. These characteristics, in turn, enhance that attitude's capacity to predict later behavior" (p. 405). In the present view this works not because of self-perceptions, as the authors claim (Fazio & Zanna, 1981), but because of the additional information supplied by direct experience.

Likewise, other evidence comes from a careful study of interpersonal attraction, from which Taylor (1975) concluded: "Under conditions where one is asked one's attitude about an inconsequential issue, one's behavior, or more properly feedback about one's behavior, may quite markedly affect the attitude one expresses; however, when one's future behavior is affected by the expression of an attitude, that attitude seems to be weighted more carefully, and more available information is brought to bear on deciding what one believes" (Taylor, 1975, p. 131). Thus, attitudes bear a directive relationship to behaviors only when what is adaptive can be known and is relevant to the individual (see Schwartz, 1973; Snyder, in press).

In many studies that have failed to detect attitude-behavior consistency, researchers have created acute transformations of what is adaptive and have therefore engendered situations in which the subject engages in a temporary assessment of what is adaptive rather than performance of what is known to be adaptive from abstractions of adaptive experience. Most laboratory social psychology experiments fall into this category. In other such studies researchers have paid insufficient attention either to personal (.e.g self-monitoring) or to situational moderators of the attitude-behavior link (Snyder & Monson, 1975; Snyder & Swann, 1976). Many of these moderators, such as opportunity and ability, have been identified by Fishbein & Ajzen (1975) and by Schuman & Johnson (1976).

Let us briefly examine person influences on consistency. One interesting line of research on personality moderation of attitude-behavior consistency has been carried out by Snyder and his associates (Snyder, in press). They started out with the hypothesis that individuals who are high self-monitors, people who attend to and respond to situational cues with great acuity, should display less attitude-behavior consistency than individuals who are low self-monitors, people who have a more integrated, unified self-view. Snyder & Swann (1976) confirmed this basic hypothesis in one study, showing that the attitude-behavior correlation was .42 for low self-monitors and .03 for high self-monitors. Only the former correlation attained statistical significance. Snyder (in press) observes that others have also reported the same pattern of correlations (Bercher & Richard, 1978; Zanna, Olson, & Fazio, 1980; Zuckerman & Reis, 1978). Wicker (1969) has identified several person variables that moderate consistency: other attitudes, competing motives, abilities (verbal, intellectual, and social), and activity level.

Situations also have been shown to influence attitude-behavior consistency. For example, Snyder (in press) reports on one study in which subjects who were made acutely aware of the relevance of their behaviors ("Think through the implications of your verdicts, mock jurors.") showed attitude-behavior consistency regardless of their degree of self-monitoring. Yet another situation difference variable that has been shown to influence attitude-behavior consistency and which relates to self-monitoring theory is objective self awareness (Carver, 1975; Gibbons, 1978; Wicklund, 1975). Wicker (1969) has contributed to this list of situational moderators of consistency, too: actual or considered presence of other people, normative prescriptions, availability of alternative behaviors, specificity of attitude objects, unforeseen extraneous events, and expected and/or actual consequences of various acts.

Consideration of Comments on Kahle & Berman (1979a)

Several studies have been designed specifically to test the social adaptation hypothesis about attitude-behavior consistency when important attitudes during a period of relative stability are involved. In the first of these studies Kahle &

Berman (1979a) tested the attitudes and behaviors of several hundred college students toward religion, consumption of alcoholic beverages, Jimmy Carter's candidacy for the Presidency of the United States, and Gerald Ford's candidacy for the same. Both attitudes and behaviors were measured five weeks apart, with the second period of measurement coming just one week before the 1976 presidential election in the United States, in which Carter and Ford were the major candidates. A great deal of attention was given to constructing psychometrically adequate measures. For each of the four topics subjects rated their agreement on a nine-point scale with at least five attitude statements (e.g. I strongly support Gerald Ford for president) and told how frequently they had engaged in at least seven behaviors (e.g. How many times in the past 14 days have you made a favorable comment about Gerald Ford). Although a few researchers construct composites similar to these for measuring attitudes, it is the exception rather than the rule that researchers realize how crucial constructing composites of behaviors can be. For all eight composites, it was shown that single-factoredness and internal consistency were adequate and that the correlation with a measure of social desirability was negligible.

Kahle & Berman computed cross-lagged panel correlations (CLPC) and tested for the differences between these correlations. As can be seen from Table 8–1, the pattern supports the hypothesis that for these attitudes during this time lag, attitudes do lead to behaviors nonspuriously. These data clearly and directly contradict self perception theory (Bem, 1972b). They also have important implications concerning the significance of attitudes in relationship to behavior.

TABLE 8–1

Attitude-Behavior Cross-Lagged Correlation Test Results

Issue	r_{A1B2}	r_{B1A2}	z[a]
Carter's Candidacy	0.53	0.18	6.29**
Ford's Candidacy	0.57	0.13	7.73**
Religion	0.57	0.49	1.84*
Drinking	0.58	0.48	2.20**

a   Pearson-Filon test for the differences between correlated correlations, following Kenny (1975).

* $p < 0.1$

** $p < 0.05$

From Kahle & Berman (1979a).

Rogosa (1980) has criticized cross-lagged panel correlation (Kenny, 1975) and, by implication, Kahle & Berman. Yet it is clear that the conclusions of Rogosa are overstated (Kenny & Campbell, in press), even though the logic he uses (see Chapter 6) basically is sound.

For researchers with data for which CLPC may be appropriate, the main implication of the Rogosa article is that researchers should inspect their autocorrelations before making inferences. Data for which the "causal" variable has the smaller autocorrelation should be viewed as inconclusive. Nonsignificantly different autocorrelations or autocorrelations in the opposite direction of this are inconsistent with Rogosa's objection. This inspection would better be viewed as another issue to consider in CLPC research similar to other issues raised by Kenny (1975) and others than as a reason to abandon CLPC. To argue that because something could in principle go awry therefore a methodology should be boycotted, as Rogosa does, would be analogous to arguing that all analysis of variance should be banned because lack of homogeneity of variance can distort inferences.

Some researchers are already doing and reporting this inspection (e.g. Eisert & Kahle, 1982; Kahle, Klingel & Kulka, 1981; Kahle, Kulka & Klingel, 1980). Although Kahle & Berman (1979a) did not discuss this issue, for all except one issue (religion) their data followed the opposite pattern necessary for Rogosa's assertions to apply (i.e. the "cause" variable, attitude, had a larger autocorrelation than the "effect" variable, behavior).

The Kahle & Berman (1979a) study is, of course, not flawless. No study is. One point on which the Kahle & Berman (1979) article is vulnerable has to do with representativeness. Their conclusions apply only "on these issues" (Kahle & Berman, 1979, p. 321), for this time lag (p. 317), and to the subjects mentioned (p. 316). The results have been replicated on other issues, in other geographic places, with other subjects of different ages and for different (longer) time lags (Andrews & Kandel, 1979; Kahle, Lingel, & Kulka, 1980), increasing the confidence in the inferences somewhat; nevertheless, for all practical purposes, an infinite number of attitudes, behaviors, people, places, time lags, and historic periods could be sampled. Even such a specific concept as "religious behavior" has an (almost) infinite number of potential empirical manifestations. Kahle & Berman measured only 32 behaviors and 33 attitudes to capture their four issues, an average of about eight of each per issue, and even these measurements were not based on probabilistic sampling. Nonrepresentativeness is such a common problem in social psychology that most people do not explicitly mention it, assuming that all readers are aware of that problem. Kahle & Berman (p. 321) do note that they have not listed all alternative problems, and, since the issue has been raised, it is worth mentioning explicitly that all research reports, including Kahle & Berman's, are but one drop in the ocean of all possible manifestations of the phenomenon of interest, which is why one can never totally "prove" anything abstract through induction and empiricism.

Another problem with the Kahle & Berman article has to do with the operational definition of behavior. We address this question empirically in another article (Kahle, Klinger. & Kulka, 1981). For the moment let us examine the issue logically. What did Kahle & Berman measure in these self-reports of behavior? For one thing, their measures used multiple measures of each behavioral construct. Although most definitions of behavior-attitude relationships suggest multiple behavioral implications of any given attitude, in fact most empirical studies measure only one variable. Secondly, Kahle & Berman assessed internal consistency and single factoredness of their behavioral scales. Reliability is not identical to validity, but it is a *sine qua non* of validity, although most studies do not report internal consistencies of behavioral measures. Thirdly, Kahle & Berman constructed conceptually commensurate attitude-behavior scales, which is often not the case, even though this problem is important in psychology generally (cf. Bem, 1979). Fourth, Kahle & Berman attempted to collect specific and specificity-commensurate (Ajzen & Fishbein, 1977) attitude-behavior scales. Finally, Kahle & Berman ruled out social desirability (p. 318). To my knowledge, no attitude-behavior study has shown lack of validity, given that it has measured behaviors with self-reports when multiple measures of the construct (with internal consistency, single factoredness, conceptual commensurability, specificity and specificity commensurability, and no social desirability) were present. The Kahle & Berman assumption of validity is at least tenable. Again, to conclude that the measures do or do not reflect what an observer would see is to infer from silence.

Beyond this discussion, however, remains the more metaphysical question: what is behavior? Marking on paper *is* behavior (cf. Ericsson & Simon, 1980). A self-report *is* a behavior. It is not at all clear that other-observed gross motor behavior (e.g. attendance at a political rally or ingratiation of a professor before an examination) is always "more real" than self-observed marks on a piece of paper (voting or an anonymous course evaluation) (cf. Schuman & Johnson, 1977). Furthermore, it may be that the very processes by which self-observations and other-observations occur are fundamentally different (Jones & Nisbett, 1971). A more specific statement of the hypothesis of Kahle & Berman might be: "person X's attitudes cause person X's behaviors".Person Y's observations of person X's behaviors therefore are not directly implicated in the hypothesized causal link. To the extent that other causal factors intervene in Y's observations, the relationship between X's attitudes and Y's observations of X's behaviors will be attenuated. Of course, factors can also intervene between self-observed behaviors and self-reported behaviors (e.g. social desirability). The point is that the issue is not simple.

Research by Kahle, Klingel, & Kulka (1981)

Research Plan

A study by Kahle, Klingel, & Kulka (1981) provides additional evidence of the behavioral regulation emanating from attitudinal adaptation abstractions (cf. also Eisert & Kahle, 1982; Kahle, Kulka, & Klingel, 1980). In this study an adaptive attitude led to self-reported behaviors across several different time lags.

The topic of interest was adolescents' "outgoingness toward other people", which should be quite adaptive given the evidence extolling the virtues of emersion in a wide social support network (e.g. Berkman & Syme, 1979; Cobb, 1976; Gurin, Veroff, & Feld, 1960; Litwak & Szelenyi, 1969; Lowenthal & Haven, 1968; Veroff, Douban, & Kulka, 1981) and of adolescent popularity (Coleman, 1963; Douvan & Adelson, 1963; Sebald, 1968). Thus, we would expect that outgoing attitudes should be antecedent to and guide outgoing behaviors. This study was also conceptually similar to Kahle & Berman (1979a), and thus it may help to clarify some unresolved issues from that study. Among the additional issues that this study attempted to address were: (1) A time lag of two months was the only time lag that Kahle & Berman employed. A proponent of equal but reciprocal causation between attitudes and behaviors would expect that the causal relationship between attitudes and behaviors would vary depending upon the time lag. Consequently, the Kahle et al. (1981) study utilized multiple time lags. (2) The second study attempted to validate the self-report behavioral measure. (3) The content of the topics used in the Kahle & Berman study (politics, religion, and drinking) differ from the content of the topic of outgoingness, a topic with a more abstract attitudinal object. (4) The second study used subjects from a different age group and a different geographic region.

Results

The cross-lagged panel correlation differences from the Kahle, Klingel, & Kulka study presented in Table 8–2 suggest that Michigan high school students of Kahle, Klingel, & Kulka display the same basic causal relationship between attitudes and behaviors for outgoingness as the Nebraska college students did for politics, drinking, and religion (Kahle & Berman, 1979a) and as other students have shown on drugs (Andrews & Kandel, 1979; Bentler & Speckart, 1979; Jessor & Jessor, 1977). Furthermore, this causal relationship is generally replicated at several different time lags, contrary to the "equal but reciprocal" causation prediction, which would predict different directions of causation at different lags.

The question of the optimal time lag for detecting a causal relationship between attitudes and behaviors is perhaps one of the issues addressed in a most interesting manner by these data. Results of this study suggest that predictability may have eroded somewhat as the time lag lengthened. In comparison with the

TABLE 8–2

Cross-lagged Correlations between Outgoing Attitudes (A) and Outgoing Behaviors (B)

Semester Pair	n	r_{A1B2}	r_{B1A2}	z^a
2 year lag				
Spring 10th–Spring 12th	114	0.557	0.424	1.852*
1½ year lag				
Spring 10th–Fall 12th	133	0.552	0.396	1.982**
Fall 11th–Spring 12th	156	0.439	0.392	< 1.64
1 year lag				
Spring 10th–Spring 11th	134	0.600	0.379	2.853**
Fall 11th–Fall 12th	139	0.551	0.357	2.514**
Spring 11th–Spring 12th	184	0.577	0.401	2.792**
½ year lag				
Spring 10th–Fall 11th	121	0.740	0.398	4.675**
Spring 11th–Fall 12th	185	0.596	0.533	< 1.64
Fall 12th–Spring 12th	167	0.565	0.429	1.962**

Note. One additional time pair, Fall 11th–Spring 11th, was too unstationary to examine.

[a] Pearson-Filon test, following Kenny (1975).

* $p < 0.1$, two-tailed test.

** $p < 0.05$, two-tailed test.

From Kahle, Klingel, & Kulka (1981)

two-month time lag in the Kahle & Berman (1979a) study; in which the larger cross-lagged correlation was always larger than either of the synchronous correlations (which was not true in the present study), it may be that even the shortest lag (of six months) assessed here was longer than optimal. Or this difference between the present study and the Kahle & Berman study may be due to differences other than time lag length, such as issue content or subject population. On the other hand, the replicability of the CLPC differences implies that the phenomenon identified by Kahle & Berman may be fairly robust across a variety of time lags, and such replicability is welcome in CLPC research (Calsyn & Kenny, 1977).

Self-report Validation Plan

An assumption of this longitudinal study (and almost all self-report studies) is that the self-reports of behavior actually correspond to behavior. In constructing the self-report measures Kahle, Klingel, & Kulka attempted to avoid faults of measurement that tend to decrease the validity of self-reports. For example, they used a composite rather than a single item (Fishbein & Ajzen, 1974; Weigel & Newman, 1976). They attempted to establish reliability (Cronbach, 1951). They measured the behavioral self-reports at a commensurate level of specificity as the attitude self-reports (Ajzen & Fishbein, 1977; Weigel, Vernon, & Tognacci, 1974). They ruled out statistically any significant causal relationship ($p < .1$) between outgoing behaviors and a measure of social desirability (Crowne & Marlowe, 1964). And they used reversed items (Crano & Brewer, 1973). Nevertheless, some skeptics may additionally demand observational evidence of the validity of the behavioral measures.

In order to test whether the general and diffuse concept of *outgoing behavior*, which was operationalized in the self-report measures, related to actual observations of behavior, three separate cross-sectional studies with independent operationalizations of outgoing behavior were conducted during the first three semesters of the longitudinal study. These studies are especially important because they represent the first CLPC study of attitude-behavior consistency with validated self-report measures of behavior. Although each study only tapped a small number of the myriad possible empirical manifestations of outgoing behavior, as did the self-reports of outgoing behavior in the longitudinal study, evidence of a significant relationship between self-reports of behavior would increase our confidence in the results of the longitudinal study. Because of the considerable expense involved in collecting multiple-act observational data, these studies were only cross-sectional and additionally involved sample sizes smaller than 100. Either of these facts eliminated the possibility of using the observational composites in cross-lagged comparisons and forced them to rely on descriptive data. The three observational studies may be summarized as follows:

1. Dyadic Interaction. The subjects were 40 participants from the longitudinal study who were paired in order to create dyads of subjects with discrepant levels of outgoingness. Subjects solved three dilemmas via dyadic discussion and reported their solutions to the experimenter. The dilemmas involved: (1) what to do when denied admission to an essential drivers' education class because of a lost application, (2) how to help a friend unjustly expelled from school because of an unwilling involvement in a fight, and (3) how to initiate a school scuba diving club. Subjects knew that the experimenter tape recorded their conversations. The interactions took place in an informal setting at the subjects' schools. Discussions typically lasted 20 minutes, with a break in the action each time the subjects returned to the absent experimenter to relate a solution to a dilemma.

Various types of information were coded from transcripts of the tape recordings of the interactions, and from these coding categories a composite score of outgoingness was constructed by summing the relevant category frequencies for each subject. Coders were blind to subjects' level of outgoingness. The category with the largest corrected item-total correlation was "frequency of interaction control", which was defined as any attempt by the respondent to control the direction of the discussion. Generally one member of the dyad would assert dominance, attempting to lead the discussion in a different direction through such behaviors as attempting to initiate or to close off discussion. Examples of this category include, "Let's get back on track", or "Wait a second, how about . . ."

Four other categories completed this composite: (1) "Opinion requested", defined as a subject actively seeking out his partner's opinion, inference, or judgment, is exemplified by such questions as "What do you think about that idea?" or "Would that work?" (2) "Information requested" is defined as an inquiry about non-inferential, factual, descriptive, or objective information. An example would be, "Does the principal have to approve of a club?" or "How much does a private driver's ed course cost?" (3) "Disagreement" requires sufficient tact to execute effectively without destroying interpersonal communication that it may also be considered an example of outgoingness. As a coding category it includes only active and open disagreement, such as "No, I don't think so . . ." or "I don't agree". (4) "Attempts to control relation of solution" is defined as a verbal effort to determine which of the partners will relate their problem solution to the experimenter, such as "You do it", or "No. I'll tell him". Jones (1979) reported additional information about other aspects of this study.

2. Group Discussions. Sixteen participants from the longitudinal cohort, half of whom came from each school, participated in a discussion group at their school for eight one-hour sessions. Subjects in each school who had diverse levels of outgoingness were selected in such a way as to avoid the inclusion of close friends.

A graduate student led all discussion groups by suggesting a topic for discussion at the beginning of each session. She sought to avoid directing the discussion or encouraging any specific group member to participate. She tried to foster diversity in the ideas expressed. At each group discussion two observers sat at a table near the circle of chairs in which subjects sat, watching and observing the interactions. The discussion leader brought milk and doughnuts to each session to help promote an informal atmosphere.

The topics of discussion were selected to apply to diverse experiences of the boys, both inside and outside of school (e.g. "What do you think of teaching as a profession?" and "How has your relationship with your parents changed?"), both retrospectively and prospectively (e.g. "How have you changed in the last few years", and "What sort of skills would you like to develop if you had the opportunity?"), both descriptively and philosophically (e.g. "What is it like to be a student at your school?" and "Do you see yourselves as part of a revolution or period of change?"), and both socially near and diverse (e.g. "What kinds of things do you and your friends do together?" and "What is it like to grow up in your community?").

The two observers who watched the interactions as they occurred later coded responses from a tape recording of the session. The coding category with the highest corrected item-total correlation was the "mean number of acts of initiation per session". Any verbal act not preceded by another person's request for an opinion, suggestion, or orientation was defined as an act of initiation. This category would include active attempts to initiate conversation, mention personal experiences, and invite interaction, such as the unsolicited comment, "I saw you taking out the garbage yesterday". The second item in this composite tallied the mean number of acts per session that each subject directed toward the leader. A third category was the mean number of supportive or friendly acts by each subject during each session. All positive acts directed toward someone else as a person (not the content of verbal interaction) were included in this category, such as expressions of concern, warmth, encouragement, or helpfulness. An example of this category: "Hi, have a doughnut". The final category again was "disagreeing". Any act that resisted, questioned, or posed an alternative to a position, opinion, or suggestion previously made by another person would be considered a disagreement, such as: "No! Let's meet during third hour so I can miss biology". All these category frequencies were standardized and summed to form an outgoing behavior composite. Newman (1979) has described this study more thoroughly.

3. Tracking. The seventeen subjects here all were participants in the longitudinal study, and almost all of them had participated in the group discussion study as well. Undergraduate male observers followed each boy for two days, coding interactions as they took place. Observers established sufficient rapport with subjects to avoid unduly interrupting the normal daily activities of the boys. Newman (1976) detailed more fully the rationale used in the design of this study.

Five coding categories constituted the items summed to form the composite here. The highest corrected item-total correlation was for the "number of interactions initiated by the subject". Because an outgoing person should interact with diverse, dissimilar people, two other coding categories were the "number of interactions with teachers and adults" and the "number of interactions with girls". Finally, the tone of interaction was considered by including the categories "number of positive affective style interactions" and "number of neutral affective style interactions".

Validation Study Results

The internal consistency of each of the observational composites was, respectively .54, .91, and .84. The self-report with observation correlations with correction for attenuation were, respectively, .56, .64, and .73. All of these correlations were significant beyond the .05 level prior to correction for attenuation.

The results of this study, then, clearly imply a certain degree of predictive utility from attitudes toward behaviors. The assumption that attitudes hardly ever lead to behaviors (Wicker, 1969), seems unfounded. Nevertheless, much variance in even these studies remains mystery, and many studies have done far more poorly.

Conclusions

Block (1977) has characterized much of the personality research, which is cited as evidence of the poor utility of trait measures, as "litter-ature", and the same generalization also applies for much of the attitude research. Many of the studies cited as evidence of the poor predictive utility of attitudes reflect poorly conceived and poorly executed research. What we learn from this research is not that attitudes and behaviors are unrelated, but rather that it is important for research on attitudes that is expected to be informative about behaviors as well to utilize careful measurement. Both laboratory and survey researchers often pretend that what we have learned from 50 years of attitude research does not apply to their research designs. The basic principles of measurement (cf. Crano & Brewer, 1973) should always be applied.

Yet when methodologically acceptable studies are employed, many reviewers infer that attitudes and behaviors are related. Schuman & Johnson (1976) do note two studies, which they explicitly describe as a noncomprehensive listing, that show a relationship between attitudes and behaviors. Ajzen & Fishbein (1977) identify at least 15 studies showing a positive relationship in their review, and Calder & Ross (1973) find at least 7 more studies showing a consistency between attitudes and behaviors. Any assertion that attitudes and behaviors are unrelated would minimally have to account for all of these studies. And it is quite likely that many other studies also show strong attitude-behavior consistency. It is notable in this context that the three reviews involve only one study in common (Goodmonson & Glaudin, 1971) among the studies that are methodologically acceptable. Apparently different reviewers find different studies to meet their criteria of acceptable.

One final question for proponents of the hypothesis that attitudes and behaviors are unrelated: Do the journals select studies to publish randomly? Of course not. In attitude-behavior research, there is reason to believe that studies showing attitudes leading to behavior may be difficult to publish since that is the expected result. "Dog bites man" is not news or a scientific breakthrough. Only "man bites dog" or "behaviors cause attitudes" are regularly represented in publications.

CHAPTER 9

Scope of interactions: conclusions

AS with situations, interactions are discussed far more frequently than they are carefully defined. *Interaction* is accepted as an important concept by many psychologists, but the generally sloppy level of definition of it insures that many ostensible proponents of the concept in fact disagree with one another quite strongly. It is hoped that the following discussion will clarify the concept of interaction as it is employed in social adaptation theory and will promote more careful usage in the future.

Concepts of Interaction

Olweus (1977) contributed a widely-cited distinction among 4 concepts of interaction: (1) *Interaction* may mean simply combine or connect. Persons and situations come together in a unidirectional influence on behavior. (2) A second meaning concentrates on interdependency between the person and the situation. This concept frequently characterizes the writings of proponents of the psychological or perceived aspects of the environment. (3) The reciprocal action definition summarizes the notion that both the person and the situation have an on-going influence on one another. "Environmental events affect the person's responses, which in turn affect the environment, which again influences the person's responses, etc." (Olweus, 1977, p. 225). (4) The final definition Olweus summarizes is statistical interaction.

Although Olweus only mentions interaction in statistical theory as the literal analysis of variance interaction, Southwood (1978) has identified at least five different senses of the concept of statistical interaction within the general linear model as it is used in social science. Many psychologists and other social scientists fail to appreciate the full diversity of concepts of statistical interaction that one can test, even when using only analysis of variance. For example, many researchers fail to distinguish between two types of 3 x 2 ANOVA interaction. If one has an independent variable with two levels (say, A and B) and another independent variable with three levels (say, 1, 2, and 3), one could test two

123

different interactions: (A1, A2, and B3 versus B1, B2, and A3) or (A1, B2, and B3 versus B1, A2, and A3). Most data analysis programs arbitrarily test only one of these hypotheses unless otherwise instructed, but often theory dictates one pairing as far more important than the other. For example, in a 3 x 2 design Kahle (1980) trichotomized locus of control in a college population, fully expecting middles to behave as if they were internals since college populations have twice as many internals as the general population. Researchers should define their interactions with care, since the results of this study would have been different had the program tested the wrong hypothesis about interaction.

Buss (1977) also proposed several types of interactions, in order to clarify contemporary usage. In his system four types of functional relationships that have been proposed among persons, situations, and behaviors must be considered. The first two suggest that behavior can be a function of either the person, $B = f(P)$, or the situation, $B = f(S)$. The former assertion is the classic person-oriented assertion, and the second is the classic situation-oriented assertion. To claim that both assertions are true is to defend a mechanistic interactionism, similar to the mechanistic interactionism advocated by Engler (1975). One may also consider only the relationship between the person and the situation, regardless of behavior, and how these two interact. The classic cognitivist would claim that people influence their situations, $S = f(P)$. The social learning theory position at times has been that the situation shapes behavior, $P = f(S)$. Together these two positions coalesce into an organismic interactionism, which Buss attributed to Mischel. Note that the mechanistic and the organismic interactionisms differ substantially in terms of defining what interacts and in terms of defining the variables of interest. For the mechanistic position the behavior is the dependent variable, and the person and the situation do not interact with each other. For organismic interactionism behavior is not of interest, but the person and the situation do indeed interact in determining each other.

Howard (1979) noted that these two types of interactionism do not inherently have to be viewed as mutually exclusive. She proposed yet a third type of interactionism, combinatory, in which all of the relationships of both mechanistic and organismic interactionism apply, in which the environment and the person both influence each other and both can influence behavior. Nothing in the logic of mechanistic interactionism prohibits organismic interactionism from also being possible, and certainly nothing in organismic interactionism excludes consideration of behavior. One might speculate that neo-behaviorist Mischel would hardly consider behavior to be unimportant. And Endler in other places (e.g. Magnusson & Endler, 1977) also advocates nonmechanistic interactionism. Therefore, combinatory interactionism seems plausible.

Howard proposes yet a fourth type of interaction to the three that have already been considered, a complete interactionism, which adds two more structural equations to the four that have already been included. To complete all possible causal connections between the person, situation, and behavior, she speculates that the person may be influenced by behavior, $P = f(B)$, as in self-perception theory, and behavior may change the environment, $S = f(B)$, as when people build houses. Although this model is overidentified in the structural equation sense of the term, Howard proposes a means to overcome this problem and provides a rationale for the plausibility of the existence of all six possible paths. The irony of person-situation psychology is that most theorists, including social adaptation theory, probably have a type of complete interactionism in mind when developing postulates but that most available methodologies, with their snap-shot nature, probably allow only for direct tests of the mechanistic interactionism.

Kulka (1979) added even more conceptual complexity to the issue of the nature of interactions when he examined the concept only within one specific hypothesis: that good outcomes accrue when persons and environments fit one another. By attending only to persons and situations, Kulka limited his discussion to two of the six paths from the Howard discussion, specifically the two involved in "social learning" (not Kulka's term) interactionism. He noted that the fit between person and situation may be (1) continuous or noncontinuous, (2) monotonic or nonmonotonic, (3) one-directional or two-directional, (4) linear or nonlinear, and (5) symmetrical or nonsymmetrical. These distinctions are, of course, not all true dichotomies since a number imply more than two levels, but, if they were only dichotomies, 32 possible types of person-situation interactions could be expected ($2 \times 2 \times 2 \times 2 \times 2$).

Conclusions about Interaction

Kulka's examples implied that all 32 combinations are plausible relationships. If one considers that Kulka limited his attention to person-situation interactions and ignored person-behavior interactions and situation-behavior interactions, as well as higher order interactions (e.g. person x person x situation) interactions, the range of possible interaction types, for all practical purposes, begins to approach limitlessness. It therefore would seem unwise, and also inaccurate, to identify one type of interaction as *the* type of interaction. Certainly several types of interactions have been empirically manifested. The far more useful task at this point in the history of social psychology would be to begin to document the types of person-situation interactions that occur within various circumstances and begin to develop a classification system for the chronicling of interactions.

The social adaptation view of the nature of interaction, of course, sprouts from Piaget's equilibration model. Continuous assimilation, accommodation, and organization animate interactions. In structural equation terms this view is similar to complete interactionism, although measuring the moving equilibrium with stationary scales may often create misleading results.

Although the relationship between person and situation has been described as *interaction* here, it may in one sense be termed more appropriately *transaction* (Riegel & Meacham, 1978). In this view *interaction* implies that elements (e.g. persons and situations) are primary, whereas in *transactions* elements are derived from activity, are summaries to describe prior adaptive abstractions and to predict future ones. This view has been described particularly clearly in one passage, although the passage was incorrectly described as contrary to Piagetian theory:

> Memories are constructed in order to represent knowledge of past experience. As a derivative of these basic activities also a social context is constructed through the attribution of meaning to the environment. Thus, the system does not merely consider the individual rememberer but also includes the memories and the social context. Neither the rememberer nor the memories are stable entities, for both depend on the continuing activity of the system; as the system functions, the rememberer and the memories are changed (Riegel & Meacham, 1978, p. 25).

This type of transaction may be viewed as interaction within the context of the present theory.

Moessinger (1978) has recently clarified Piagetian (and therefore social adaptation) equilibration theory. First, the nature of the metaphor must be considered. The equilibrium is in the sense of climbing the slope of entropy, not in mechanical, chemical, or thermodynamic senses of the term. Equilibration in this sense implies a certain tendency toward augmentation, not just change. Secondly, the types of interaction leading to augmentative equilibrium must be clarified. The equilibration may result from an interaction between a subject and "reality", between subsystems as in the coordination of schemata, or between subsystems and the totality. Thus, equilibration is not a process that occurs on just one level.

This perspective on interactionism points to one particular problem in any interactional theory: no two people have exactly the same memories, schemata, abstractions, or structures since no two people have exactly the same experiences nor are exposed to exactly the same situations. When we use abstract terms to describe people, such as trait terms, we are assuming persons and situations of sufficient similarity that common descriptions may be useful. Frequently, however, this assumption may only be partially true. Traits are not like Platonic Ideas with some perfect existence in the generic form (Hogan, DeSoto, & Solano, 1978). When we measure attitudes, for example, two people may hold quite similar attitudes for .quite different reasons. Consider the civil libertarian and the highly conservative factory worker who both believe that fascist politicians should be allowed to speak. These two people are indeed similar on this one issue, and various references to these two people as similar in this regard may be useful. However, since the situational contributions to their attitudes may reflect quite different experiences, the similarity on this particular issue may tend to obscure very important different views on other issues between these two people. The links are probabilistic rather than mono-lithic. To say that two people share an attitude or trait implies that they are probably more similar to each other than to other people with whom they do not share that attitude or trait, but it does not imply they are identical in any regard.

An especially useful discussion of interactions has been presented by Bronfen-brenner (1977). He identified several theoretical propositions that seem reason-able but commonplace, but he insightfully illustrated how much methodology cannot tap the full complexity of human behavior often described in currently popular psychological theories. He then suggested dimensions along which im-proved methodologies should progress and phenomena that methodologies should allow to be researched, in order to be truly interactive. For him an "ecological" or interactive experiment must allow for reciprocity of processes, the interdependence of multiple participants, the significance of the physical environment, the interactions among different settings, the larger context of settings, and the life-span progress of role transitions. Clearly his views move interactionism in the direction of a more careful analysis of human behavior in its full complexity.

Criticisms of Interactionism

All theories eventually spawn critics, and interactionism is no exception. A brief consideration of several recent relatively eloquent criticisms is in order.

Gadlin & Rubin (1979) have proposed that interactionism represents the inevitable psychological theory to emerge at this point in history. In their view human nature changes every several generations, and psychological theory will tend to document these shifts. Industrialization, capitalism, urbanization, and bureaucratic technology have transformed human nature from inner to external to interactive over the last two centuries. Although their argument is well de-veloped, it seems throughout their essay that they are confusing content and function. Many aspects of human behavior do indeed shift from time to time as a result of historical, economic, and social forces from larger society, and these changes are not trivial. But any change in behavior does not necessarily reflect a shift in human nature, for it may very well be that the equilibration model can account for the historic shifts in the content of behavior without implicating changes in the basic functions of human cognition. Nothing about adaptation dictates an independence from historic, economic, and larger social forces.

Sampson (1981) has presented a scathing critique of both interactionism and Piagetian theory. Many of his criticisms are based on misunderstandings of the equilibration model and of Piagetian theory in general. Contrary to his assertion that in Piagetian theory only the person is active, not the environment, it should by now be clear that for Piaget any action influences both the environment and the person. This is true whether the action comes or acts upon the environment.

Interaction in adaptation theory necessarily assumes multiple reciprocal influences between the person and the environment. Therefore, it is invalid to suggest that only the person can influence the world, and not vice versa. Furthermore, the suggestion that Piagetian theory denies the existence of reality apart from the perceiver is also a misconception. The perceiver certainly does construct abstractions about the world, but these constructions necessarily bear some relationship to the reality, tending to approximate it ever more closely.

Final Thoughts

This chapter completes our second complete loop through the dialectical spiral. In the first loop we considered theories of attitude change and their predominant polarization into either person-oriented or situation-oriented perspectives. We completed that loop by proposing an extension and elaboration of Piaget's person-situation interaction theory into the realm of attitude change, suggesting that it synthesizes the antithetical polarities of current popular theories of attitude change. In the second dialectical loop we have considered the implications of the proposed synthesis for the current status of the person in attitude psychology, for the current status of the situation, and finally for the nature of the interaction.

Interactionism has stimulated a great deal of discussion during the past two decades within the area of personality research. Many of the more recent statements reflect a theoretical progression of remarkable improvement over the earliest statements and a methodological examination that has been in need ever since the popularization of analysis of variance. The explicit application of interactionism to the domain of attitude change research should also benefit psychological thinking and should lead researchers to consider new ideas and methodologies carefully. Researchers and theorists alike should recognize the flaw of inflexibly assuming that the person alone or the situation alone determines attitudes and attitude-relevant behavior. To ignore at least half of the influence on psychological construct is to limit the capacity of that construct needlessly. If the attitude construct is to retain the centrality it has enjoyed in the last half century (cf. Allport, 1935), then its interactive significance must receive attention, and its relationship to the process of social adaptation must be made clear.

Social adaptation, more than most theories of attitude change, fits in well with the larger body of knowledge about people. Adaptation has proved a useful concept in other human sciences, such as anthropology and biology. Likewise, Piagetian theory has been important in other areas of psychology, such as cognitive psychology, developmental psychology, and the helping professions. If one considers social adaptation theory a neo-structuralist perspective, the relationship of social adaptation to other areas of knowledge also becomes clearer. Exercises that synthesize and organize knowledge are scientifically adaptive, much as the organization of experiential knowledge is individually adaptive.

References

Adorno, R.W., Frenkel-Brunswik, E., Levinson, D.J. & Sanford, R.N. (1950) *The authoritarian personality*. New York: Harper and Row.

Ajzen, I. & Fishbein, M. (1974) Factors influencing intentions and the intention-behavior relation. *Human Relations*, 27, 1—15.

Ajzen, I. & Fishbein, M. (1977) Attitude-behavior relations: A theoretical analysis and review of empirical research. *Psychological Bulletin*, 84, 888—918.

Ajzen, I. & Fishbein, M. (1980) *Understanding attitudes and predicting social behavior*. Englewood Cliffs, N.J.: Prentice Hall.

Alker, H.A. (1972) Is personality situationally specific or intrapsychically consistent? *Journal of Personality*, 40, 1—16.

Alker, H.A. (1977) Beyond ANOVA psychology in the study of person-situation interactions. In D. Magnusson & N.S. Endler (Eds.), *Personality at the crossroads: Current issues in interactional psychology*. Hillsdale, N.J.: Lawrence Erlbaum Ass.

Allport, G.W. (1935) Attitudes. In C. Murchison (Ed.), *Handbook of Social Psychology*. Worchester, Mass.: Clark University Press.

Allport, G.W. (1966) Traits revisited. *American Psychologist*, 21, 167—176.

Andrews, K.H. & Kandel, D.B. (1979) Attitudes and behavior: A specification of the contingent consistency hypothesis. *American Sociological Review*, 44, 298—310.

Angyal, A. (1941) *Foundations for a science of personality*. Cambridge: Harvard University Press.

Appley, M.H. & Moeller, G. (1963) Conforming behavior and personality variables in college women. *Journal of Abnormal and Social Psychology*, 66, 284—290.

Apsler, R. (1975) Effects of embarrassment on behavior toward others. *Journal of Personality and Social Psychology*, 32, 145—153.

Argyle, M., Furnham, A. & Graham, J.A. (1981) *Social situations*. Cambridge: Cambridge University Press.

Argyle, M. & Little, B.R. (1972) Do personality traits apply to social behavior? *Journal for the Theory of Social Behavior*, 2, 1—35.

Aronson, E. (1969) The theory of cognitive dissonance: A current perspective. In L. Berkowitz (Ed.), *Advances in experimental social psychology*, (Vol. 4), New York: Academic Press.

Aronson, E., Blaney, N., Stephan, C., Sikes, J. & Snapp, M. (1978) *The jigsaw classroom*, Beverly Hills, CA: Sage.

Averill, J.R. (1973) The dis-position of psychological disposition. *Journal of Experimental Research in Personality*, 6, 275—282.

Bandura, A., Blanchard, E.B. & Ritter, B. (1969) Relative efficiency of desensitization and modeling approaches for inducing behavioral, affective, and attitudinal changes. *Journal of Personality and Social Psychology*, 13, 173—199.

Barber, T.X. & Silver, M.J. (1968) Fact, fiction, and the experimenter bias effect. *Psychological Bulletin Monograph Supplement*, 70, 1—29.

Barlett, D.L., Drew, P.B., Fahle, G. & Watts, W.A. (1974) Selective exposure to a presidential campaign appeal. *Public Opinion Quarterly,* 38, 264—271.

Bartlett, F.C. (1932) *Remembering.* Cambridge: Cambridge University Press.

Baumrind, D. (1964) Some thoughts on ethics of research: After reading Milgram's "behavioral study of obedience". *American Psychologist,* 19, 421—423.

Becherer, R.C. & Richard, L.M. (1978) Self-monitoring as a moderating variable in consumer behavior. *Journal of Consumer Research,* 5, 159—162.

Bem, D.J. (1965) An experimental analysis of self-persuasion. *Journal of Experimental Social Psychology,* 1, 199—218.

Bem, D.J. (1967) Self-perception: An alternative interpretation of cognitive dissonance phenomena, *Psychological Review,* 74, 183—200.

Bem, D.J. (1970) *Beliefs, attitudes, and human affairs.* Belmont, Ca: Brooks/Cole.

Bem, D.J. (1972) Constructing cross-situational consistency in behavior: Some thoughts on Alker's critique of Mischel. *Journal of Personality,* 40, 17—26. (a)

Bem, D.J. (1972) Self-perception theory. In L. Berkowitz (Ed.), *Advances in experimental social psychology* (Vol. 6). New York: Academic. (b)

Bem, D.J. (1979) Assessing persons and situations with the template matching technique. In L.R. Kahle (Ed.), *New directions for methodology of behavioral science* No. 2: *Methods for studying person-situation interactions.* San Francisco: Jossey-Bass, 1—16.

Bem, D.J. & Allen, A. (1974) On predicting some of the people some of the time: The search for cross-situational consistencies in behavior. *Psychological Review,* 81, 506—520.

Bem, D.J. & Funder, D.C. (1978) Predicting more of the people more of the time: Assessing the personality of situations. *Psychological Review,* 85, 485—501.

Bem, D.J. & Lord, C.G. (1979) Template matching: A proposal for probing the ecological validity of experimental settings in social psychology. *Journal of Personality and Social Psychology,* 37, 833—846.

Bentler, P.M. & Speckart, G. (1979) Models of attitude-behavior relations. *Psychological Review,* 86, 452—464.

Bentler, P.M. & Speckart, G. (1981) Attitudes "cause" behaviors: A structural equation analysis. *Journal of Personality and Social Psychology,* 40, 226—238.

Berelson, B. & Janowitz, M. (Eds.) (1966) *Reader in public opinion and communication.* 2nd ed. New York: Free Press.

Berkman, L.F. & Syme, S.L. (1973) Social networks, host resistance, and mortality: A nine-year follow-up study of Alameda county residents. *American Journal of Epidemiology,* 109, 186—204.

Berkowitz, L. & Cottingham, D.R. (1960) The interest value relevance of fear arousing communications. *Journal of Abnormal and Social Psychology,* 60, 37—43.

Berkowitz, L. & Lundy, R.M. (1957) Personality characteristics related to susceptibility to influence by peers or authority figures. *Journal of Personality,* 25, 306—316.

Bernstein, D.J. & Kahle, L.R. (1982) An idiographic approach to cognitive consistency. Manuscript submitted for publication.

Bettinghaus, R. (1968) *Persuasive communication.* New York: Holt, Rinehart, and Winston.

Binet, A. (1900) *La Suggestibilité.* Paris: Scheicher Fréres.

Block, J. (1971) *Lives through time*. Berkeley, Calif.: Bancroft.

Block, J. (1977) Advancing the psychology of personality: Paradigmatic shift or improving the quality of research? In D. Magnusson and N.S. Endler (Eds.) *Personality at the crossroads: Current issues in interactional psychology*. Hillsdale, NJ: Lawrence Erlbaum Ass.

Bogart, L. (1972) *Silent politics: Polls and the awareness of public opinion*. New York: John Wiley and Sons.

Bonfield, E.H. (1974) Attitude, social influence, personal norm, and intention interactions as related to brand purchasing behavior. *Journal of Marketing Research*, 11, 379–389.

Bowers, K.S. (1973) Situationism in psychology: An analysis and a critique. *Psychological Review*, 80, 307–336.

Brannon, T., Cyphers, G., Hesse, S., Hesselbart, R., Keane, R., Schuman, H., Viccaro, R. & Wright, D. (1973) Attitude and action: A field experiment joined to a general population survey. *American Sociological Review*, 38, 625–636.

Bransford, J.D. & Franks, J.H. (1972) The abstraction of linguistic ideas: A review. *Cognition*, 1, 211–240.

Brehm, J.W. (1966) *A theory of psychological reactance*. New York: Academic Press.

Brehm, S.S., Kassin, S.M. & Gibbons, F.X. (Eds.) (1981) *Developmental social psychology: Theory and research*. New York: Oxford University Press.

Brewer, W.F. (1974) There is no convincing evidence for operant or classical conditioning in adult humans. In W.B. Weimer and D.S. Polermo (Eds.), *Cognition and symbolic processes*. Potomac, MD: Erlbaum.

Brickman, P. & D'Amato, B. (1975) Exposure effects in a free-choice situation. *Journal of Personality and Social Psychology*, 32, 415–420.

Brickman, P., Coates, D. & Cohn, E. (1977) Changing relationship between commitment and happiness. Unpublished manuscript, Northwestern University.

Brickman, P., Coates, D. & Janoff-Bulman, R. (1978) Lottery winners and accident victoms: Is happiness relative? *Journal of Personality and Social Psychology*, 36, 917–927.

Brinberg, D. (1979) An examination of the determinants of intention and behavior: A comparison of two models. *Journal of Applied Social Psychology*, 9, 560–575.

Brock, T.C. (1968) Dissonance without awareness. In R.P. Abelson, E. Aronson, W.J. McGuire, T.M. Newcomb, M.J. Rosenberg & P.H. Tannenbaum (Eds.) *Theories of cognitive consistency: A sourcebook*. Chicago: Rand McNally.

Brock, T.C. & Balloun, J.L. (1967) Behavioral receptivity to dissonant information. *Journal of Personality and Social Psychology*, 6, 413–428.

Bronfenbrenner, U. (1977) Toward an experimental ecology of human development, *American Psychologist*, 32, 513–531.

Burgoon, M., Miller, G.R. & Tubbs, S.L. (1972) Machiavellianism, justification, and attitude change following counterattitudinal advocacy. *Journal of Personality and Social Psychology*, 22, 366–371.

Burnstein, E. & Vinokur, A. (1975) What a person thinks upon learning he has chosen differently from others: Nice evidence for the persuasive-arguments explanation of choice shifts. *Journal of Experimental Social Psychology*, 11, 412–426.

Buss, A.R. (1977) The trait-situation controversy and the concept of interaction. *Personality and Social Psychology Bulletin*, 3, 196–201.

Calder, B.J. & Ross, M. (1973) *Attitudes and behavior.* Morristown, NJ: General Learning Press.

Calsyn, R.J. & Kenny, D.A. (1977) Self-concept of ability and perceived evaluation of others; Cause or effect of academic achievement? *Journal of Educational Psychology,* 69, 136—145.

Campbell, A., Converse, P.E., Miller, W.E. & Stokes, D.E. (1960) *The American voter.* New York: Wiley.

Campbell, A. & Stokes, D.E. (1959) Partisan attitudes and the presidential vote. In E. Burdick & A.J. Brodbeck (Eds.), *American voting behavior.* Glencoe, Ill.: Free Press.

Campbell, D.T. (1963) Social attitudes and other acquired dispositions. In S. Koch (Ed.), *Psychology: A study of a science.* (Vol. 6), New York: McGraw-Hill.

Campbell, D.T. (1975) On the conflicts between biological and social evolution and between psychology and moral tradition. *American Psychologist,* 30, 1103—1126.

Campbell, D.T. (1977) On the genetics of altruism and the counter-hedonic components in human culture. In L. Wispé (Ed.), *Psychology of sympathy and altruism.* Cambridge, Mass.: Harvard University Press.

Campbell, D.T. & Fiske, D.W. (1959) Convergent and discriminant validation by the multi-trait-multimethod matrix. *Psychological Bulletin,* 56, 81—105.

Campbell, D.T. & Stanley, J.C. (1963) *Experimental and quasi-experimental designs for research.* Chicago: Rand McNally & Co.

Campbell, R.J. (1977—1978) Comments on "Legal issues in state mental health care: Proposals for change — civil commitment." *Mental Disability Law Reporter,* 2, 519—521.

Canning, R.R. & Baker, J.M. (1959) Effect of the group on authoritarian and nonauthoritarian persons. *American Journal of Sociology,* 64, 579—581.

Canon, L.K. (1964) Self-confidence and selective exposure to information. In L. Festinger (Ed.), *Conflict, decision, and dissonance.* Stanford, CA: Stanford University Press.

Cantor, N. (1981) Perceptions of situation: Situation prototypes and person-situation prototypes. In D. Magnusson (Ed.), *Toward a psychology of situations.* Hillsdale, N.J.: Lawrence Erlbaum.

Cartwright, D. & Harary, F. (1956) Structural balance: A generalization of Heider's theory. *Psychological Review,* 63, 277—293.

Carver, C.S. (1975) Physical aggression as a function of objective self-awareness and attitudes toward punishment. *Journal of Experimental Social Psychology,* 11, 510—519.

Centers, R., Shomer, R.W. & Rodrigues, A. (1970) A field experiment in interpersonal persuasion using authoritative influence. *Journal of Personality,* 38, 392—403.

Chapanis, N.P. & Chapanis, A. (1964) Cognitive dissonance: Five years later. *Psychological Bulletin,* 61, 1—22.

Christie, R. & Geis, F. (1968) Some consequences of taking Machiavelli seriously. In E.F. Borgatta and W.W. Lambert (Eds.). *Handbook of personality theory and research.* Chicago: Rand McNally.

Cialdini, R.B., Brauer, S.L. & Lewis, S.K. (1974) Attributional bias and the easily persuaded other. *Journal of Personality and Social Psychology,* 30, 631—637.

Cobb, S. (1976) Social support as a moderator of life stress. *Psychosomatic Medicine*, **38**, 300–314.

Cochrane, R. & Kelly, K. (1971) Personality and the differential effectiveness of an experimental value change procedure. Unpublished paper. Reported in Rokeach, M. *The nature of human values*. New York: Free Press, 1973.

Cody, M.J. (1978) *The dimensions of persuasion situations: Implications for communication research and assessments of taxonomy construction methodologies*. Unpublished doctoral dissertation, Department of Communication, Michigan State University.

Cohen, A.R. (1959) Some implications of self-esteem for social influence. In C.I. Hovland and I.L. Janis (Eds.). *Personality and persuasibility*. New Haven, CT: Yale University Press.

Coleman, J.S. (1963) *The adolescent society*. New York: Free Press.

Collins, B.E. & Hoyt, M.F. (1972) Personal responsibility-for-consequences: An integration and extension of the "forced compliance" literature. *Journal of Personality and Social Psychology*, **8**, 558–593.

Cook, T.D. & Campbell, D.T. (1979) *Quasi-experimentation: Design and analysis issues for field settings*. Chicago: Rand McNally College Publishing Co.

Cooley, C.H. (1902, Rev. ed. 1922) *Human nature and the social order*. New York: Charles Scribner's Sons.

Costa, P.T., Jr., McCrae, R.R. / Arenberg, D. (1980) Enduring dispositions in adult males. *Journal of Personality and Social Psychology*, **38**, 793–800.

Cox, D.F. & Bauer, R.A. (1964) Self-confidence and persuasibility in women. *Public Opinion Quarterly*, **28**, 453–466.

Crano, W.D. & Brewer, M.B. (1973) *Principles of research in social psychology*. New York: McGraw-Hill.

Crano, W.D., Kenny, D.A. & Campbell, D.T. (1972) Does intelligence cause achievement? A cross-lagged panel analysis. *Journal of Educational Psychology*, **63**, 258–275.

Cronbach, L. (1951) Coefficient alpha and the internal structure of tests. *Psychometrika*, **16**, 297–334.

Cronkhite, G. & Goetz, E. (1971) Dogmatism, persuasibility, and attitude instability. *Journal of Communication*, **21**, 342–352.

Crowne, D.P. & Marlowe, D. (1960) A new scale of social desirability independent of psychopathology. *Journal of Consulting Psychology*, **24**, 349–354.

Dabbs, J.M. (1964) Self-esteem, communicator characteristics, and attitude change. *Journal of Abnormal and Social Psychology*, **69**, 173–181.

Davidson, A.R. & Jaccard, J. (1979) Variables that moderate the attitude-behavior relation: Results of a longitudinal survey. *Journal of Personality and Social Psychology*, **37**, 1364–1376.

Dermer, M., Cohen, S.J., Jacobsen, E. & Anderson, E.A. (1979) Evaluative judgments of aspects of life as a function of vicarious exposure to hedonic extremes. *Journal of Personality and Social Psychology*, **37**, 247–260.

Deutscher, I. (1966) Words and deeds: Social science and social policy. *Social Problems*, **13**, 235–254.

Deutscher, I. (1973) *What we say/What we do: Sentiments and acts.* Glenview, IL: Scott, Foresman.

Diamond, S.S. & Zeisel, H.A. (1974) Courtroom experiment on juror selection and behavior. *Personality and Social Psychology Bulletin,* **1**, 276–277.

Dienstbier, R.A., Hillman, D., Lehnhoff, J., Hillman, J. & Valkenaar, M.C. (1975) An emotion-attribution approach to moral behavior: Interfacing cognitive and avoidance theories of moral development. *Psychological Review,* **82**, 299–315.

Dienstbier, R.A., Kahle, L.R. Willis, K.A. & Tunnell, G.B. (1980) The impact of moral theories on cheating: Studies of emotion attribution and schema activation. *Motivation and Emotion,* 4(3), 193–216.

Dillehay, R.C. (1972) On the irrelevance of the classical negative evidence concerning the effect of attitudes on behaviors. *American Psychologist,* **28**, 887–891.

Doherty, M.A. & Walker, R.E. (1966) The relationship of personality characteristics, awareness, and attitude in a verbal conditioning situation. *Journal of Personality,* **34**, 504–516.

Doob, L.W. (1948) *Public opinion and propaganda.* New York: Henry Holt and Co.

Douvan, E. (1974) Commitment and social contract in adolescence. *Psychiatry,* **37**, 23–36.

Douvan, E. & Adelson, J. (1966) *The adolescent experience.* New York: Wiley.

Dreben, E.K., Fiske, S.T. & Hastie, R. (1979) The independence of evaluation and item information: Impression and recall order effects in behavior-based impression formation. *Journal of Personality and Social Psychology,* **37**, 1758–1768.

Dulany, D.E. (1961) Hypotheses and habits in verbal "operant conditioning". *Journal of Abnormal and Social Psychology,* **63**, 251–263.

Duncan, O.D. (1972) Unmeasured variables in linear models for panel analysis: Some didactic examples. In H.L. Costner (Ed.), *Sociological methodology.* San Francisco: Jossey-Bass.

Duverger, M. (1972) *The study of politics.* Tr. by R. Wagoner. New York: Thomas Y. Crowell.

Eagly, A.H. & Carli, L.L. (1981) Sex of researchers and sex-typed communications as determinants of sex differences in influenceability: A meta-analysis of social influence studies. *Psychological Bulletin,* **90**, 1–20.

Eagly, A.H. & Warren, R. (1976) Intelligence, comprehension, and opinion change. *Journal of Personality,* **44**, 226–242.

Eagly, A.H., Wood, W. & Chaiken, S. (1978) Causal inferences about communications and their effect on opinion change. *Journal of Personality and Social Psychology,* **36**, 424–435.

Eddy, G.L. & Sinnett, R.E. (1973) Behavior setting utilization by emotionally disturbed college students. *Journal of Consulting and Clinical Psychology,* **40**, 210–216.

Eisert, D.C. & Kahle, L.R. (1982) Self-evaluation and social comparison of physical and role change during adolescence: A longitudinal analysis. *Child Development,* **53**, 98–104.

Ekehammar, B. (1974) Interactionism in personality from a historic perspective. *Psychological Bulletin,* **81**, 1026–1048.

Ekehammar, B., Magnusson, D. & Ricklander, L. (1974) An interactionist approach to the study of anxiety. *Scandinavian Journal of Psychology,* **15**, 4–14.

Endler, N.S. (1975) The case for person-situation interactions. *Canadian Psychological Review*, 16, 12—21.

Epstein, G.F. (1969) Machiavelli and the devil's advocate. *Journal of Personality and Social Psychology*, 11, 38—41.

Epstein, S. (1979) The stability of behavior: I. On predicting most of the people much of the time. *Journal of Personality and Social Psychology*, 37, 1097—1126.

Epstein, S. (1980) The stability of behavior: II. Implications for psychological research. *American Psychologist*, 35, 790—806.

Ericsson, K.A. & Simon, H.A. (1980) Verbal reports as data. *Psychological Review*, 87, 215—251.

Erikson, E. (1968) *Identity: Youth and Crisis*. New York: Norton.

Eysenck, H.J. (1953) *The structure of human personality*. London: Methuen.

Fazio, R.H. & Zanna, M.P. (1978) Attitudinal qualities relating to the strength of the attitude-behavior relationship. *Journal of Experimental Social Psychology*, 14, 398—408.

Fazio, R.H. & Zanna, M.P. (1981) Direct experience and attitude-behavior consistency. In L. Berkowitz (Ed.). *Advances in experimental social psychology*. Vol. 14. New York: Academic Press.

Feinman, S. (1980) The utility of evolutionary theory for the social sciences. In S.G. McNall & G.N. Howe (Eds.), *Current Perspectives in Social Theory*.

Festinger, L. (1957) *A theory of cognitive dissonance*. Stanford, CA: Stanford University Press.

Festinger, L. & Carlsmith, J.M. (1959) Cognitive consequences of forced compliance. *Journal of Abnormal and Social Psychology*, 58, 203—210.

Fire, B.J. (1957) Conclusion drawing, communication credibility and anxiety as factors in opinion change. *Journal of Abnormal and Social Psychology*, 54, 369—374.

Fishbein, M. (1980) A theory of reasoned action: Some applications and implications. In M.M. Page (Ed.), *Nebraska Symposium on Motivation*. Vol. 27. Lincoln: University of Nebraska Press.

Fishbein, M. & Ajzen, I. (1974) Attitudes toward objects as predictors of single and multiple behavioral criteria. *Psychological Review*, 81, 59—74.

Fishbein, M. & Ajzen, I. (1975) *Belief, attitude, intention, and behavior*. Reading, Mass.: Addison-Wesley.

Fishbein, M. & Coombs, F.S. (1974) Basis for decision: An attitudinal analysis of voting behavior. *Journal of Applied Social Psychology*, 4, 95—124.

Flavell, J.H. (1963) *The developmental psychology of Jean Piaget*. New York: D. Van Nostrand.

Flay, B.R. (1978) Catastrophe theory in social psychology: Some applications to attitudes and social behavior. *Behavioral Science*, 23, 335—350.

Fleming, D. (1967) Attitude: The history of a concept. *Perspectives in American History*, 1, 287—365.

Forgas, J.P. (1976) The perception of social episodes: Categorical and dimensional representations in two different social millieus. *Journal of Personality and Social Psychology*,

34, 199—209.

Frederiksen, N. (1972) Toward a taxonomy of situations. *American Psychologist,* **27**, 114—123.

Freedman, J.L. (1965) Confidence, utility, and selective exposure: A partial replication. *Journal of Personality and Social Psychology,* **2**, 778—780.

Freedman, J.L. & Sears, D.O. (1965) Selective exposure. In L. Berkowitz (Ed.), *Advances in experimental social psychology* (Vol. 2), New York: Academic Press.

Freedman, R., Hermalin, A. & Chang, M. (1975) Do statements about desired family size predict fertility? The case of Taiwan 1967—1970. *Demography,* **12**, 407—416.

Furnham, A. & Argyle, M. (1981) Introduction. In A. Furnham & M. Argyle (Eds.), *The psychology of social situations: Selected readings.* Oxford: Pergamon Press.

Fyans, J.L., Jr. & Maehr, M.L. (1979) Attribution style, task selection, and achievement. *Journal of Educational Psychology,* **71**, 499—507.

Gadlin, H. & Rubin, S.H. (1979) Interactionism: A nonresolution of the person-situation cotroversy. In A.R. Buss (Ed.). *Psychology in social context.* New York: Irvington Publishers, 213—238.

Gallup, G.H. (1973) *The Gallup poll: Public opinion 1935—1971.* Vol. 3, New York: Random House.

Gelfind, D.M. (1962) The influence of self-esteem on rate of verbal conditioning and social matching behavior. *Journal of Abnormal and Social Psychology,* **65**, 259—265.

Gibbons, F.X. (1978) Sexual standards and reactions to pornography: Enhancing behavioral consistency through self-focused attention. *Journal of Personality and Social Psychology,* **36**, 976—987.

Gibson, J.J. (1960) The concept of the stimulus in psychology. *American Psychologist,* **15**, 694—703.

Goldstein, J.H., Rosnow, R.L., Goodstadt, B.E. & Suls, J.M. (1972) The "good subject" in verbal operant conditioning research. *Journal of Experimental Research in Personality,* **6**, 29—33.

Gollob, H.F. & Dittes, J.E. (1965) Effects of manipulated self-esteem on persuasibility depending on threat and complexity of communication. *Journal of Personality and Social Psychology,* **2**, 195—201.

Goodmonson, C. & Glaudin, V. (1971) The relationship of commitment-free behavior and commitment behavior: A study of attitude toward organ transplantation, *Journal of Social Issues,* **27**, 171—183.

Gordon, G.N. (1971) *Persuasion: The theory and practice of manipulative communications.* New York: Hasting House.

Graham, J.A., Argyle, M. & Furnham, A. (1980) The goal structure of situations. *European Journal of Social Psychology,* **10**, 345—366.

Granberg, D. & Brent, E.E., Jr. (1974) Dove-hawk placements in the 1968 election: Application of social judgment and balance theories. *Journal of Personality and Social Psychology,* **29**, 687—695.

Greenberg, M.T., Marvin, R.S. & Mossler, D.G. (1977) The development of conditional reasoning skills. *Developmental Psychology,* **13**, 527—528.

Greenwald, A.G. (1965) Behavior change following a persuasive communication. *Journal of Personality, 33, 370–391.*

Greenwald, A.G. (1966) Effects of prior commitment on behavior change after a persuasive communication. *Public Opinion Quarterly, 29, 595–601.*

Greenwald, A.G. (1968) Cognitive learning, cognitive response to persuasion and attitude change. In A.G. Greenwald, T.C. Brock & T.M. Ostrom (Eds.), *Psychological foundations of attitudes.* New York: Academic Press.

Greenwald, A.G. (1975) On the inconclusiveness of "crucial" cognitive tests of dissonance versus self-perception theories. *Journal of Experimental Social Psychology, 11, 490–499.*

Gurin, G., Veroff, J. & Feld, S. (1960) *Americans view their mental health.* New York: Basic Books.

Hagan, J. (1975) Law, order, and sentencing: A study of attitude in action. *Sociometry, 38, 374–384.*

Hall, C.S. & Lindzey, G. (1970) *Theories of personality.* (2nd ed.). New York: John Wiley and Soncs.

Harrell, G.D. & Bennett, P.D. (1974) An evaluation of the expectancy value model of attitude measurement for physician prescribing behavior. *Journal of Marketing Research, 11, 269–278.*

Hartshorne, H. & May, M.S. (1928–1930) *Studies in the nature of character: Vol. I; Studies in deceit; Vol. II, Studies in self-control; Vol. III, Studies in the organization of character.* New York: Macmillan.

Harvey, J.H., Town, J.P. & Yarkin, K.L. (1981) How fundamental is "the fundamental attribution error"? *Journal of Personality and Social Psychology, 40, 346–349.*

Harvey, O.J. (1965) Some situational and cognitive determinants of dissonance resolution. *Journal of Personality and Social Psychology, 1, 349–355.*

Harvey, O.J. & Beverly, G.D. (1961) Some personality correlates of concept change through role playing. *Journal of Abnormal and Social Psychology, 63, 125–130.*

Hays, W.L. (1973) *Statistics for the social sciences.* (2nc ed.). New York: Holt, Rinehart, and Winston.

Heider, F. (1946) Attitudes and cognitive organization. *Journal of Psychology, 21, 107–112.*

Heider, F. (1958) *The psychology of interpersonal relations.* New York: John Wiley.

Heider, F. & Summel, M. (1944) An experimental study of apparent behavior. *American Journal of Psychology, 57, 243–259.*

Heise, D.R. (1969) Problems in path analysis and causal inference. In G.W. Bohrnstedt (Ed.), *Sociological Methodology, 38–73.*

Helson, H. (1959) Adaptation-level theory. In S. Koch (Ed.), *Psychology: A study of a science.* Vol. 1. New York: McGraw-Hill.

Helson, H. (1964) *Adaptation-level theory.* New York: Harger & Row.

Henle, M. (1962) On the relation between logic and thinking. *Psychological Review, 69, 366–378.*

Hogan, R., DeSoto, C.B. & Solano, C. (1977) Traits, tests, and personality research. *American Psychologist*, **32**, 255—264.

Hogarth, R.M. (1981) Beyond discrete biases: Functional and dysfunctional aspects of judgmental heuristics. *Psychological Bulletin*, **90**, 197—217.

Holland, J. (1966) *The psychology of vocational choice*. Waltham, MA: Blaisdell.

Hovland, C.I. (1959) Reconciling conflicting results derived from experimental and survey studies of attitude change. *American Psychologist*, **14**, 8—17.

Hovland, C.I. & Janis, I.L. (Eds.) (1959) *Personality and persuasibility*. New Haven, CT: Yale University Press.

Howard, J.A. (1979) Person-situation interaction models. *Personality and Social Psychology Bulletin*, **5**, 191—195.

Hunt, J. McV. (1981) The role of situations in early psychological development. In D. Magnusson (Ed.), *Toward a psychology of situations*. Hillsdale, N.J.: Lawrence Erlbaum Ass.

Hyman, H.H. & Seatsley, P.B. (1954) "The Authoritarian Personality" — A methodological critique. In R. Christie and M. Jahoda (Eds.), *Studies in the scope and method of "The Authoritarian Personality"*. New York: Free Press.

Inhelder, B. (1976) Introduction. In B. Inhelder & H.H. Chipman (Eds.), *Piaget and his school*. New York: Springer-Verlag.

Inhelder, B. & Piaget, J. (1958) *The growth of logical thinking from childhood to adolescence*. New York: Basic Books.

Inhelder, B. & Piaget, J. (1964) *The early growth of logic in the child: Classification and seriation*. London: Routledge and Kegan Paul.

Insko, C.A. (1967) *Theories of attitude change*. New York: Appleton-Century-Crofts.

Insko, C.A. (1981) Balance theory and phenomenology. In R.E. Petty, T.M. Ostrom & T.C. Brock (Eds.), *Cognitive responses in persuasion*. Hillsdale, N.J.: Lawrence Erlbaum Ass.

Insko, C.A., Arkoff, A. & Insko, V.M. (1965) Effects of high and low fear arousing communications upon opinions toward smoking. *Journal of Experimental Social Psychology*, **1**, 256—266.

Insko, C.A., Thilbaut, J.W., Moehle, D., Wilson, M., Diamond, W.D., Golmore, R., Solomon, M.R. & Lipsetz, A. (1980) Social evolution and the emergence of leadership. *Journal of Personality and Social Psychology*, **39**, 431—448.

Insko, C.A., Worchel, S., Sanger, E. & Arnold, S.E. (1973) Effort, objective self-awareness, choice, and dissonance. *Journal of Personality and Social Psychology*, **28**, 262—269.

Jaccard, J. (1979) Personality and behavioral prediction: An analysis of behavioral criterion measures. In L.R. Kahle (Ed.). *New directions for methodology of behavioral science* No. 2: *Methods for studying person-situation interactions*. San Francisco: Jossey-Bass.

Jaccard, J.J. & Davidson, A.R. (1975) A comparison of two models of social behavior: Results of a sample survey. *Sociometry*, **38**, 491—517.

James, W. (1884) What is an emotion? *Mind*, **9**, 188—205.

Janis, I.L. (1954) Personality correlates of susceptibility to persuasion. *Journal of Personality*, **22**, 504—518.

Janis, I.L. (1955) Anxiety indices related to susceptibility to persuasion. *Journal of Abnormal and Social Psychology*, **51**, 663—667.

Janis, I.L. & Feshbach, S. (1953) Effects of fear arousing communication. *Journal of Abnormal and Social Psychology*, **48**, 78—92.

Janis, I.L. & Field, P.B. (1956) A behavioral assessment of persuasibility: consistency of individual differences. *Sociometry*, **19**, 241—259.

Janis, I.L. & Field, P.B. (1959) Sex differences and personality factors related tp persuasibility. In C.I. Hovland and I.L. Janis (Eds.), *Personality and persuasibility*. New Haven, CT: Yale University Press.

Janis, I.L. & Hoffman, D. (1970) Facilitating effects of daily contact between partners who make a decision to cut down on smoking. *Journal of Personality and Social Psychology*, **17**, 25—35.

Janis, I.L. & Rife, D. (1959) Persuasibility and emotional disorder. In C.I. Hovland and I.L. Janis (Eds.), *Personality and persuasibility*. New Haven, CT: Yale University Press.

Jensen, R.E. & Moore, S.G. (1977) The effect of attribute statements on cooperativeness and competitiveness in school-age boys. *Child Development*, **48**, 305—307.

Jessor, R. & Jessor, S.L. (1973) The perceived environment in behavioral science. *American Behavioral Scientist*, **16**, 801—829.

Jessor, R. & Jessor, S.L. (1977) *Problem behavior and psychosocial developments: A longitudinal study on youth*. New York: Academic Press.

Johnson, H.H. , Torcivis, J.M. & Poprick, M.A. (1968) Effects of source credibility on the relationship between authoritarianism and attitude change. *Journal of Personality and Social Psychology*, **9**, 179—183.

Jones, E.E. (1976) How do people perceive the causes of behavior? *American Scientist*, **64**, 300—305.

Jones, E.E. & Davis, K.E. (1965) From acts to dispositions: The attribution process in person perception. In L. Berkowitz (Ed.), *Advances in experimental social psychology*. Vol. 2. New York: Academic Press.

Jones, E.E. & Gerard, H.B. (1967) *Foundations of social psychology*. New York: Wiley.

Jones, E.E. & Nisbett, R.E. (1971) *The actor and the observer: Divergent perspectives of the causes of behavior*. Morristown, N.J.: General Learning Press.

Jones, W.H. (1979) Exploratory behavior of adolescents in a dyadic, problem solving situation. In J.G. Kelly (Ed.), *Adolescent boys in high school: A psychological study of coping and adaptation*. Hillsdale, NJ: Lawrence Erlbaum.

Jordan, N. (1953) Behavioral forces that are a function of attitudes and of cognitive organization. *Human Relations*, **6**, 273—287.

Joseph, J.M., Gaes, G. & Tedeschi, J.T. (September, 1975) *A consistency need: When dissonance fails and impression management succeeds*. Paper presented at the meeting of the American Psychological Association, Chicago.

Juster, F.T. (1964) *Anticipations and purchases: An analysis of consumer behavior*. Princeton, NJ: Princeton University Press.

Kahle, L.R. (1978) Dissonance and impression management as theories of attitude change. *Journal of Social Psychology*, **105**, 53—64.

Kahle, L.R. (1979) Attitudinal entailment and resistance to change. *Journal of Social Psychology*, **106**, 99–109.

Kahle, L.R. (1980) Stimulus condition self-selection by males in the interaction of locus of control and skill-chance situations. *Journal of Personality and Social Psychology*, **38**, 50–56.

Kahle, L.R. (Ed.). *Social values and social change: Adaptation to life in America.* In preparation.

Kahle, L.R. & Berman, J.J. (1979) Attitudes cause behaviors: A cross-lagged panel analysis. *Journal of Personality and Social Psychology*, 37, 315–321. (a)

Kahle, L.R. & Berman, J.J. (1979) Cross-lagged panel correlation and personality. In L.R. Kahle (Ed.), *New directions for methodology of behavioral science* (No. 2): *Methods for studying person-situation interaction.* San Francisco: Jossey-Bass. (b)

Kahle, L.R. Kenny, D.A. & Berman, J.J. (1982) In defense of theoretical precision and methodological diversity: A comment on Bentler & Speckart. Manuscript submitted for publication.

Kahle, L.R., Klingel, D.M. & Kulka, R.A. (1981) A longitudinal study of adolescent attitude-behavior consistency. *Public Opinion Quarterly*, **45**, 402–414.

Kahle, L.R., Kulka, R.A. & Klingel, D.M. (1980) Low adolescent self-esteem leads to multiple interpersonal problems: A test of social adaptation theory. *Journal of Personality and Social Psychology*, **39**, 496–502.

Kahle, L.R. & Page, M.M. (1976) The deprivation-satiation effect in attitude conditioning without deprivation but with demand characteristics. *Personality and Social Psychology Bulletin*, **2**, 470–473.

Kahle, L.R. & Sales, B.D. (1978) Attitudes of clinical psychologists toward involuntary civil commitment law. *Professional Psychology*, **9**, 428–439. (a)

Kahle, L.R. & Sales, B.D. (1978) Personalization of the outside envelope in mail surveys. *Public Opinion Quarterly*, **42**, 547–550. (b)

Kahle, L.R. & Sales, B.D. (1980) Due process of law and the attitudes of professionals toward involuntary civil commitment. In P.D. Lipsitt & B.D. Sales, *New directions in Psycholegal research.* New York: Van Nostrand Reinhold.

Kahle, L.R., Sales, B.D. & Nagel, S. (1978) On unicorns blocking commitment law reform. *Journal of Psychiatry and Law*, **6**, 89–105.

Kahle, R. (1977) Opinion leader attitudes on media-business relations. In B. Rubin (Ed.), *Big business and the mass media.* Lexington, MA: Lexington Books.

Kahn, D. (1972) Mechanisms of change in the development of cognitive structures, *Child Development*, **43**, 833–844.

Kahneman, D. & Tversky, A. (1972) Subjective probability: A judgment of representativeness. *Cognitive Psychology*, **3**, 430–454.

Kahneman, D. & Tversky, A. (1973) On the psychology of prediction. *Psychological Review*, **80**, 237–251.

Kamenetsky, J., Burgess, G.G. & Rowan, T. (1956) The relative effectiveness of four attitude assessment techniques in predicting a criterion. *Educational and Psychological Measurement*, **16**, 187–194.

Kantor, J.R. (1959) *Interbehavioral psychology*. Bloomington: Principia Press.

Katz, D. (1960) The functional approach to the study of attitudes. *Public Opinion Quarterly*, 24, 163—204.

Katz, D., Cartwright, D., Eldersveld, S. & Lee, A.M. (Eds.) (1954) *Public opinion and propaganda*. New York: The Dryden Press.

Katz, D., McClintock, C. & Sarnoff, I. (1957) The measurement of ego defence as related to attitude change. *Journal of Personality*, 25, 465—474.

Katz, D. & Stotland, E. (1959) A preliminary statement of a theory of attitude structure and change. In S. Koch (Ed.), *Psychology: A study of a science*. (Vol. 3), New York: McGraw-Hill.

Kelley, H.H. (1967) Attribution theory in social psychology. In D. Levine (Ed.), *Nebraska Symposium on Motivation*. (Vol. 15). Lincoln: University of Nebraska Press.

Kelley, H.H. (1971) *Attribution in social interaction*. Morristown, NJ: General Learning Press.

Kelley, H.H. (1972) *Causal schemata and the attribution process*. Morristown, NJ: General Learning Press.

Kelley, H.H. & Stahelski, A.J. (1970) The social interaction basis of cooperators' and competitors' beliefs about others. *Journal of Personality and Social Psychology*, 16, 66—91.

Kelly, G.A. (1963) *A theory of personality: The psychology of personal constructs*. New Yrok: W.W. Norton.

Kelman, H.C. (1958) Compliance, identification, and internalization: Three processes of attitude change. *Journal of Conflict Resolution*, 2, 51—60.

Kelman, H. (1961) Processes of opinion change. *Public Opinion Quarterly*, 25, 57—78.

Kelman, H.C. (1967) Human use of human subjects: The problem of deception in social psychological experiments. *Psychological Bulletin*, 67, 1—11.

Kelman, H.C. (1968) *A time to speak: On human values and social research*. San Francisco: Jossey-Bass.

Kelman, H.C. (1972) The rights of the subject in social research: An analysis in terms of relative power and legitimacy. *American Psychologist*, 27, 989—1016.

Kelman, H.C. (1974) Attitudes are alive and well and gainfully employed in the sphere of action. *American Psychologist*, 29, 310—324.

Kenrick, D.T. & Stringfield, D.O. (1980) Personality traits and the eye of the beholder: Crossing some traditional philosophical boundries in the search for consistency in all of the people. *Psychological Review*, 87, 88—104.

Kenny, D.A. (1973) Cross-lagged and synchronous common factors in panel data. In A.S. Goldberger & O.D. Duncan (Eds.), *Structural equation models in the social science*. New York: Sminar Press.

Kenny, D.A. (1975) Cross-lagged panel correlation: A test for spuriousness. *Psychological Bulletin*, 72, 887—903.

Kenny, D.A. (1979) *Correlation and causality*. New York: Wiley.

Kenny, D.A. & Campbell, D.T. Methodological issues in the analysis of temporal data. In K. Gergan and S. Gergen (Eds.), *Historical social psychology*. Hillsdale, N.J.: Lawrence Erlbaum Ass. in press.

Kenny, D.A. & Harackiewicz, J.M. (1979) Cross-lagged panel correlation: Practice and promise. *Journal of Applied Psychology, 64,* 372–379.

Kiesler, C.A. (1971) *The psychology of commitment.* New York: Academic Press.

Kiesler, C.A., Collins, B.E. & Miller, N. (1969) *Attitude change: A critical analysis of theoretical approaches.* New York: John Wiley.

Kiesler, C.A. & Munson, P.A. (1975) Attitudes and opinions. *Annual Review of Psychology, 26,* 415–456.

King, B.T. (1959) Relationships between susceptibility to opinion change and child-rearing practice. In C.I. Hovland and I.L. Janis (Eds.), *Personality and persuasibility.* New Haven: Yale University Press.

Kiritz, S. & Moos, R.H. (1974) Physiological effects of social environments. *Psychosomatic Medicine, 36*(2), 96–114.

Kish, L. (1965) *The survey sample.* New York: Wiley.

Kleck, R.E. & Weston, J. (1967) Dogmatism and response to opinion-consistent and opinion-inconsistent information. *Journal of Personality and Social Psychology, 5,* 249–252.

Kohlberg, L. (1966) A cognitive developmental analysis of children's sex-role concepts and attitudes. In E. Maccoby (Ed.), *The development of sex differences.* Stanford: Stanford University Press.

Kothandapani, V. (1971) Validation of feeling, belief, and intention to act as three components of attitude and their contribution to prediction of contraceptive behavior. *Journal of Personality and Social Psychology, 19,* 321–333.

Krause, M.S. (1970) Use of social situations for research purposes. *American Psychology, 25,* 748–753.

Kruglanski, A.W. (1975) The human subject in the psychological experiment: Fact and artifact. In L. Berkowitz (Ed.), *Advances in experimental social psychology.* Vol. 8. New York: Academic Press.

Kruglanski, A.W. (1979) Causal explanation, teleological explanation: On radical particularism in attribution theory. *Journal of Personality and Social Psychology, 37,* 1447–1457.

Kuhn, D. (1972) Mechanisms of change in the development of cognitive structures. *Child Development, 43,* 833–844.

Kuhn, D. & Ho, V. (1977) The development of schemes for recognizing additive and alternative effects in a "natural experiment" context. *Developmental Psychology, 13,* 515–516.

Kulka, R.A. (1979) Interaction as person-environment fit. In L.R. Kahle (Ed.), *New directions for methodology of behavioral science. No. 2: Methods for studying person-situation interactions.* San Francisco: Jossey-Bass, 55–72.

Kulka, R.A. (1981) Idiosyncrasy and circumstance: Choices and constraints in the research process. *American Behavioral Scientist, 24* (6), in press.

Kulka, R.A., Kahle, L.R., & Klingel, D.M. (1982) Aggression, deviance, and personality adaptation as antecedents and consequences of alienation and involvement in high school. *Journal of Youth and Adolescence, 11,* 261–279.

Kutner, B., Wilkens, C. & Yarrow, P.R. (1952) Verbal attitudes and overt behavior involving racial prejudice. *Journal of Abnormal and Social Psychology, 47,* 647–652.

Lamm, H. & Meyers, D.G. (1978) Group-induced polarization of attitudes and behavior. In L. Berkowitz (Ed.), *Advances in experimental social psychology,* Vol. 11. New York: Academic Press.

LaPiere, R.T. (1934) Attitudes vs. action. *Social Forces,* 13, 230–237.

Leon, G.R., Gillum, B., Gillum, R. & Gouze, M. (1979) Personality stability and change over a 30-year period. *Journal of Consulting and Clinical Psychology,* 47, 517–524.

Leventhal, H. & Niles, P.A. (1964) A field experiment on fear around with data on the validity of questionnaire measures. *Journal of Personality,* 32, 459–479.

Leventhal, H., Singer, R.P. & Jones, S.H. (1965) The effects of fear and specificity of recommendation upon attitudes and behavior. *Journal of Personality and Social Psychology,* 2, 20–29.

Levonian, E. (1970) Need for control data in studies of self-esteem and persuasibility. *Psychological Reports,* 27, 527–544.

Lewin, K. (1935) *A dynamic theory of personality: Selected papers.* New York: McGraw-Hill.

Lewin, K. (1936) *Principles of topological psychology.* New York: McGraw-Hill.

Lieberman, S. (1965) The effects of changes of roles on the attitudes of role occupants. In M.R. Rosenzweig & L.W. Porter (Eds.), *Basic studies in social psychology.* New York: Holt, Rinehart, & Winston, 485–494.

Likert, R. (1932) A technique for the measurement of attitude. *Archives of Psychology,* 140, 1–55.

Linder, D.E., Cooper, J. & Jones, E.E. (1967) Decision freedom as a determinant of the role of incentive magnitude in attitude change. *Journal of Personality and Social Psychology,* 6, 245–254.

Linton, H. & Graham, E. (1959) Personality correlates of persuasibility. In C.I. Hovland and I.L. Janis (Eds.), *Personality and persuasibility.* New Haven, CT: Yale University Press.

Liska, A.E. (1974) Emergent issues in the attitude-behavior consistency controversy. *American Sociological Review,* 39, 261–272.

Litwak, E. & Szeleny, I. (1969) Primary group structures and their functions: Kin, neighbors, and friends. *American Sociological Review,* 34, 465–481.

Livesley, W.J. & Bromley, D.B. (1973) *Person perception in childhood and adolescence.* London: Wiley.

Lowenthal, M.F. & Haven, C. (1968) Interaction and adaptation: Intimacy as a critical variable. *American Sociological Review,* 33, 20–30.

Maddi, S.R. (1972) *Personality theories: A comparative analysis.* (Revised ed.) Homewood, IL: The Dorsey Press.

Magnusson, D. (1981) Wanted: A psychology of situations. In D. Magnusson (Ed.), *Toward a psychology of situations.* Hillsdale, N.J.: Lawrence Erlbaum.

Magnusson, D. & Endler, N.S. (Eds.) (1977) *Personality at the crossroads: Current issues in interactional psychology.* Hillsdale, N.J.: Lawrence Erlbaum.

Mandler, J.M. & Johnson, N.S. (1977) Remembrance of things parsed: Story structure and recall. *Cognitive Psychology,* 9, 111–151.

Mandler, J.M. & Parker, R.E. (1976) Memory for descriptive and spatial information in complex pictures. *Journal of Experimental Psychology: Human Learning and Memory*, 2, 38—48.

Manis, M. & Moore, J.C. (1978) Summarizing controversial messages: Retroactive effects due to subsequent information. *Social Psychology Quarterly*, 41, 62—68.

Markus, H. (1977) Self-schemata and processing information about the self. *Journal of Personality and Social Psychology*, 35 63—78.

Marple, C.H. (1933) The comparative susceptibility of three age levels to the suggestion of groups versus expert opinion. *Journal of Social Psychology*, 4, 176—186.

Maslach, C. (1971) The "truth" about false confessions. *Journal of Personality and Social Psychology*, 20, 141—146.

Masling, J. (1966) Role-related behavior of the subject and psychologist and its effects upon psychological data. In D.L. Levine (Ed.), *Nebraska Symposium on motivation*. Lincoln: University of Nebraska Press.

Maykovich, M.X. (1975) Correlates of racial prejudice. *Journal of Personality and Social Psychology*, 32, 1014—1020.

McGuire, W.J. (1960) Cognitive consistency and attitude change. *Journal of Abnormal and Social Psychology*, 60, 345—353.

McGuire, W.J. (1964) Inducing resistance to persuasion: Some contemporary approaches. In L. Berkowitz (Ed.), *Advances in experimental social psychology*. Vol. 1. New York: Academic Press.

McGuire, W.J. (1968) The nature of attitudes and attitude change. In G. Lindzey and E. Aronson (Eds.), *The handbook of social psychology*. Vol. 3. (2nd ed.) Reading, MA: Addison-Wesley. (a)

McGuire, W.J. (1968) Personality and attitude change: An information processing theory. In A.G. Greenwald, T.C. Brock, and T.M. Ostrom (Eds.), *Psychological foundations of attitudes*. New York: Academic Press. (b)

McGuire, W.J. (1968) Personality and susceptibility to social influence. In E.F. Borgatta and W.W. Lambert (Eds.), *Handbook of personality theory and research*. Vol. 3 (2nd ed) Reading, MA: Addison-Wesley. (c)

McGuire, W.J. (1968) Theory of the structure of human thought. In R. Abelson, E. Aronson, W. McGuire, T. Newcomb, M. Rosenberg & P. Tannenbaum (Eds.), *Theories of cognitive consistency: A sourcebook*. Chicago: Rand McNally. (d)

McGuire, W.J. (1973) The yin and yang of progress in social psychology: Seven koan. *Journal of Personality and Social Psychology*, 26, 446—456.

McGuire, W.J. (1976) The concept of attitudes and their relation to behavior. In H.W. Sinaiko & L.A. Broedling (Eds.), *Perspectives on attitude assessment: Surveys and their alternatives*. Champaign, IL: Pendleton.

McGuire, W.J. (1981) The probabilogical model of cognitive structure and attitude change. In R.E. Petty, T.M. Ostrom & T.C. Brock (Eds.), *Cognitive responses in persuasion*. Hillsdale, NJ: Lawrence Erlbaum Ass.

McMillen, D.L. & Geiselman, J.H. (1974) Effect of cognitive dissonance on alpha wave production. *Personality and Social Psychology Bulletin*, 1, 150—151.

Meier, N.C. & Saunders, H.W. (1949) *The polls and public opinion: The Iowa conference on attitude and opinion research sponsored by the University of Iowa, Opwa City*. New York: Henry Holt and Company.

Meyer, J.S., Dechenne, T. & Albano, L.J. (1981) Cognitive consistency in the development of social attitudes. *Developmental Psychology*, 17, 494—498.

Miller, G.R. & Steinberg, M. (1975) *Between people: A new analysis of interpersonal communication*. Chicago: Science Research Associates.

Miller, N. (1965) Involvement and dogmatism as inhibitors of attitude change. *Journal of Experimental Social Psychology*, 1, 121—132.

Miller, R.L., Brickman, P. & Bolen, D. (1975) Attribution versus persuasion as a means for modifying behavior. *Journal of Personality and Social Psychology*, 31, 430—441.

Minard, R.D. (1952) Race relations in the Pocahontas coal field. *Journal of Social Issues*, 8, 29—44.

Minsky, M. (1975) A framework for representing knowledge. In P. Winston (Ed.), *The psychology of computer vision*. New York: McGraw-Hill.

Mischel, W. (1968) *Personality and assessment*. New York: Wiley.

Mischel, W. (1969) Continuity and change in personality. *American Psychologist*, 24, 1012—1018.

Mischel, W. (1973) On the empirical dilemmas of psychodynamic approaches: Issues and alternatives. *Journal of Abnormal Psychology*, 82, 335—344. (a)

Mischel, W. (1973) Toward a cognitive social learning reconceptualization of personality. *Psychological Review*, 80, 252—283. (b)

Mischel, W. (1976) *Introduction to personality*. 2nd ed. New York: Holt, Rinehart, and Winston.

Mischel, W. (1977) On the future of personality measurement. *American Psychologist*, 32, 246—254.

Mischel, W. (1979) On the interface of cognition and personality: Beyond the person-situation dabate. *American Psychologist*, 34, 740—754.

Moltz, H. & Thistlethwaite, D. (1955) Attitude modification and anxiety reduction. *Journal of Abnormal and Social Psychology*, 50, 231—237.

Moessinger, P. (1978) Piaget on equilibration. *Human Development*, 21, 255—267.

Murphy, G. (1947) *Personality: A biosocial approach to origins and structure*. New York: Harper.

Murray, H.A. (1951) Toward a classification of interaction. In T. Parsons and E.A. Shils (Eds.), *Toward a general theory of action*. Cambridge: Harvard University Press.

Nadler, E.B. (1959) Yielding, authoritarianism, and authoritarian ideology regarding groups. *Journal of Abnormal and Social Psychology*, 58, 408—410.

Newcomb, T.M. (1953) An approach to the study of communicative acts. *Psychological Review*, 60, 393—404.

Newman, B.M. (1976) The study of interpersonal behavior in adolescence. *Adolescence*, 11(41), 127—142.

Newman, B.M. (1979) Interpersonal behavior and preferences for exploration in adolescent boys: A small group study. In J.G. Kelly (Ed.), *Adolescent boys in high school: A*

Psychological study of coping and adaptation. Hillsdale, NJ: Lawrence Erlbaum.

Nisbett, R.E. (1980) The trait construct in lay and professional psychology. In L. Festinger (Ed.), *Retrospections on social psychology.* New York: Oxford Univ. Press, 109–130.

Nisbett, R.E. & Gordon, A. (1967) Self-esteem and susceptibility to social influence. *Journal of Personality and Social Psychology, 5,* 268–276.

Nisbett, R. & Ross, L. (1980) *Human inference: Strategies and shortcomings of social judgment.* Englewood Cliffs, NJ: Prentice-Hall.

Nisbett, R.E. & Wilson, T.D. (1977) Telling more than we can know: Verbal reports on mental processes. *Psychological Review, 84,* 231–259.

Noris, E.L. (1965) Attitude change as a function of open or closed-mindedness. *Journalism Quarterly, 42,* 571–575.

O'Donnell, J.M. & Brown, M.J.K. (1973) The classical conditioning of attitudes: A comparative study of ages 8 to 18. *Journal of Personality and Social Psychology, 26,* 379–385.

Olweus, D.A. (1977) Critical analysis of the "modern" interactionist position. In D. Magnusson and N.S. Endler (Eds.), *Personality at the crossroads: Current issues in interactional psychology.* Hillsdale, NJ: Lawrence Erlbaum Ass., 221–234.

Orne, M.T. (1962) On the social psychology of the psychological experiment. *American Psychology, 17,* 776–783.

Osgood, C.E., Suci, G.J. & Tannenbaum, P.H. (1957) *The measurement of meaning.* Urbana, IL: University of Illinois Press.

Osgood, C.E. & Tannenbaum, P.H. (1955) The principle of congruity in the prediction of attitude change. *Psychological Review, 62,* 42–55.

Oskamp, S. (1977) *Attitudes and opinions.* Englewood Cliffs, NJ: Prentice-Hall.

Ostrom, T.M. & Upshaw, H.S. (1968) Psychological perspective and attitude change. In A.G. Greenwald, T.C. Brock & T.M. Ostrom (Eds.), *Psychological foundations of attitudes.* New York: Academic Press.

Page, M.M. (1969) Social psychology of a classical conditioning of attitudes experiment. *Journal of Personality and Social Psychology, 11,* 177–186.

Page, M.M. (1970) Demand awareness, subject sophistication, and the effectiveness of a verbal "reinforcement". *Journal of Personality, 38,* 287–301. (a)

Page, M.M. (1970) Role of demand awareness in the communicator credibility effect. *Journal of Social Psychology, 82,* 57–66. (b)

Page, M.M. (1972) Demand characteristics and the verbal operant conditioning experiment. *Journal of Personality and Social Psychology, 23,* 372–378.

Page, M.M. (1974) Demand characteristics and the classical conditioning of attitudes experiment. *Journal of Personality and Social Psychology, 30,* 468–476.

Page, M.M. & Kahle, L.R. (1976) Demand characteristics in the satiation-deprivation effect on attitude conditioning. *Journal of Personality and Social Psychology, 33,* 553–562.

Passini, F.T. & Norman, W.T. (1966) A universal conception of personality structure? *Journal of Personality and Social Psychology, 4,* 44–49.

Peabody, D. (1966) Authoritarianism scales and response bias. *Psychological Bulletin, 65,* 11–23.

Pelz, D.C. & Andrews, F.M. (1964) Detecting causal priorities in panel study data. *American

Sociological Review, 29, 836—848.

Pepitone, A. & DiNubile, M. (1976) Contrast effects in judgments of crime severity and the punishment of criminal violators. *Journal of Personality and Social Psychology*, 33, 448—459.

Pervin, L. (1976) A free-response description approach to the analysis of person-situation interaction. *Journal of Personality and Social Psychology*, 34, 465—474.

Pervin, L.A. (1978) Definitions, measurements, and classification of stimuli, situations, and environments. *Human Ecology*, 6, 71—105.

Pervin, L.A. (1981) The relation of situations to behavior. In D. Magnusson (Ed.), *Toward a psychology of situations*. Hillsdale, N.J.: Lawrence Erlbaum.

Peterson, D.R. (1965) Scope of generality of verbally defined personality factors. *Psychological Review*, 72, 48—59.

Peterson, D.R. (1979) Assessing interpersonal relationships in natural settings. In L.R. Kahle (Ed.), *New directions for methodology of behavior science No. 2: Methods for studying person-situation interactions*. San Francisco: Jossey-Bass.

Petty, R.E. & Cacioppo, J.T. (1977) Forewarning, cognitive responding, and resistance to persuasion. *Journal of Personality and Social Psychology*, 35, 645—655.

Petty, R.E. & Cacioppo, J.T. (1981) *Attitudes and persuasion: Classic and contemporary approaches*. Dubuque, Iowa: Wm. C. Brown.

Petty, R.E. Ostrom, T.M. & Brock, T.C. (Eds.) (1981) *Cognitive responses in persuasion*. Hillsdale, NJ: Lawrence Erlbaum Ass.

Piaget, J. (1924) Les traits principaux de la logique de l'enfant. *Journal de psychologie*, 21, 48—101.

Piaget, J. (1926) *The language and thought of the child*. New York: Harcourt & Brace.

Piaget, J. (1928) *Judgment and reasoning in the child*. New York: Harcourt & Brace.

Piaget, J. (1929) *The child's conception of the world*. London: Routledge & Kegan Paul.

Piaget, J. (1930) *The child's conception of physical causality*. London: Routledge & Kegan Paul.

Piaget, J. (1932) *The moral judgment of the child*. London: Kegan Paul.

Piaget, J. (1950) *Introduction à l'épistémolgie génetique*. Paris: Presses Universitaires de France.

Piaget, J. (1952) *The origins of intelligence in children*. New York: Internat. Univ. Press.

Piaget, J. (1968) *Le Structuralisme*. (Translated by C. Maschler and published in English as: *Structuralism*. New York: Basic Books, 1970) Presses Universitaires de France.

Piaget, J. (1970) *Genetic epistemology*. New York: Columbia University Press.

Piaget, J. (1971) *Psychology and epistemology: Towards a theory of knowledge*. New York: Viking.

Piaget, J. (1976) Piaget's theory. In B. Inhelder & H.H. Chipman (Eds.), *Piaget and his school*. New York: Springer-Verlag.

Piaget, J. & Inhelder, B. (1969) *The psychology of the child*. New York: Basic Books.

Piaget, J. & Inhelder, B. (1975) *The origin of the idea of chance in children*. London: Routledge & Kegan Paul.

Polanyi, M. (1958) *Personal knowledge: Towards a post-critical philosophy.* Chicago: University of Chicago Press.

Poppleton, P.K. & Pilkington, G.W. (1963) A comparison of four methods of scoring an attitude scale in relation to its reliability and validity. *British Journal of Social and Clinical Psychology,* 3, 36—39.

Posner, M.I. (1969) Abstraction and the process of recognition. In G.H. Bower and J.T. Spence (Eds.), *The psychology of learning and motivation* (Vol. 3). New York: Academic Press.

Potter, H.W. & Klein, H.R. (1957) On nursing behavior. *Psychiatry,* 20, 39—46.

Powell, F.A. (1962) Open- and closed-mindedness and the ability to differentiate source and message. *Journal of Abnormal and Social Psychology,* 65, 61—64.

Powell, N.J. (1951) *Anatomy of public opinion.* New York: Prentice Hall.

Presser, S. (1981) *The use of survey data in basic social science research.* Paper presented at the annual meeting of the National Academy of Science.

Rajecki, D.W. (1982) *Attitudes: Themes and advances.* Sunderland, Mass.: Sinover.

Reardon, K.K. (1981) *Persuasion: Theory and context.* Beverly Hills, CA: Sage.

Reiss, I.L. (1967) *The social context of premarital sexual permissiveness.* New York: Holt, Rinehart, & Winston.

Rickard, S. (1972) The assumptions of causal analyses for incomplete causal sets of two multilevel variables. *Multivariate Behavioral Research,* 7, 317—359.

Riegel, K.F. & Meacham, J.A. (1978) Dialectics, transaction, and Piaget's theory. In L. Pervin (Ed.), *Perspectives in interactional psychology.* New York: Plenum.

Ring, K. (1967) Experimental social psychology: Some sober questions about frivolous values. *Journal of Experimental Social Psychology,* 3, 113—123.

Rogers, C.R. (1959) A theory of therapy, personality, and interpersonal relationships as developed in the client-centered framework. In S. Koch (Ed.), *Psychology: A study of a science,* Vol. 3, *Formulations of the Person and the Social Context.* New York: McGraw-Hill, 184—256.

Rogosa, D. (1980) A critique of cross-lagged correlation. *Psychological Bulletin,* 88, 245—258.

Rokeach, M. (1960) *The open and closed mind.* New York: Basic Books.

Rokeach, M. (1973) *The nature of human values.* New York: Free Press.

Rokeach, M. (1979) Some unresolved issues in theories of beliefs, attitudes, and values. In M.M. Page (Ed.), *Nebraska symposium on motivation: Beliefs, attitudes, and values.* Vol. 27. Lincoln: University of Nebraska Press.

Rokeach, M. & Kliejunas, P. (1972) Behavior as a function of attitude-toward-object and attitude-toward-situation. *Journal of Personality and Social Psychology,* 22, 194—201.

Roll, C.W., Jr. & Cantril, A.H. (1972) *Polls: Their use and misuse in politics.* New York: Basic Books.

Romer, D. (1981) A person-situation causal analysis of self-reports of attitudes. *Journal of Personality and Social Psychology,* 41, 562—576.

Rosenberg, M.J. (1965) When dissonance fails: On eliminating evaluation apprehension from attitude measurement. *Journal of Personality and Social Psychology,* 1, 28—42.

Rosenberg, M.J. (1969) The conditions and consequences of evaluation apprehension. In

R. Rosenthal & R. Rosnow (Eds.), *Artifact in behavioral research.* New York: Academic Press.

Rosenberg, M.J. & Abelson, R.P. (1960) An analysis of cognitive balancing. In M.J. Rosenberg *et al., Attitude organization and change.* New Haven, CT: Yale University Press.

Rosenthal, R. (1966) *Experimenter effects in behavioral research.* New York: Appleton-Century-Crofts.

Rosnow, R.L. (1981) *Paradigms in transition: The methodology of social inquiry.* New York: Oxford University Press.

Ross, L. (1977) The intuitive psychologist and his [sic] shortcomings: Distortions in the attribution process. In L. Berkowitz (Ed.), *Advances in experimental social psychology.* Vol. 10. New York: Academic Press.

Ross, M. & Schulman, R.F. (1975) Increasing the salience of initial attitudes: Dissonance vs. self-perception theory. *Journal of Personality and Social Psychology, 28,* 138–144.

Runyan, W.M. (1978) The life course as a theoretical orientation: Sequences of person-situation interaction. *Journal of Personality, 46,* 569–593.

Rychlak, J.F. (1968) *A philosophy of science for personality theory.* Boston: Houghton-Mifflin.

Rychlak, J.F. (1973) *Introduction to personality: A theory-construction approach.* Boston: Houghton-Mifflin.

Sadler, O. & Tesser, A. (1973) Some effects of salience and time upon interpersonal hostility and attraction during social isolation. *Sociometry, 36,* 99–112.

Sales, B.D. & Kahle, L.R. (1980) Law and attitudes toward the mentally ill. *International Journal of Law and Psychiatry, 3(4),* 391–403.

Sampson, E.E. (1981) Cognitive psychology as ideology. *American Psychologist, 36,* 730–743.

Sarason, I.G. (1958) Interrelationships among individual difference variables, behavior in psychotherapy, and verbal conditioning. *Journal of Abnormal and Social Psychology, 56,* 339–344.

Sarason, I.G., Smith, R.E. & Diener, E. (1975) Personality research: Components of variance attributable to the person and the situation. *Journal of Personality and Social Psychology, 32,* 199–204.

Schank, R.C. & Abelson, R.P. (1977) *Scripts, plans, goals, and understanding.* Hillsdale, NJ: Erlbaum.

Schlenker, B.R. (1974) Attitude statements following commitment to proattitudinal actions. *Personality and Social Psychology Bulletin, 1,* 138–140.

Schlenker, B.R. (1975) Liking for a group following an initiation: Impression management or dissonance reduction? *Sociometry, 38,* 99–118. (a)

Schlenker, B.R. (1975) Self-presentation: Managing the impression of consistency when reality interferes with self-enhancement. *Journal of Personality and Social Psychology, 38,* 1030–1037. (b)

Schlenker, B.R. & Schlenker, P.A. (1975) Reactions following counterattitudinal behavior which produces positive consequences. *Journal of Personality and Social Psychology, 31,* 962–971.

Schlenker, B.R., Soraci, S., Jr. & Schlenker, P. (1974) Self-presentation as a function of performance expectations and performance anonymity. *Personality and Social Psychology Bulletin*, 1, 152–154.

Schneider, J.M. (1968) Skill versus chance activity preference and locus of control. *Journal of Consulting and Clinical Psychology*, 32, 333–337.

Schneider, J.M. (1972) Relationship between locus of control and activity preferences: Effects of masculinity, activity, and skill. *Journal of Consulting and Clinical Psychology*, 38, 225–230.

Schuman, H. & Johnson, M.P. (1976) Attitudes and behavior. *Annual Review of Sociology*, 2, 161–207.

Schwartz, S.H. (1973) Normative explanations of helping behavior: A critique, proposal, and empirical test. *Journal of Experimental Social Psychology*, 9, 349–364.

Schwartz, S.H. & Tessler, R.C. (1972) A test of a model for reducing measured attitude-behavior discrepancies. *Journal of Personality and Social Psychology*, 24, 225–236.

Sebald, H. (1968) *Adolescence: A sociological analysis*. New York: Appleton-Century-Crofts.

Sherif, C.W., Sherif, M. & Nebergall, R.E. (1965) *Attitude and attitude change: The social judgment-involvement approach*. Philadelphia: W.B. Saunders.

Sherif, M., Harvey, O.J., Hoyt, B.J., Hood, W.R. & Sherif, C.W. (1961) *Intergroup conflict and cooperation: The Robbers Cave experiment*. Norman: University of Oklahoma Book Exchange.

Sherif, M. & Sherif, C.W. (1967) Attitude as the individual's own categories: The social judgment-involvement approach to attitude and attitude change. In C.W. Sherif & M. Sherif (Eds.), *Attitude, ego involvement, and change*. New York: John Wiley and Sons.

Silverman, B.I. & Cochrane, R. (1971) The relationship between verbal expressions of behavioral intention and overt behavior. *Journal of Social Psychology*, 84, 51–56.

Silverman, I. (1964) Differential effects of ego threat upon persuasibility for high and low self-esteem subjects. *Journal of Abnormal and Social Psychology*, 69, 567–572. (a)

Silverman, I. (1964) Self-esteem and differential responsiveness to success and failure. *Journal of Abnormal and Social Psychology*, 69, 115–119. (b)

Silverman, I. (1970) Reply to Levonian. *Psychological Reports*, 27, 545–546.

Silverman, I. (1977) *The human subject in the psychological laboratory*. New York: Pergamon Press.

Silverman, I., Ford, L.H. & Morganti, J.B. (1966) Inter-related effects of social desirability, sex, self-esteem, and complexity of argument of persuasibility. *Journal of Personality*, 34, 555–568.

Silverman, I., Shulman, A.D. & Wiesenthal, D. (1970) Effects of deceiving and debriefing psychological subjects on performance in later experiments. *Journal of Personality and Social Psychology*, 14, 203–212.

Silverman, I.W. (1979) Two tests of Piaget's equilibration model: A replication and an extension. *International Journal of Behavioral Development*, 2, 225–233.

Simon, J.L. (1978) *Basic research methods in social science*. (2nd ed.). New York: Random House.

Singer, P. (1981) *The expending circle: Ethics and sociobiology.* New York: Parrar, Staus, & Giroux.

Singh, U.P. (1970) Sex and age differences in persuasibility. *Journal of Social Psychology,* 82, 269—270.

Sistrunk, F. & McDavid, J.W. (1971) Sex variable in conforming behavior. *Journal of Personality and Social Psychology,* 17, 200—207.

Skolnick, P. & Heslin, R. (1971) Quality versus difficulty: Alternative interpretations of the relationship between self-esteem and persuasibility. *Journal of Personality,* 39, 242—251.

Smith, M.B., Bruner, J.S. & White, R.W. (1956) *Opinions and personality.* New York: Wiley.

Snyder, M. (1979) Self-monitoring processes. In L. Berkowitz (Ed.), *Advances in Experimental Social Psychology.* (Vol. 13). New York: Academic Press.

Snyder, M. (1981) On the influence of individuals on situations. In N. Cantor & J.F. Kihlstrom (Eds.), *Cognition, social interaction, and personality.* Hillsdale, NJ: Lawrence Erlbaum Ass.

Snyder, M. When believing means doing: Creating links between attitudes and behaviors. In M.P. Zanna, C.P. Herman & E.T. Higgens (Eds.), *Variability and consistency in social behavior: The Ontario Symposium.* Hillsdale, NJ: Lawrence Erlbaum Ass. in press.

Snyder, M. & Ebbesen, E.B. (1972) Dissonance awareness: A test of dissonance theory versus self-perception theory. *Journal of Experimental Social Psychology,* 8, 502—517.

Snyder, M. & Monson, T.C. (1975) Persons, situations, and the control of social behavior. *Journal of Personality and Social Psychology,* 32, 637—644.

Snyder, M. & Swann, W.B., Jr. (1976) When actions reflect attitudes: The politics of impression management. *Journal of Personality and Social Psychology,* 34, 1034—1042.

Snyder, M. & Tanke, E.D. (1976) Behavior and attitude: Some people are more consistent than others. *Journal of Personality,* 44, 510—517.

Southwood, K.E. (1978) Substantive theory and statistical interaction: Five models. *American Journal of Sociology,* 83, 1154—1203.

Speare, A., Jr. (1974) Residential satisfaction as an intervening variable in residential mobility. *Demography,* 11, 173—188.

Spielberger, C.D. (1962) The role of awareness in verbal conditioning. In C.W. Eriksen (Ed.), *Behavior and awareness.* Durham, NC: Duke University Press.

Spielberger, C.D., Berger, A. & Howard, K. (1963) Conditioning of verbal behavior as a function of awareness, need for social approval, and motivation to receive reinforcement. *Journal of Abnormal and Social Psychology,* 67, 241—246.

Staats, A.W., Minke, K.A., Martin, C.H. & Higa, W.R. (1972) Deprivation-satiation and strength of attitude conditioning: A test of attitude-reinforcer-discriminative theory. *Journal of Personality and Social Psychology,* 24, 178—185.

Staats, C.K. & Staats, A.W. (1957) Meaning established by classical conditioning. *Journal of Experimental Psychology,* 54, 74—80.

Stang, D.J. (1974) Methodological factors in mere exposure research. *Psychological Bulletin,* 81, 1014—1025.

Steffensmeier, R.H. & Steffensmeier, D.J. (1975) Attitudes and behavior toward hippies: A field experiment accompanied by home interviews. *Sociology Quarterly*, 16, 393–400.

Steiner, I.D. & Johnson, H.H. (1964) Relationships among dissonance reducing responses. *Journal of Abnormal and Social Psychology*, 68, 38–44.

Steiner, I.D. & Rogers, E.D. (1963) Alternative responses to dissonance. *Journal of Abnormal and Social Psychology*, 66, 128–136.

Stephenson, W. (1953) *The study of behavior: Q-technique and its methodology*. Chicago: University of Chicago Press.

Stone, V.A. (1969) Individual differences and inoculation against persuasion. *Journalism Quarterly*, 46, 267–273.

Stricker, L. (1967) The true deceiver. *Psychological Bulletin*, 68, 13–20.

Strickland, B.R. (1977) Internal-external control of reinforcement. In T. Blass (Ed.), *Personality variables in social behavior*. Hillsdale, NJ: Lawrence Erlbaum.

Sullivan, H.S. (1953) *The interpersonal theory of psychiatry*. New York: Norton.

Suppes, P. (1970) *A probabilistic theory of causality*. Amsterdam: North-Holland Publishing.

Taffel, C. (1955) Anxiety and the conditioning of verbal behavior. *Journal of Abnormal and Social Psychology*, 51, 496–501.

Taylor, S.E. (1975) On inferring one's attitudes from one's behavior: Some delimiting conditions. *Journal of Personality and Social Psychology*, 31, 126–131.

Taylor, S.E. & Fiske, S.T. (1978) Salience, attention, and attribution: Top of the head phenomena. In L. Berkowitz (Ed.), *Advances in experimental social psychology*. (Vol. 11). New York: Academic Press.

Tedeschi, J.T., Schlenker, B.R. & Bonoma, T.V. (1971) Cognitive dissonance: Private ratiocination or public spectacle? *American Psychologist*, 26, 685–695.

Terkel, S. (1980) *American dreams: Lost and found*. New York: Pantheon Books.

Tesser, A. (1978) Self-generated attitude change. In L. Berkowitz (Ed.), *Advances in experimental social psychology*. Vol. 11. New York: Academic Press.

Thibaut, J., Friedland, N. & Walker, L. (1974) Compliance with rules: Some social determinants. *Journal of Personality and Social Psychology*, 30, 792–801.

Thomas, W.I. (1907) *Sex and society: Studies in the social psychology of sex*. Chicago: University of Chicago Press.

Thomas, W.I. & Znaniecki, F. (1927) *The Polish peasant in Europe and America* (Vol. 1). New York: Alfred A Knopf.

Thurstone, L.L. (1928) Attitudes can be measured. *American Journal of Sociology*, 33, 529–544.

Tittle, C.R. & Hill, R.J. (1967) Attitude measurement and prediction of behavior: An evaluation of conditions and measurement techniques. *Sociometry*, 30, 199–213.

Tomlinson-Keasey, C., Eisert, D.C., Kahle, L.R., Hardy-Brown, K. & Keasey, C.B. (1979) The structure of concrete operational thought. *Child Development*, 50, 1153–1163.

Touhey, J.C. (1973) Individual differences in attitude change following two acts of forced compliance. *Journal of Personality and Social Psychology*, 27, 96–99.

Triandis, H.C. (1971) *Attitude and attitude change*. New York: John Wiley.

Triandis, H.C. (1977) *Interpersonal behavior*. Monterey, CA: Brooks/Cole.

Triandis, H. (1979) Values, attitudes, and interpersonal behavior. In M.M. Page (Ed.),

Nebraska Symposium on Motivation (Vol. 27). Lincoln: University of Nebraska Press.

Tunnell, G.B. (1977) Three dimensions of naturalness: An expanded definition of field research. *Psychological Bulletin*, **84**, 426–437.

Tunnell, G. (1980) Intraindividual consistency in personality assessment: The effect of self-monitoring. *Journal of Personality*, **48**, 220–232.

Turiel, E. (1977) Social-convention and morality: Two distinct conceptual and developmental systems. In C.B. Keasey (Ed.), *Nebraska Symposium on Motivation* (Vol. 25). Lincoln: University of Nebraska Press.

Underwood, B. & Moore, B.S. (1981) Sources of behavioral consistency. *Journal of Personality and Social Psychology*, **40**, 780–785.

Vaillant, B.E. (1977) *Adaptation to life*. Boston: Little, Browne & Co.

Veevers, J.E. (1971) Drinking attitudes and drinking behavior: An exploratory story. *Journal of Social Psychology*, **85**, 103–109.

Veroff, J., Douvan, E. & Kulka, R.A. (1981) *The inner American: A self-portrait from 1957 to 1976*. New York: Basic Books.

Wachtel, P.L. (1973) Psychodynamics, behavior therapy, and the implacable experimenter: An inquiry into the consistency of personality. *Journal of Abnormal Psychology*, **82**, 324–334.

Wagman, M. (1955) Attitude change and authoritarian personality. *Journal of Psychology*, **40**, 3–24.

Warner, L.G. & DeFleur, M.C. (1969) Attitude as an interactional concept: Social constraint and social distance as intervening variables between attitudes and action. *American Sociological Review*, **34**, 153–169.

Weber, S.J. & Cook, T.D. (1972) Subject effects in laboratory research: An examination of subject roles, demand characteristics, and valid inference. *Psychological Bulletin*, **77**, 273–295.

Webb, E.J., Campbell, D.T., Schwartz, R.D. & Sechrest, L. (1966) *Unobtrusive measures: Nonreactive research in the social sciences*. Chicago: Rand McNally.

Weigel, R.H. & Newman, L.S. (1976) Increasing attitude-behavior correspondence by broadening the scope of the behavioral measure. *Journal of Personality and Social Psychology*, **33**, 793–803.

Weigel, R.H., Vernon, D.T.A. & Tognacci, L.N. (1974) The specificity of the attitude as a determinant of attitude-behavior congruence. *Journal of Personality and Social Psychology*, **30**, 724–728.

Weinstein, A.G. (1972) Predicting behavior from attitudes. *Public Opinion Quarterly*, **36**, 355–360.

Weisz, J.R. (1980) Developmental change in perceived control: Recognizing non-contingency in the laboratory and perceiving it in the world. *Developmental Psychology*, **16**, 385–390.

Weisz, J.R., Yeates, K.O. & Robertson, D. (1981) Perceived contingency of skill and chance events in the lab and in the field: A developmental study. Unpublished manuscript. University of North Carolina at Chapel Hill.

Weisz, J.R. & Zigler, E. (1979) Cognitive development in retarded and nonretarded persons:

Piagetian tests of the similar sequence hypothesis. *Psychological Bulletin,* **86**, 831—851.

Whiteman, M. (1967) Children's conceptions of psychological causality. *Child Development,* **38**, 143—155.

Whittaker, J.O. (1965) Consistency of individual differences in persuasibility. *Journal of Communications,* **15**, 28—34.

Whittaker, J.O. & Meade, R.D. (1967) Sex and age variables in persuasibility. *Journal of Social Psychology,* **73**, 47—52.

Wicker, A.W. (1969) Attitudes versus action: The relationship of verbal and overt behavioral responses to attitude objects. *Journal of Social Issues,* **25** (4), 41—78.

Wicklund, R.A. (1978) Objective self-awareness. In L. Berkowitz (Ed.), *Advances in experimental social psychology.* Vol. 8. New York: Academic Press.

Wicklund, R. & Brehm, J. (1976) *Perspectives on cognitive dissonance.* Hillsdale, NJ: Lawrence Erlbaum Ass.

Wiest, W.M. (1965) A quantitative extension of Heider's theory of cognitive balance applied to interpersonal perception and self-esteem. *Psychological Monographs,* **79** (14, Whole No. 607).

Wilson, E.O. (1975) *Sociobiology: The new synthesis.* Cambridge, MA: Harvard Univ. Press.

Wish, M., Deutsch, M. & Kaplan, S. (1976) Perceived dimensions of interpersonal relations. *Journal of Personality and Social Psychology,* **33**, 409—420.

Wright, J.M. & Harvey, O.J. (1965) Attitude change as a function of authoritarianism and punitiveness. *Journal of Personality and Social Psychology,* **1**, 177—181.

Wyer, R.S., Jr. (1970) Quantitative prediction of belief and opinion change: A further test of a subjective probability model, *Journal of Personality and Social Psychology,* **16**, 559—570.

Wyer, R.S. & Goldberg, L. (1970) A probabilistic analysis of the relationships between beliefs and attitudes. *Psychological Review,* **77**, 100—120.

Wylie, R. (1979) *Self-concept: Theory and research on selected topics.* Rev. ed. Vol. 2. Lincoln: University of Nebraska Press.

Zajonc, R.B. (1968) Attitudinal effects of mere exposure. *Journal of Personality and Social Psychology Monograph,* **9**, (2, Pt. 2).

Zajonc, R.B. (1980) Feeling and thinking: Preferences need no inferences. *American Psychologist,* **35**, 151—175.

Zanna, M.P., Kiesler, C.A. & Pilkonis, P.A. (1970) Positive and negative attitudinal affect established by classical conditioning. *Journal of Personality and Social Psychology,* **14**, 321—328.

Zanna, M.P., Olson, J.M. & Fazio, R.H. (1980) Attitude-behavior consistency: An individual difference perspective. *Journal of Personality and Social Psychology,* **38**, 432—440.

Zuckerman, M. & Reis, H.T. (1978) A comparison of three models for predicting altruistic behavior. *Journal of Personality and Social Psychology,* **36**, 498—510.

Zunich, M. (1962) Relationship between maternal behavior and attitudes toward children. *Journal of Genetic Psychology,* **100**, 155—165.

Name Index

Abelson, R. P. 5, 9, 46
Adelson, J. 115
Adorno, R. W. 68
Ajzen, I. 6, 8, 64, 105–9, 114, 117
Albano, L. J. 63
Alker, H. A. 54
Allen, A. 46, 90
Allport, F. 77, 78, 90
Allport, G. W. 4, 34, 54, 128
Anderson, E. A. 52
Andrews, K. H. 28, 109, 113, 115
Appley, M. H. 70, 72
Apsler, R. 49
Argyle, M. 37, 93, 96, 97, 102
Aristotle 56
Arkoff, A. 61
Aronson, E. 12, 44, 79
Asch, S. 98

Baker, J. M. 67
Bales, R. 98
Balloun, J. L. 84
Bandura, A. 25
Barber, T. X. 79
Barlett, D. L. 84
Bartlett, F. C. 5
Bauer, R. A. 60, 69
Baumrind, D. 81
Bem, D. J. 3, 4, 25, 26, 27, 29, 41, 46, 54, 71, 82, 90, 103, 112, 114
Bentler, P. M. 28, 115
Bercher 111
Berelson, B. 88
Berkman, L. F. 115
Berkowitz, L. 67, 68
Berman, J. J. 28, 49, 84, 87, 88, 111, 112, 114, 115, 117
Bernstein, D. J. 15
Bettinghaus, R. 53

Beverly, G. D. 67, 68
Binet, A. 53
Blanchard, E. B. 25
Blaney, N. 79
Block, J. 44, 54, 120
Blumer, J. 78
Bogart, L. 77, 78
Bolen, D. 29
Bonoma, T. V. 1, 31, 109
Bowers, K. S. 42, 49, 54, 55
Brannon, T. 109
Bransford, J. D. 5
Brauer, S. L. 73
Brehm, J. W. 12, 14, 37
Brent 46
Brewer, M. B. 117, 120
Brewer, W. F. 23, 24
Brickman, P. 12, 29, 52, 84
Brinberg, D. 108
Brock, T. C. 16, 17, 84
Bromley, D. B. 4, 63
Bronfenbrenner, U. 86, 127
Brown, M. J. K. 23
Bruner, J. S. 18, 19
Bunker, A. 103
Burgoon, M. 63, 68
Burnstein, E. 17
Buss, A. R. 124

Cacioppo, J. T. 8, 16, 101
Calder, B. J. 12, 106, 120
Calsyn, R. J. 117
Campbell, D. T. 4, 40, 89, 91, 107, 113
Canning, R. R. 67
Carli, L. L. 70
Carlsmith, J. M. 12, 26, 99
Carter, J. 112
Cartwright, D. 9, 10
Carver, C. S. 111

Subject Index